# SEX DIFFERENTIATION AND SCHOOLING

*Heinemann Organization in Schools Series*

General Editor: Michael Marland

# Sex Differentiation and Schooling

*edited by*

MICHAEL MARLAND
*Head, North Westminster Community School*

*with contributions by*

JACKIE BOULD
EILEEN M. BYRNE
CAROL S. DWECK
ELIZABETH FENNEMA
BARRIE HOPSON
CAROL NAGY JACKLIN

BARBARA G. LICHT
EMILY PATTERSON
LISA A. SERBIN
DALE SPENDER
MARGARET B. SUTHERLAND

HEINEMANN EDUCATIONAL BOOKS
LONDON

Heinemann Educational Books Ltd
22 Bedford Square, London WC1B 3HH
LONDON EDINBURGH MELBOURNE AUCKLAND
HONG KONG SINGAPORE KUALA LUMPUR NEW DELHI
IBADAN NAIROBI JOHANNESBURG
EXETER (NH) KINGSTON PORT OF SPAIN

First published 1983

**British Library CIP Data**

Sex differentiation and schooling—(Organization
   in schools series)
   1. Sex discrimination in education—Great
   Britain      2. Sex role
   I. Marland, Michael      II. Series
   370.19'345         LC212.3.G7

ISBN 0 435 80592 4

Printed and bound in Great Britain by Biddles Ltd, Guildford

# Contents

# Acknowledgements

The genesis of this book lies in an Aspen Foundation seminar, 'Roles of Men and Women'. I had the privilege of being one of the UK delegates, and at this week-long multi-disciplinary international seminar in West Berlin re-focused my approach to education. I should like to thank the Aspen Foundation and the Moderator, Florence Howe, of the Feminist Press, New York.

I am happy to acknowledge the very great help of the Ford Foundation, New York, in making arrangements for the American contributors to the Organization in Schools Courses conference from which this book grew, and for funding their travel to the UK. I should especially like to thank the Programme Officer for the Education Programme, Terry Tinson Saario, for her advice and support, and for making her very wide knowledge and understanding available to me in planning the conference and later this book.

The Inner London Education Authority granted me a sabbatical term, and the English-Speaking Union honoured me with a Senior Walter Hines Page scholarship to study this topic in a large number of USA high schools. I am very grateful to both those bodies, and to the many hosts, principals, academics and teachers who helped me so generously in America. In particular I wish to thank Carol Nagy Jacklin of the Psychology Department, Stanford University, for her insight, knowledge and encouragement.

I was also helped by a series of discussions organized at Woodberry Down School, ILEA, when I was the head, which included Professor Tessa Blackstone, Professor Harvey Goldstein, Shirley Hase, Jeanette Hebbert, Wilfred Knowles, Ian Leslie, Professor Marten Shipman, and Sally Sly. Additional help in the final stages of preparing the book was given by Alison Leake.

Although this is not a book of the conference, it does owe a particular debt to the conference under the same title run by Organization in Schools Courses at Churchill College, Cambridge. The management of that course, from which the book came, was superbly handled by Ben Marland, Linda Parsons, Emily Patterson and Folly Perry, who worked together to make a most complex conference most successful. I was grateful for funding of part of the cost by the Equal Opportunities Commission. The substantial and inevitable deficit of the conference was met by Organization in Schools Courses.

Michael Marland

# 1 School as a Sexist Amplifier

*Michael Marland*

## The challenge

Boys and girls come to schools with a host of individual differences and
an even greater range of individual potentialities. They are met at all
ages by teachers who have strong, if only partly articulated, views on
what constitutes the pupils' 'girlishness' or 'boyishness'. We teachers
consciously or otherwise put part of the reason for these imagined
differences between boys and girls down to the approach of parents, as
teachers are apt to do in so many matters. Further, we presume that
parents would approve of our images of the differences between the
sexes.

Actually Carol Nagy Jacklin's chapter makes it clear that girls and
boys are more likely to be regarded as individuals by their parents than
by others. It is true that other adults in a variety of sharp or subtle ways
teach girls and boys how to be and, even more important, how not to be
if they are to gain their sex identity. (See also Maccoby and Jacklin,
1974, pp. 303–48.) That, though, is hardly a reason for professional
teachers doing the same.

What is not 'nurture' is often declared to be 'nature' and schools
act as though they believe there are fundamental differences in cognitive, emotional, and attitudinal endowments. Indeed, as a major
survey concludes: 'Much discussion has been wasted and many
theories generated from differences that do not actually exist' (Wittig
and Petersen, 1979, p. 338). Yet teachers persist in seeing girls as good
at some kinds of learning and boys at others. These teachers respond
to the imagined differences between the sexes by selecting learning
material (from infant picture book to sixth-form or twelfth-grade textbook), subject content and topics that reflect those views; uncon-

sciously using language that embodies them; making practical arrangements, from the division of tasks in the youngest class to the option or elective advice for the oldest students, that amplify them; and having an entire repertoire of ways of reacting to, controlling, questioning, rewarding and punishing which relate to a greater than realized extent to sex and not to person.

It is usually not realized how deeply this sexism penetrates the details of the texture of the most ordinary classroom activities, from what teachers do to what they say. For instance, videotapes of teachers in the USA of sixth- and eleventh-grade pupils (11- and 16-year-olds) showed that both women and men teachers talked more about men than about women (Barron and Marlin, 1971). Lisa Serbin shows the expectations of teachers in Chapter 3; Barbara Licht and Carol Dweck in Chapter 6 show how these differences radically alter the way children are treated; and Dale Spender in Chapter 7 shows how the very language of schooling embodies these differences.

Of course it is not only the teachers: girls and boys meet other pupils who themselves bring similar external expectations and use them as one of their main ways of identifying their peers. Thus they teach each other how to be to retain approval of their peers and also teach each other how *not* to be.

This interaction with peer, teacher, and school organization takes place typically in schools so under-powered and under-planned that they not only allow the expectations of differences to flourish, but even use them as ways of relating, as tools for social control, and as ways of trying to motivate children.

The mass of carefully researched evidence in this book show not only that schools treat boys and girls differently, but that they actually make girls and boys more different than the forces of society would otherwise do. Schools act as amplifiers for society's stereotypes. Frequently, though, they do not know what is happening, indeed do not have adequate data on the different performance levels of boys and girls at different stages in their schooling, on the sex breakdown of option (or elective) groups, or the destination of school-leavers.

The sufferers are the girls and boys who have learning opportunities denied them, skills withdrawn from them, possible interests thwarted, their perception of the identity of others warped and, perhaps most important of all, their view of themselves and their potential distorted. Because they are the sufferers, so is the society in which they will lead their adult lives – and bring up their children.

An oft-quoted platitude of education is that all of us working as educators are doing so to help individuals become more truly themselves. Behind even the humblest of actions in a school is the vision of releasing and developing the potential talent, character, personality and self of each pupil. The history of education can be seen as a series of movements to free people from the accident of their birth, and to allow them to take their future into their own hands; this is as true of the accidents of birth, of wealth, class, race, locality (especially rural or urban), and even intelligence as it is of the concern of this book, of sex. Therefore, this concern is not external to education, or some externally imposed current fashion. It is not a minor side issue to be looked at when there are no pressing worries around, but part of the long-standing major, central ambition of educators. There is in this last part of the century a fusion of this educational goal with the important feminist movement, so that both movements are driving towards the same target: to ensure that pupils are given the educational opportunity that they need as individuals, not as imposed on them as a crude and arbitrary result of the accident of their birth.

## The difficulties

There is more chance of intervention if we analyse the very real difficulties that face any school hoping to work towards altering the situation. There seem to be seven separate but related problems:

1  Schools should be, and try to be, responsive to society. Both the right wing and the left wing of political thought agree on this. The American High School 'common, free, and locally controlled' may not be as locally controlled these days as in times of less Federal intervention (Tyack, 1968 and Marland, 1980), and the pressures for central control of the curriculum may be increasing in the UK, but in the USA schools are still heavily influenced by local people, and in the UK the community school movement is in many ways endeavouring to increase this influence (Poster, 1982). Here is the problem: to be open to local influence is to be open to local prejudice. Similarly, the more sensitive the school is to society's views, the harder it is for the school to work against them.

2  Much of a school's influence of pupils in creating or strengthening sex stereotypes belongs to the deep layers of the hidden curriculum, and is not only obscure but also often intangible. Lisa Serbin, Barbara Licht, Carol Dweck, and Dale Spender, for instance, show the power of the hidden curriculum. Because it is not a planned, articulated, ostensible part of the school, it is difficult to work on; there are no accessible channels of influence or control.

3  There is a real risk of creating fresh stereotypes. We can get caught in a deterministic trap of our own making. We argue that society and schools have made girls thus and boys thus. We then too easily accept this description as a situation to which we must respond. For instance, should we respond to the fact that girls often turn away from science by suggesting a solution that repeats the stereotype, and thus increases it: put the scientific content under the label (always a strange one anyway) of 'domestic science'? Or in choosing books, should we recognize the insistent masculinity of current choices by extending stereotyping and making matters worse by

searching for 'feminine' books? It is this sympathetic but essentially limiting reaction to the recognition of the results of stereotyping that sadly increases the effects of stereotyping in mixed schools. Similarly, some thinkers respond to the existing power of man in society by labelling certain modes of working and gaining power as 'masculine' (for example, the lecture). In elevating 'female' methods of working (for example the cooperative discussion group), they are surely creating fresh sexual stereotypes.

4   This risk is contributed to by the strong habit of statistical over-simplification, which leads to strengthening stereotype while investigating it. This comes from the over-reliance on the mean (or 'average', as such over-simplifiers are wont to call the measure). The mean is a concentration of the spread of results onto one figure, which then takes on a life of its own. It is a measure of concentration, not one of dispersal. It masks the spread of results, and gives no idea how far away from the mean the majority of readings may lie. This is particularly dangerous in considering the characteristics of pupils for it masks the fact that more pupils in the two different categories may be like each other than within one of the categories. In speaking of 'the average boy' or 'the average girl', we are suppressing the important fact that there is more difference between some girls than there is between most girls and most boys. The same error leads us to talk of 'girls' characteristics' and 'boys' characteristics', and thus avoid more precise definition of these characteristics, and to avoid realizing that treating people by their sex is repeating stereotyping, as well as probably being inaccurate. Thus, in Chapter Two, Carol Jacklin's figures on 'rough and tumble play' show that 'the majority of the boys were in the same range as the girls'. In Chapter 6, Carol Dweck is at pains to speak about qualities not sex. *Thus any school structure that wishes to work on deficiencies should do so by grouping by characteristic not by sex.* For instance, to create boys' foreign language groups to help with difficulties in language learning is to overlook that there are girls hidden by the average figure who have exactly the same problems.

5   There is also what I have to call the problem of unexpected side-effects. Many movements to improve aspects of school – both curricular and pastoral – bring with them side-effects unrelated to the main aim of the change and thus unexamined by those proposing the change. Because of the quasi-political enthusiasm that energizes much curriculum argument, one factor only becomes dominant. This leads to any unfocused aspects being completely overlooked, and I suspect that because the question of sexual differentiation has not been questioned or investigated much in the past, a number of changes introduced with good reasons have led to many girls being under-favoured. For example:

Single-sex to mixed schools     — stereotypes  likely  to  be
                                  stronger in the latter

| | |
|---|---|
| 'Theoretical' to 'practical' science lessons | — girls with little practical or experimental experience penalized |
| Unstructured essays to multiple-choice or structured questions in examinations | — boys with limited language powers given a help |
| From classic heritage literature to free choice of contemporary | — effects of masculine predominance exaggerated |
| Primary school timetabled day made more flexible | — mathematics given less stress, and thus the weak left weaker |
| Subject choice made freer | — sex-stereotypical choice made more common. |

It is probable that the overall effect of quite separate changes has in fact been to increase the effect of societal and personal prejudices in schooling in the last quarter of a century.

6 The career structure of the teaching profession on both sides of the Atlantic is heavily male dominated. Although there is only anecdotal evidence that men make boy-oriented decisions in school planning, there is ample evidence that the lack of role models for growing girls affects their aspirations. This problem is so deeply entrenched that it is difficult to see how it can be changed quickly. (I discuss medium-term changes in Chapter 4.)

7 Significant changes require whole-school approaches, and in all the countries referred to in this book educational developments are notoriously narrow in their impact and schools lack the organizational strength to consider, devise or implement whole-school approaches (for example, HM Inspectorate, 1981). Thus subject departments devise syllabuses, argue for resources and plan from a specific and limited 'departmental' point of view. There is little or no overall curriculum planning, and little or no interrelatedness between the aspects of counselling, pastoral care, learning resources and curriculum planning. In the USA 'Title IX' (see page 235) has had a strong effect, but it too has been unable to help schools beyond looking at segments at a time. *For a proper response to the question of sex differentiation and schooling, a coherent whole-school approach is required from school management and in curriculum planning for all aspects of schooling.*.

## This book

In devising this book I have tried to commission major studies that will be helpful to heads, curriculum planners, leaders of pastoral teams, and heads of departments in schools, as well as those outside schools who influence them: advisers, inspectors, local education authority administrators, elected politicians, parents and interested members of the public. (There are, of course, gaps: a major one in my view being that there is no account of the relationship of the topic to the study of foreign languages.) The book aims to focus research and thought to assist those who want to take action.

I have had seven specific ideas in mind in preparing this volume:

1  Its theme is 'sex differentiation' not just 'what happens to girls'. It is true that at the moment most of the studies of schooling and sexual differentiation take girls as their focus, but actually both boys and girls suffer badly from the present situation.

2  Throughout, the contributors and I have tried to get behind the broad generalizations, and to go back to basic detail. That is one of the reasons why I have commissioned chapters by those working on actual investigations of what happens to pupils.

3  The book considers all ages of schooling, but not higher education. Its main focus is on the compulsory years.

4  We have tried not to latch too readily on a single scapegoat. It is too easy to dub as the villains the examiners, the publishers, the primary schools, or whoever. The blame is multifarious.

5  The book is not concerned only with surface actions. The subjects taken and the qualifications gained are, of course, immensely important, but so too is the way girls and boys are led by schooling to see themselves and the other sex. Both boys and girls suffer from the limited perceptions of human personality that can be imposed by the powerful hidden curriculum.

6  The book hopes to be positive. Our stance is that if there is careful examination of the facts, strategies can be devised to make changes.

7  The differences between education systems in different countries are very great, but all share the weakness of sex differentiation. This book therefore is concerned with and refers to many parts of the world. Although much of the data and many of the arguments are closely focused on the UK or the USA, there is considerable reference also to Australia, Canada, New Zealand, and the European countries. In each case terms for those countries are used as appropriate.

The present situation is unfair on both boys and girls: not only are girls kept out of technology, engineering, mathematics and physics, but boys are in effect kept away from modern languages, literature, child development, nutrition, and much that they need to know about their future lives. Worse than that, the very view that boys and girls are given of themselves and of others is warped by a system that is committed to individual regard for individual needs in every other respect but fixes girls and boys into patterns that may not suit them as individuals. In terms of power, western schooling can be seen as perpetuating and increasing the subordination of women, asking what they are for and not what they can do. It is presently a man's world in the school, even when there is a predominantly female population. In political terms women are the losers. In human terms all people are also losers.

# References

Barron, N.M. and Marlin, M.J. (1971). *Sex of the Speaker and the Grammatical Case Gender of Referenced Persons*. Technical Report N. C153. Columbia: Centre for Research in Social Behaviour, University of Missouri.

HM Inspectorate (1981). *Curriculum 11–16: A Review of Progress*. HMSO.

Maccoby, Eleanor Emmons and Jacklin, Carol Nagy (1974). *The Psychology of Sex Differences*. Stanford: Stanford University Press.

Marland, Michael (1980). *Education for the Inner City*. Heinemann Educational Books.

Poster, Cyril (1982). *The Community School*. Heinemann Educational Books.

Tyack, Donald (1968). *The One Best System*. Cambridge, Mass.: Harvard University Press.

Wittig, Michele Andrisin and Petersen, Anne C. (1979). *Sex-related Differences in Cognitive Functioning*. Academic Press.

# 2    Boys and Girls Entering School

*Carol Nagy Jacklin*

In what ways are boys and girls different when they enter school? Are teachers presented with already shaped and formed 'boy' and 'girl' packages or are the schools the shaping agents of sex differences? If teachers do get children already formed differently by sex, she or he may need to use differential teaching methods to pursue the goal of equal educational opportunities for both sexes. Does the legal and moral obligation to work for equal educational opportunities mean that the teacher ends up with equal products? For example, does the inability of the schools to produce the same number of boys and girls interested in mathematics mean that the teacher and schools have failed or simply that the teachers did the best they could, given the limitations of the material they receive from the parents and culture.

We can deliberate these issues more productively once we determine what sex differences children actually have at the start of schooling, and that is what I will attempt to describe here in reviewing studies done by many researchers on the first five years of life, and covering the results to date of the Stanford Longitudinal Study. This study, in collaboration with Eleanor Maccoby, has been a specific attempt to follow three groups of children from birth until they enter formal schooling at about 6 years old. One of the aims of the study has been to try to determine the development of sex differences over this six-year period. We have observed the children and their parents repeatedly, and we have in addition five sex steroid hormone scores, assayed from the umbilical cord plasma at birth for each child. Thus we have one measure of biological contribution to sex differences and many socialization measures.

The chapter is divided into three parts: (1) what sex differences are evident from birth (which will include physical and behavioural differences); (2) what sex differences are found in parenting in the pre-school years; and (3) what other environmental influences are known to impinge on the children before school. The research is not evenly divided in these areas. I have tried to indicate areas where research is in progress, where research is much needed, and some of the general problems inherent in research in sex differences.

Although I have divided the paper into biological and socialization sections, this is a false dichotomy. There can be and are biological influences that are not evident at birth. For example, such physical attributes as thickness of beard growth for males are biologically determined before birth and yet not manifest until late adolescence. With similar complexity, the time course of socialization effects may also be variable. The chapter divisions are only for organizational convenience.

## Sex differences from birth

One poorly understood sex difference evident even before birth is the greater vulnerability of boys. (See Maccoby and Jacklin, 1974 for a review.) More boys than girls die before birth from many causes. In our own work, we have found that the length of labour is on the average about one and a half hours longer for boy children than for girl children. This in turn may be related to the fact that there are greater numbers of boys in all categories of birth defects.

There is considerable current research on whether obstetric medication given to mothers has effects on behaviour of the children both at birth and for several years after (Brackbill, 1979). It is known that the amount of obstetric medication varies with the length of labour. However, there may be other factors as well operating on birth defects that we do not have information about and other vulnerabilities before or near birth. Birth defects, whatever their cause, may have repercussions on educationally related behaviour in the pre-school and school years.

Boys are found in much greater numbers in groups of hyperactive children. The ratios of girls to boys in these populations differ from 1 girl to 5 boys up to 1 girl to 20 boys. Similarly, speech problems are much more frequent in boys than girls. Reading problems, too, which are found in the same kind of lopsided ratio in girls and boys are suspected to be related to this general vulnerability problem. I will return to these issues later.

A second sex difference at birth is the presence of sex steroid hormones. Although it is believed that our primary sex characteristics are determined by sex steroid hormones during the third month after conception, it may also be that sex differences in behaviour are related to hormone differences before and near birth. There are striking sex differences in the sex steroid hormone testosterone at three months after conception and these differences attenuate but remain clear at birth.

The important question is whether sex steriod hormones at birth are associated with particular behaviours, either behaviours at birth or behaviours later in life. Some researchers (for example, Dalton, 1968 and Hutt, 1972) believe that such a connection may exist with cognitive abilities and hormones at birth. We are working on this very issue, but our results are not yet in. One complication that we have documented is that sex steroid hormones at birth differ depending on your birth order, or ordinal position. That is, we have found that progesterone, oestrone and oestradiol are present in much greater amounts in first borns than later born boys and girls. Testosterone is present in greater amounts in first born than later born boys. Girls' testosterone levels do not depend on ordinal position (Maccoby et al., 1979).

This birth order result is suggestive of other work in cognitive abilities. Zajonc and his colleagues (Zajonc, 1976; Zajonc and Markus, 1975) have argued that birth order differences in cognitive abilities come from a difference in the environment of first borns and later borns. Zajonc's 'confluence' model tries to measure the amount of adult or child verbal interaction children have and the amount of teaching a child does of other children. Using these factors, he had been very good at describing the birth order effects found in cognitive abilities. However, we now may have uncovered a confounding variable. This is not to say that environmental components are unimportant, but only that hormonal effects must also be investigated.

There is another kind of behaviour that may be linked to sex steroid hormones. These are tentative findings because we have so far seen only thirty boys and twenty-two girls at birth who have grown old enough for this assessment. We will have a larger sample analysed within the next year. Thus for present purposes we should treat these findings as hypotheses to be replicated. The behaviour in question is rough-and-tumble play, and the children we observed at four and a half years old (nursery-school age in the U S). In our study, we defined rough-and-tumble play as playful attack, plus wrestling. Playful attack was the number of times a child physically jumped on, hit or pushed another child or hit or pushed with an object while smiling or laughing. (There were almost no instances of hostile physical attack.) Rough-and-tumble play is one of the most substantial sex differences we have obtained so far in our longitudinal work. For the boys, rough-and-tumble play occurred in 14 per cent of the time intervals, for girls, in only 4½ per cent. This difference is highly significant. Even so, it should be noted that there is a great deal of overlap in the distributions. There is a group of boys (about 20 per cent) for whom rough-and-tumble play occurs more frequently than is seen in any of the girls; but the majority of the boys were in the same range as the girls. It is worth noting that the behaviour is a large sex difference but is actually *not* being shown by the majority of males.

Three hormones at birth are related to rough-and-tumble play at four and a half years old. Testosterone, oestrogen and progesterone all show the same pattern; they seem to activate boys and calm girls. The exception to this pattern is seen with androstenedione, which has an activating effect for both sexes. We do not know why androstenedione should have a different relationship to the behaviour of girls than the other hormones do; we are currently exploring this issue.

Hormones at birth then, may influence behaviour of pre-school age children. We are left with many more questions than answers in this area. But understanding the complexity of the problem may be a step towards real answers.

## Behaviour at birth

Are there sex differences in behaviour at birth? There have been many candidates of suggested behaviours that might differentiate the sexes, but very few have held up to empirical test. There are some complicating factors after birth. Circumcision is one of them. Some researchers believe that if you compare only uncircumcised (or pre-circumcised) males with females, sex differences disappear. Unfortunately, most of the studies do not differentiate circumcised from uncircumcised males. In our own work, we have observed only males prior to circumcision or after a minimum of eight hours following circumcision. Comparing this sub-sample of males with females, very few sex differences appear.

We have tested three of the behaviours most believed to differentiate the sexes: *tactile sensitivity, prone head reaction* and *grip strength*. It is alleged that females are more sensitive to touch at birth. We have been unable to obtain this finding with any of our three independent samples of infants. However, we have found very slight sex differences in two other infant behaviours both associated with strength. Prone head reaction measures the height and duration of the head lift when the infant is placed in a prone position. Although we did not find significant differences in any one of our three samples of newborns, when the three samples are combined (Rosenthal, 1978) we do find an overall sex difference in prone head reaction. Again this is a small group difference. Many newborn girls lifted their heads higher than many newborn boys. Still overall there were average differences. We have not yet been able to trace any connection between prone head reaction at birth to other behaviour at a later age, but neverthless this is a difference at birth. The third behaviour we investigated was grip strength. Grip strength was measured with a small fish scale that had a rubber ring easily grasped by a newborn attached to the end of the scale. The infant was placed on his/her back and the rubber ring was pressed into his/her palm. All infants responded reflexively by grasping the ring. The scale was lifted directly upward by the experimenter, slowly and steadily until the infant released the ring. The scale was designed so that the highest weight reached when the ring was released remained registered until the scale was reset. This measure of grip strength was only used in two samples of infants. In one group there were no sex differences. In the other group boys were higher in grip strength at a level which approached, but did not achieve, statistical significance. When the groups were combined, there was a slight overall sex difference. In all then, although many behaviours have been tested as possible sex differences at birth, only two measures, both measures of muscle strength, appear to differentiate the sexes. These two measures, prone head reaction and responsive grip strength are very small sex differences. That is, in some groups we did not find differences, but when groups are combined a statistical difference appears. What is very clear is the overlap or similarity; put another way, knowing the child's sex will not help predict the child's muscle strength.

## Parents' behaviour towards girls and boys

In some senses, the behavioural differences (or similiarities) at birth reviewed above constitute the packages the parents receive. We must conclude that on many dimensions newborns are very different but the packages the parents receive do not differ much depending on whether the child is a boy or a girl. But do the parents know this? In some interesting research (Rubin et al., 1974) parents were asked what their sons and daughters were like right after the babies were born. The parents said the children were different depending on the child's sex. Daughters, in contrast to sons, were rated as softer, finer featured, littler and more inattentive. Sons were rated as more alert, stronger, hardier, better coordinated and larger featured. Both mothers and fathers rated their children in these sex-stereotypic ways. However, fathers' ratings were more extreme in their stereotyping than mothers. The babies in this study were weighed and measured and no sex differences emerged. We can conclude that parental expectations are different right from birth. Some research done in our laboratory indicates that after parents have had experience with their children, they become less sex-role stereotypic. We administered a modified version of this rating scale to one group of parents when their children were 6 months old and a second group when their children were 2 years 9 months old. Parents of childen of these ages rate their childen differently but not depending on the sex of the child. Having experience with one's own children seems to mitigate the sex-stereotypic responses.

What about behaviour with children? Are there differences in the ways pre-school age boys and girls are treated by their parents? Measuring behaviour of more than one person in interaction is a difficult thing. There is always the problem of who started the interaction and who is running it. For example, in a study of our longitudinal children at 12 months old interacting with their fathers (we set up a playroom with many things for the children to get into) we found that fathers were prohibiting more behaviour of their sons than their daughters. However, we also found that sons were getting into much more mischief than daughters. This could be described as differential behaviour, but it does not have the flavour of differential behaviour at all. We wanted to see whether fathers would be harder on their sons or daughters – would fathers verbally and physically prohibit the behaviour of their sons or their daughters to a different extent?

A second problem is that in the area of group differences in the social sciences it is relatively easy to publish positive findings, but difficult to publish null findings. That is, if a study finds a sex difference, it is easier to get into print, and then into abstracts and indexes, than a study which does not find a difference. Thus we know that there is a bias against negative findings. With these caveats in mind I will nevertheless try to review the relevant studies.

There is an interesting study (Smith and Lloyd, 1978) on parent differential treatment of boys and girls and the age of their own children depending on whether they believe they are interacting with a boy or a girl. Six-month-old children were dressed as a boy or a girl and given names appropriate to their dress. If the adults thought they were playing with a boy, large body movements on the part of the child were interpreted as a playful motion and the adults responded with play. If a similar movement was made by a supposed girl, the adults interpreted it as a frightened movement and gave the child support and cuddled 'her'.

Again, this work has not been done on parents playing with their own children; it would be impossible to do such a study. Similar work, though, is in progress (Smith, personal communication) with parents playing with their own children and recording movements of the child with parents' responses to the movements.

The work to date, on differential treatment of boys and girls under school age by parents has not been able to document many differences (see Maccoby and Jacklin, 1974 for a review). It is clear with older children that there are differential treatments. For example, with 7- or 8-year-olds, parents are more likely to know where their girls are than their boys, and some cross-cultural work has indicated that boys are allowed to be farther away from home than girls. But in the first five or six years of life, differential treatment is difficult to pin down.

There is one area where differential socialization has been documented which may have wide implications. We do know that boys and girls are given different kinds of toys and, more importantly, fathers initiate sex-appropriate play with children when sex-typed toys are available. Further, at some ages but not others, if boys are playing with 'girl' toys they will be punished for it (Langlois and Downs, 1980).

Mothers are more likely to play with 'girl' toys when they are with their sons or their daughters and neither mothers nor fathers punish daughters when they are doing cross-sex-toy play. It is of some interest that the fathers and not the mothers are more likely to punish boys for cross-sex-toy play. Much of the differential socialization studies have concentrated on the mothers, reasoning that mothers spend more time with the children. With further work on the fathers, more differential socialization may become evident.

For completeness, I want to mention one area of study I have not reviewed. There have been a number of studies which ask parents of adult children to think back to their child-rearing years and describe how they treated their sons and daughters. The children of these parents are often also asked to remember their childhoods and describe their parents' behaviours. Sex-role stereotyped responses are more likely in these retrospective studies than in studies which observe child-rearing while it is occurring. Since the parents' memories and the children's memories of child-rearing differ, and since both accounts differ from observational studies of child-rearing, I am dissatisfied with the methodology and do not believe it is a fruitful way to understand parenting.

## Other environmental influences

### Peers

In some work with 2 year 9 month old children (Jacklin and Maccoby, 1978) playing with an unfamiliar peer, we found some curious results. Both boys and girls, when playing with same-sex peers are socially very active. There was a lot of interactive play, sharing and competing for toys, vocal commands to each other and vocal prohibitions. There were some differences in boy and girl same-sex pairs: there was more aggression, hitting and threatening in the boy-boy pairs and more offers of toys in the girls' pairs, but on the whole, the differences were outweighed by the similarities. What was striking by contrast, was the play of mixed-sex pairs at this age. In these pairings there was very little interaction. We had asked the parents to bring their children to our playroom in play clothes, and although some of these were clearly sex-typed by clothes, we were unable to tell the sex of the children in about half of the cases. Somehow the children seemed to be able to tell, although they never asked each others' names. We have analysed the behaviour of boys and girls to try to understand the different behaviours in the same and the mixed-sex pairs and have found one interesting difference. If boys use a vocal prohibition such as 'mine' or 'no', their partner is very likely to withdraw or retreat whether their partner is a boy or girl. However, when a girl uses a vocal prohibition, if her partner is a girl she will retreat, but if her partner is a boy, he is not likely to retreat. We do not know what accounts for this difference, whether, for example, boys' vocal prohibitions are louder. Whatever the cause, the effect seems to be a difference in same versus mixed-sex play at a very young age.

One other difference in early peer behaviour is the size of the groups that boys and girls play in. In a laboratory nursery school, it was found (Waldrop and Halverson, 1975) that the average size of boy groups was five, while the girls' groups were likely to have two or three members. Are these group size differences due to the fact that boys are taught group games or given more encouragement in group games as compared to the girls? Or are group games devised because of boys preferring to play in larger groups? We do not know and more work needs to be done before we will be able to decide this question.

## The media

Another source of socialization influence on boys and girls before they get to school is the media. A number of studies have shown that books, radio, and television programmes all portray many more boys and men than girls and women. (See Maccoby and Jacklin, 1974, for a review.) In addition, what the women and men are portrayed doing, and the consequences of their actions are very different. For example, one study of television drama for children and adults found that when women were shown in leading roles, they were able to act by virtue of some supernatural power or magic rather than by their own abilities. In another study, it was found that if women were shown married and working (common in life, but uncommon on television), their marriages were unhappy. But men shown working and married were happy.

Children's books, too, provide stereotypic and unrealistic views of the world. In one study, I found that girls and women were almost completely absent from difficult reading books, and when women were shown in the easier readers, they were almost always mothers in the homes, while men were shown in a variety of jobs and roles. Although children's attention is held by television programmes, recent research has shown that any complication of plot and moral are lost on the youngest viewers. More research needs to be done to determine how much the youngest children are understanding of the media messages. It is likely that the general reinforcement of the stereotypic male and female roles still shines through.

## Non-parent adults

One source of sex-role socialization that has not been studied, but which has long been my favourite hypothesis, is the influence of non-parent family members and family friends. Differential socialization of boys and girls may be occurring by non-parent adults and by older children as well. In general, we do the greatest stereotyping with people, children and adults, that we know the least. It therefore seems reasonable to believe that aunts and uncles and family friends may be heavily stereotyping children and having an influence on the children's behaviour which far outweighs the amount of time children may be with these individuals. The amount of time a person spends with a child may not be directly related to the amount of influence that person has. I described earlier more sex-role socialization by fathers than mothers, and fathers may spend much less time with their children but may still have great influence. I will even hypothesize further that those fathers who do the most stereotyping with sex-appropriate toys may be the fathers who spend the least amount of time with their children.

Many other influences may be affecting sex-role socialization of boys and girls, but thus far we have not pinned down these influences. One hypothesis is that adult family or non-family members, who spend less time with the children, do more sex-role stereotyping.

## Summary

A boy may have had more difficulty at birth, which may have implications for speech and reading. It must be noted that only a few children will be affected by the greater male vulnerability. The great majority of children will not differ in this respect. There may be differences in sex-steroids at birth but these seem to have a greater differential effect according to the child's birth order than the child's sex. Behaviour at birth does not differ in tactile sensitivity but does to a negligible extent in muscle strength. The largest sex difference we have been able to document is rough-and-tumble play at 4 to 5 years old. I have tried to emphasize that although this behaviour is a large sex difference, most boys are like most girls and do not show very much rough-and-tumble play.

What of parent behaviour? Given the difficulties of studying social interaction, we cannot always sort out which behaviours are a function of the parent and which a function of the child. Yet, we have found that parents' treatment of young boys and girls is very similar. Parents do make different attributions about their children at birth, and do treat other people's children differently by their supposed sex. But given experience with their own children, the differential attributions (by sex) disappear. One area in which differential treatment by fathers has been documented is sex-stereotypic-toy play. Fathers initiate same-sex-toy play and punish cross-sex-toy play, particularly with sons.

Early peer interactions differ somewhat by the sex of the child. One study found that girls play in smaller groups than boys, and we have found same-sex play to differ from cross-sex play in young children.

Books and television programmes portray different models of male and female behaviour, but it is not clear how much this directly influences the pre-school child. Again more research is needed.

In general intelligence, attention span, cognitive abilities and task orientation boys and girls are alike when they enter school. These are all areas relevant to school behaviour that do not differentiate the sexes. In sum, boys and girls entering school are much more similar than they are different. Although we have been able to demonstrate some small sex differences, there is mostly overlap of the sexes even in the differences described.

What then is a teacher committed to helping children become educated to do? And what can researchers and policy-makers do to help teachers? I believe we must teach teachers to respond to individual differences and not group differences. We all categorize information to help us deal with information. We tend to categorize people on obvious dimensions. Again, the less we know about individuals, children or adults, the more we stereotype and categorize. We have learned that short/tall is not a distinction that is useful for predicting educational outcomes; we must similarly learn that male/female is not a useful distinction for predicting educational outcomes. If we allow the use of this distinction to continue, self-fulfilling prophecy takes over and teachers will contribute to the maintenance of the *status quo*. An emphasis on individual variation and conscious fighting of the tendency to use group differences will allow teachers to maximize individual freedom and growth.

# References

Brackbill, Y. (1979). 'Obstetrical medication and infant behavior', in J. Osofsky (ed.), *Handbook of Infant Development*. New York: John Wiley.

Dalton, K. (1968). 'Ante-natal progesterone and intelligence'. *British Journal of Psychiatry*, vol. 114, pp. 1377–82.

Hutt, C. (1972). *Males and Females*. Harmondsworth: Penguin Books.

Jacklin, C.N. and Maccoby, E.E. (1978). 'Social behaviour in same-sex and mixed-sex dyads'. *Child Development*, vol. 49, pp. 557–69.

Langlois, J. and Downs, C. (1980). 'Mothers, fathers and peers as socialization agents of sex-typed play behavior in young children'. *Child Development*, vol. 7, pp. 1237–47.

Maccoby, E.E. and Jacklin, C.N. (1974). *Psychology of Sex Differences*. Stanford: Stanford University Press.

——, Doering, C.H., Jacklin, C.N. and Kraemer, H. (1979). 'Concentrations of sex hormones in umbilical-cord blood: their relation to sex and birth order of infants'. *Child Development*, vol. 50, pp. 632–42.

Rosenthal, R. (1978). 'Combining results of independent studies'. *Psychological Bulletin*, vol. 85, pp. 185–93.

Rubin, J.Z., Provenzano, F.J. and Luria, Z. (1974). 'The eye of the beholder: parents' views on sex of newborns'. *American Journal of Orthopsychiatry*, vol. 44, no. 4, pp. 512–19.

Smith, C. and Lloyd, B. (1978). 'Maternal behavior and perceived sex of infant: revisited'. *Child Development*, vol. 49, pp. 1263–5.

Waldrop, M.F. and Halverson, C.F. Jr. (1975). 'Intensive and extensive peer behavior: Longitudinal and cross-sectional analysis', *Child Development*, vol. 46, pp. 19–26.

Zajonc, R.B. (1976). 'Family configuration and intelligence'. *Science*, vol. 192, pp. 227–36.

—— and Markus, G.B. (1975). 'Birth order and intellectual development'. *Psychological Review*, vol. 82, pp. 74–88.

# 3 The Hidden Curriculum: academic consequences of teacher expectations

*Lisa A. Serbin*

In every classroom there is an unofficial curriculum, a part of the learning experience that is determined by the teacher's attitudes and behaviour rather than by a formal syllabus. Because teachers are often unaware of the ways in which the educational experience of boys and girls differs, the reinforcing of sex typing in the classroom is often referred to as a 'hidden curriculum'. In other words, teachers themselves are generally unaware of their own expectations and behaviours that effectively sustain and reinforce conformity to sex-role stereotypes, and which encourage the development of quite different academic abilities and behaviours in their male and female students.

The research in which my colleagues and I have been engaged for the past eight years has focused on differences in the educational experiences of boys and girls. By observing the actual daily process of classroom learning, we have attempted to describe the different ways in which boys and girls receive attention and instruction and the different ways they are taught to behave in learning situations. We have also tried to determine objectively the consequences of these differential experiences and, finally, to develop effective programmes for reversing sex-stereotyped behaviour patterns, designed for use at pre-school and primary level classrooms. In this chapter I have summarized some of the results of our research, and describe the implications of these findings for classroom programmes.

# Sex roles today

The term 'sex role' is used in this chapter to refer to the collection of behaviours, occupations and personality characteristics which are popularly regarded as sex typical, or as primarily appropriate for one sex or the other. Sex roles are thus distinct from sex differences or sex-related phenomena (characteristics or behaviours in which males and females differ), and from gender identity (which will be used to refer to the sex to which the child believes him/herself to belong). The term 'sex typing' will be used to indicate the degree to which an individual conforms to a male or female sex role. The term 'sex stereotyping', or simple 'stereotyping', is often used interchangeably with 'sex role' or 'sex typing', but here it will be used only in the narrower sense of making a *judgement* about characteristics, behaviour or performance primarily or solely on the basis of sex. Thus, for example, a child who plays primarily with toys typically viewed as male-preferred or male-appropriate will be described as sex-typed. A teacher who says, 'I don't really expect much from the girls in math class' is engaging in sex stereotyping.

## Sex-role characteristics and consensus

Numerous studies have demonstrated that adults show high levels of agreement in describing male and female roles, whether they are categorizing occupations, personality traits or activities (Broverman, Vogel, Broverman, Clarkson and Rosenkrantz, 1972; Edelsky, 1976; Urberg and Labouvie-Vief, 1976). They also show strong agreement in categorizing children's play activities, social behaviours and personality characteristics as being primarily typical of one sex or the other (for example, Ricks and Pyke, 1973; Masters and Wilkinson, 1976). The accuracy of these classifications, even when the raters have presumably had little opportunity for observation, can be high. In one study with college students (Connor and Serbin, 1977), a list of thirty-five classroom play activities was given to thirty-five undergraduates, who were asked to indicate whether each activity was more likely to be engaged in by males or by females. For all but three activities presented, a majority of the college students accurately predicted which sex was more likely to engage in each activity. In this case, it is highly unlikely that the students were basing their judgements upon actual observations of pre-schoolers with each of these toys. They simply were aware of cultural expectations: boys play with blocks and trucks, girls paint, play with dolls, and so forth. Children also seem to be aware of sex-role standards and expectations from a very early age, in some cases as young as 2 or 3 (Thompson, 1975; Flerx et al., 1976; Kuhn et al., 1978). Three-year-olds can correctly identify toys as male- or female-preferred, and 5-year-olds are able to label social behaviours and personality characteristics consistently with adult stereotypes

(Vener and Snyder, 1966; Nadelman, 1974; Williams et al., 1975).

Given the increasing de-emphasis on traditional stereotyping in early education and in society in general which has taken place over the past decade, the uniformity with which sex roles are described by adults and children is somewhat surprising. It appears that the learning of traditional sex-role concepts remains one of the earliest and most consistent aspects of socialization.

## Aspects of sex roles and sex typing in children

Three aspects of sex roles in children have been extensively studied: play activities, social behaviours and conceptual knowledge and comprehension of sex roles and gender concepts.

## Sex roles and sex differences in young children's behaviour

Studies of pre-schoolers' free play behaviour consistently find significant sex differences in the frequency of participation in certain activities (for example, Parten, 1933; Fagot and Patterson, 1969; Connor and Serbin, 1977). While sex preferences for specific toys and games may vary between groups of pre-school children, certain patterns emerge with great consistency. Female-preferred activities include play with dolls, doll furniture and clothing, kitchen and housekeeping activities, and drawing, painting and other fine motor craft activities. Male-preferred activities include play with blocks and other three-dimensional construction materials, trucks and other transportation toys, and climbing and riding activities. Thus children's actual play preferences during the pre-school period do, at least to some extent, conform to sex-role expectations.

## Social behaviours

A variety of social behaviours involving interaction with peers or adults has also been studied as part of sex-role behaviour in children. The extent of play with same-sex peers has been viewed, by both researchers and applied clinicians, as one indicator of a child's degree of sex typing. It has been assumed that play with same-sex peers leads to practice of specific interpersonal skills and roles, and is related to sex typing of play activities. Psychoanalytic theory presents this phenomenon as a normal and necessary outcome of the resolution of the Oedipal conflict, and thus as a normal characteristic of the 'latency' period (which roughly corresponds to the elementary school years). Observational studies confirm that children play increasingly in same-sex groups during the pre-school years (Parten, 1933; Fagot and Patterson, 1969; Waterhouse and Waterhouse, 1973). Most 3- to 5-year-old children however, seem to play, at least occasionally, with children of the opposite sex; some have no preference in playmates and others play more frequently with members of the opposite sex.

Other aspects of sex-role-related social behaviour which have been studied in young children include problem behaviours such as aggression and dependency. Activity level, distractability, sociability and teacher orientation are also commonly included within descriptions of sex-role behaviour. These behaviours are culturally regarded as forming part of masculine and feminine sex roles by both adults and children. The presence or absence of actual sex differences in these characteristics in pre-school children is a matter of some controversy. With the exception of aggression, which is consistently observed more frequently in boys than in girls, few of these sex-role characteristics are reliably observed to show sex differences in pre-schoolers' behaviour (Jacklin, in this volume; Maccoby and Jacklin, 1974). In observational studies, girls are found to be more frequently proximal to the teacher in a classroom setting, while boys are more often observed to 'disrupt' the classroom in various ways, such as by fighting, destroying materials and ignoring directions (Serbin, O'Leary, Kent and Tonick, 1973). The correlates and potential consequences of conformity to sex-role prescriptions for social behaviour are discussed below.

## Sex roles and mental health

In reviewing the literature on behaviour disorders in children, some very consistent sex differentiated patterns emerge. Boys are consistently found to score higher on ratings, by teachers and parents, of conduct-related disorders, which include disruptive, overactive, and inattentive patterns of classroom behaviour; while girls obtain higher scores on the 'personality disorder' dimensions, including anxiety, fears, and shyness (Quay and Werry, 1974; Clarizio and McCoy, 1976). The finding that girls and boys develop different types of problem behaviours raises immediate speculations about biological sex differences. However, in considering whether environmental factors may be involved, our observational studies suggest that different contingencies, shaping or maintaining problem behaviour, may be applied to boys' and girls' behaviour. Further, sex-role stereotypes and expectations, as taught to and learned by very young children, contain elements which, if adopted in an extreme or rigid fashion, could produce severe behavioural, cognitive and/or academic problems for both sexes. Traditional masculine and feminine roles directly mirror the sex-related patterns of behavioural problems that are reported in the literature. Aggression, high-activity levels and disruptive behaviour by boys, and dependent, passive, timid or shy behaviour by girls are salient aspects of traditional sex roles, and are in fact characteristics typically included in adults' expectations for young children's behaviour. Expectations of this type may become self-fulfilling through a variety of influences, especially when children themselves are aware of adults' differential expectations for girls' and boys' behaviour.

In terms of actual referral rates, boys are much more likely than girls to be referred to clinics during the school years (Woody, 1969; Clarizio and McCoy, 1976). One explanation is that highly active, inattentive and aggressive behaviour, which is more typical of boys, is disruptive of home and school environments. Elementary school-aged boys are also more likely than girls to be referred because of severe reading problems and other learning disabilities, which may be found in conjunction with attention and behaviour problems (Stone and Rowley, 1964; Wender, 1971). Since these patterns involve direct conflicts and difficulties in the school setting, the problems of boys may have a higher visibility and, hence, a higher probability of referral than the problem of girls.

It has been suggested (Serbin, 1972; Lee, 1973; Levitin and Chananie, 1972; Guttentag and Salasin, 1977) that the conformity of young girls to their prescribed sex role, including dependency, passivity and compliance, does not conflict with the adult expectations for appropriate behaviour in young children, and may even facilitate school performance and achievement in the elementary and junior high school grades. However, conformity to a feminine sex role may also limit intellectual or cognitive development by restricting the child's exposure to certain types of experience or learning situations (Bem and Bem, 1973; Fagot and Littman, 1976). The various effects of conformity to a feminine sex role on girls' academic performance have been examined in a study by Doherty and Culver (1976) in which it was found that highly sex-typed girls have lower I.Q. scores than less rigidly conforming children but that, within I.Q. levels, more conforming girls tended to have higher class rankings (due, perhaps, to greater compliance in completion of assigned readings and homework). Maccoby (1966) hypothesizes that the highly dependent child, who remains near adults and does not explore the surrounding environment when young, may become deficient in spatial and perceptual-analytic ability. Work by Todd and Nakamura (1970) suggests that dependent children utilize informational feedback less efficiently than independent children in that they are more likely to respond on the basis of the affective component of an adult's response and are therefore less likely to profit from the objective, informational component. Nevertheless, relatively few children are referred to mental health clinics because of excessive dependency (Woody, 1969; Clarizio and McCoy, 1976), perhaps because dependent children do not create the type of disturbance which might draw attention to them.

One other important finding in studies of incidence of behavioural and psychological disorders and referral rates is that, despite the fact that girls show higher frequencies of psychoneurotic and personality problems in studies within populations of referred and of non-referred children, boys are consistently *referred* more often than girls for *all* types of behaviour and psychological disorders (Quay and Werry, 1974; Clarizio and McCoy, 1976). One possible explanation for this inconsistency, given the differential sex-role expectations adults hold of children, is that different problem identification and labelling patterns are applied to the behaviour of boys and girls when referrals for psychological services are made. For example, the rate of referrals for dependent behaviour may be low for young girls because, except in extreme cases, passivity and dependence are accepted as 'normal' behaviour for them. Similar behaviour, in males of the same age, may be viewed as atypical or abnormal, and may result in referral for psychological services.

Are boys being readily labelled as having psychological problems by intolerant parents and school personnel (Hanson, 1959; Bentzen, 1963; Austin et al., 1971)? Are girls' problems going untreated due to a variety of social labelling factors which reduce the probability of problem identification and referral? Many factors may affect the conditions under which a specific pattern of behaviour is labelled 'normal' or 'abnormal' (Krasner and Ullman, 1973). A school environment which requires passive, compliant, attentive behaviour, while sex-role expectations and environmental contingencies teach boys that such behaviour is inappropriate for them, may combine to create a substantial problem for many boys during the school years. For girls, the relationship fo sex-role conformity to mental health problems may be more clearly apparent during adolescence and adulthood.

There is a dramatic increase in referral rates for females beginning in adolescence, when they begin to outnumber males in psychiatric referrals, primarily for psychoneurotic disorders (Landau, 1973a, b; Gove and Tudor, 1973; Dohrenwend and Dohrenwend, 1976). This increase at adolescence may reflect self-referrals for problems which were overlooked earlier by others. There is also the possibility that this is the age-group which begins to experience stress or conflict between traditional sex-role socialization for dependence and passivity and new demands to cope with adult responsibilities and the necessity of making independent decisions. Role conflicts between 'feminine' behaviours, considered acceptable and even appropriate in young children, and those expected of an independent, functioning adult woman today, may well be responsible for increased psychological problems as females mature (Gayton et al., 1978; Fodor, 1974; Powell and Reznikoff, 1976). Numerous studies report an association between sex-role conformity and many forms of mental health problem in adolescent and adult women (for example, Heilbrun et al., 1974; Hjelle and Butterfield, 1974; Burchardt and Serbin, 1982). Finally, depression, which is a primary reason for adult women's referrals, may be related to early sex-role socialization (Guttentag and Salasin, 1977; Radloff, 1978). Several cognitive theories of depression suggest that a dependent or helpless mental attitude, a characteristic included in the traditional female sex role, may predispose an individual towards a depressive reaction to environmental stress (Beck, 1967; Radloff, 1975; Seligman, 1975; Hammen and Padesky, 1977).

Further studies on the development of sex roles and behaviour disorders in children will be necessary to understand directly how these processes may affect each other. At present, though, it appears that traditional theories and assumptions regarding the positive association between 'appropriate' sex-role adoption or conformity and mental health must be re-examined. In studies with adults, the concept of psychological 'androgyny', or flexible behaviour not restricted by sex-role prescriptions, has received a great deal of recent attention. There is some evidence that such individuals are more flexible and adaptive in problem-solving situations, and may have fewer mental health problems (Burchardt and Serbin, 1982). In children, the concept of androgyny has only recently begun to be discussed, and no reliable measures of this construct, or studies comparing sex-typed with more flexible children, are yet available. Given the many issues regarding the effects of sex typing and sex-role socialization on children's behavioural and psychological development, it seems likely that researchers will be examining this problem in the near future.

## Sex differences in academic performance and cognitive skills

### Language skills, reading, and sex roles

Sex differences in cognitive skills and in academic performance have been extensively studied. Girls appear to develop stronger reading and formal language skills at an earlier age than boys (Maccoby and Jacklin, 1974). Boys, far more often than girls, are referred for 'learning disabilities', typically involving problems in reading and/or writing (Clarizio and McCoy, 1976). The higher incidence of boys' difficulties in learning to read is frequently attributed to biological factors, such as slower maturation and/or greater incidence of minimal brain damage or dysfunction (Bentzen, 1963; Garai and Scheinfeld, 1968; Wender, 1971; Buffery and Gray, 1972; Hutt, 1972). Such factors are said to result in boys having shorter attention spans, higher activity levels, greater distractability and more frequent perceptual problems, all of which may interfere with classroom learning. An alternate hypothesis is that the typical socialization of males may predispose them to difficulties in classroom learning. Dwyer (1973), in a study carried out for the Educational Testing Service, notes that girls, rather than boys, have a high incidence of reading problems and learning disabilities in German schools. She suggests that academic achievement is viewed as a masculine activity in Germany, but as a feminine activity in North America (see also, Johnson, 1973–74). Other authors have complained that North American schools are 'female oriented' and not tolerant of the behavioural and learning styles characteristic of boys (Sexton, 1969; Biber et al., 1972; Hill et al., 1974). In one study, McNeil (1964) demonstrated that boys learned to read as readily as girls when individualized teaching machines were employed, but did not do as well as girls when taught in a standard classroom situation. If, in fact, boys are taught to conform to masculine sex-role behaviour, they would be predicted to do poorly in a typical elementary school classroom. Aggressive, inattentive, active behaviour, or even independence and exploration, would bring them into constant conflict with expectations for appropriate school behaviour, and might interfere with their learning. This could lead, in severe cases, to referral for psychological services or other remediation.

## Mathematics and science

Girls typically do well academically in comparison with boys. However, the fact that large numbers of women avoid mathematics and science courses in the latter years of high school and in post-secondary education has been of increasing concern to psychologists, educators, sociologists and other students of human behaviour. This deficit in mathematics and science education has serious implications for the career options available to women (Sells, 1973). Many potential sources for this deficit have been documented: mathematics anxiety (Tobias and Donady, 1976), sex-stereotyped wording of mathematical problems, and of science and mathematics textbooks (Carey, 1958; Graf and Riddell, 1972), lack of parental encouragement (Fox, 1975), teacher influences (Ernest, 1976; Fennema, 1976; Pederson et al., 1975) and negative attitudes towards mathematics and science related subjects (Fennema and Sherman, 1977). All of these factors appear to be directly related to sex-role socialization. A less direct influence is the failure of girls to develop the cognitive skills necessary for high levels of mathematics and science achievement.

One potentially relevant sex difference in cognitive functioning is in the ability to solve visual-spatial problems (Maccoby and Jacklin, 1974). Tests of visual-spatial skills involve the ability to perform mental rotations of visual stimuli, to mentally transform two-dimensional forms into three dimensions, or to complete or dissect complex visual stimuli. Performance on tests of visual-spatial ability, especially on those measuring spatial visualization (mental rotations and/or dimensional transformation), correlates with mathematical ability and achievement test scores (Fennema and Sherman, 1977). Sex differences in visual-spatial problem solving, which develops gradually prior to sex differences in mathematics course enrolment and in mathematics achievement, may contribute to girls falling behind, and subsequently avoiding mathematics and related science and technological courses.

Many researchers have suggested that genetic or other physiological factors contribute to the sex difference in visual-spatial skill (Stafford, 1961; Broverman, Klaiber, Kobayashi and Vogel, 1968; Hartlage, 1970; Bock and Kolakowski, 1973; Wittig, 1976). While there is considerable argument currently over the genetic model which best accounts for familiar patterns of visual-spatial ability, one hypothesis that has been suggested (Fain, 1976) is that the extent to which an individual develops his/her visual-spatial problem-solving ability may be related to sex. That is, in males there is a greater chance that genetic tendencies towards high visual-spatial skills will be expressed. Sherman (1967) has proposed that environmental factors, specifically the differential play experiences of boys and girls, may provide differential amounts of practice in visual-spatial skills. Different rates of play with sex-typed toys, such as blocks and models, which require the use of these skills, might result in the development, over time, of a practice deficit in girls, who have less exposure to this type of play material.

Evidence supporting Sherman's suggestion comes from several recent studies performed in our laboratory. First, in two separate correlational studies (Connor and Serbin, 1977; Serbin and Connor, 1979), rates of play with male- and female-preferred toys were related to the development of specific cognitive abilities. Consistent sex differences in visual-spatial abilities are not yet present in 3- to 5-year-old children. These differences do not begin to appear until the age of 6 or 7. If a relationship is found between sex typing of play and visual-spatial abilities in pre-schoolers, this might indicate that play with certain toys contributes to the development of these skills. That is, over time, if the male-preferred (and sex-typed) toys involve the use of these skills more than toys that females prefer, boys should begin to develop greater visual-spatial skills as a result of greater exposure. The findings of our two correlational studies were supportive of this hypothesis. In the first (Connor and Serbin, 1977), high rates of play with male-preferred toys in the pre-school classroom were significantly related to performance on two visual-spatial tests (Preschool Embedded Figures, Coates, 1972; WPPSI Block design, Wechsler, 1967). A second study of extreme groups of children (those above the median in rate of masculine play and below the median in rate of feminine play, and those showing the opposite pattern) revealed that high masculine boys and girls had stronger visual-spatial skills than verbal skills (WPPSI vocabulary sub-test) while high feminine boys and girls showed the reverse pattern (Serbin and Connor, 1979). No overall sex difference in either visual-spatial or verbal skills was found for these samples. Thus, at an age before male superiority in visual-spatial problem-solving is found, a relationship between rates of play with 'boys' toys' and visual-spatial problem solving is present.

Further evidence for differential practice effects comes from two experimental studies (Connor, Serbin and Schackman, 1977; Connor, Schackman and Serbin, 1978) in which elementary school girls were found to benefit from practice and training on a visual-spatial task (Embedded Figures, Witkin et al., 1971) more than boys did. In fact, sex differences present in the control groups of these studies were eliminated or even reversed by a brief (10 to 20 minute) training procedure. These studies present evidence that girls do in fact have a practice deficit in visual-spatial problem-solving, and that low rates of play with male-preferred toys may contribute to this deficit.

## The consequences: careers and pre-professional training

Given the sex differences in cognitive problem-solving and school achievement which exist, it is hardly surprising that boys and girls should aspire to and enter different professions. As early as the preschool period, girls and boys verbalize different career aspirations (Looft, 1971; Barclay, 1974; Vondracek and Kirchner, 1974; Papalia and Tennent, 1975), and show an awareness of the differences in adult work activities of males and females (Flerx et al., 1976; Garrett et al., 1977; Marantz and Mansfield, 1977). Recent attempts to reduce sex-stereotyping of careers and roles by young children, which will be discussed later in this chapter, are of interest, but have not been widely applied, nor consistently demonstrated to be effective.

Three factors tend to enforce sex differences in rates of job entry: discrimination against applicants of one sex or the other, sex-stereotyping of the activity by potential applicants, and failure of one sex or the other to achieve the necessary academic background or other prerequisite skills. As we have seen, sex differences in basic cognitive problem-solving skills may contribute to this latter factor. The first factor, discrimination, has been the subject of much investigation and legal action over the past decade. The second two factors, which relate directly to early sex-role socialization, have not proved to be as directly remediable by specific legislative action. Despite anti-discrimination legislation, in effect throughout North America and most of Europe, children continue to learn sex stereotypes, and differential reinforcement and practice of specific skills and behaviours by girls and boys continues. Of course, overt discrimination preventing children from developing specific skills also continues.

# Sources of sex differentiation in the school environment

## Children's books and readers

Frequent trips to the bookshop and local library by myself and my students have convinced me that, despite much discussion of sex stereotyping among children's publishers and authors, the books currently available for pre-schoolers and school-aged children continue to contain much information about 'appropriate' sex-role behaviour. Studies on this subject date back to a classic survey of children's third-grade readers by Child, Potter and Levine (1946) which revealed extensive differentiation of male and female behaviour as well as a general de-emphasis on females in roles outside the home. More recent studies of children's books show maintenance of such role presentations into the 1970s (Saario et al., 1973; Women on Words and Images, 1976). A recent study by a class of my undergraduate students found traditional sex roles portrayed in 80 per cent of the story books in local libraries and bookshops (in a total sample of approximately five hundred picture books). Male characters consistently outnumbered females in stories occurring outside the home (a majority); male worker/female housekeeper roles were consistently shown; males were leaders, had adventures, led expeditions, and were more effective in accomplishing their goals. Females who ventured into achievement or competitive roles were often unsuccessful, or decided in the end to return to traditional roles. Male incompetence in household work was, however, a popular theme. Less traditional books and stories are available. Screening of bookshops and libraries revealed many examples of non-stereotypic materials. Clearly, though, such books remain the exception.

## Effects of sex stereotyping in children's story materials and readers

Are children sensitive to sex typing in story material? This question was recently addressed in a series of studies by my colleague, Jane Connor, and myself. Story materials were presented to elementary school and pre-school children, varying the sex of the characters in the stories. Elementary school children differentially approved of behaviour which was sex-role congruent and rated role-congruent behaviour as more effective (Connor, Serbin and Ender, 1978). They also preferred to read about characters of their own sex, and were more likely to want to 'try out' activities modelled by characters of their own sex (Connor and Serbin, 1978). Pre-schoolers paid less visual attention when teachers read stories involving males in helpless, fearful and unselfconfident roles than when the stories were presented with female characters. They also recalled more sex-role congruent than incongruent behaviour by the story characters (Serbin, Citron and Connor, unpublished MS.). These results are consistent with those of Koblinsky, Cruse and Sugawara (1978) who found greater recall of sex-role appropriate behaviour in elementary school children. Extremely incongruent behaviour, however, such as a male 'ballerina', may attract more attention than sex-role congruent presentations (Jennings, 1975). These findings indicate that children are aware of and sensitive to sex stereotypes in stories, and that their attentional patterns and learning are related to the congruence of such material with sex-role norms. Thus, material which is incongruent may not be readily absorbed. In older children, liking for stories is closely related to the character's sex and the role 'appropriateness' of his/her behaviour. Hence, children's response to classroom material indicates their sensitivity to sex-role stereotypes, and their preference for material which is congruent with the sex-role standards they have learned. It also suggests that occasional exposure to incongruent materials may not have sufficient impact to weaken children's concepts of sex appropriateness of behaviour, and that incongruent materials may be less effective as teaching materials than more traditional materials.

The possibility of using less traditional story and curriculum materials, over time, to reduce sex stereotyping by children has been frequently suggested. Studies on this topic are limited to date, and have had mixed results (Flerx et al., 1976; Guttentag and Bray, 1976). However, since children are sensitive to the sex roles portrayed in literary materials, this continues justifiably to be an issue of concern to parents and teachers.

## Teacher influences

There are a variety of ways in which teachers may influence the sex-role behaviour of children. Differential teacher response, cueing, expectations and evaluation of sex-role behaviours has been widely reported (Levitin and Chananie, 1972; Serbin, O'Leary, Kent and Tonick, 1973; Etaugh, Collins and Gerson, 1975; Fagot, 1977a; Perdue and Connor, 1978). Labelling of behaviour as sex-role appropriate or inappropriate may also occur, along with introducing activities differentially to boys and girls (Serbin, Connor and Iler, 1979). Much of this behaviour has, in the past, been deliberate. Based on Freudian theories, the importance of practising sex-role appropriate activities was traditionally stressed, especially in the pre-school and primary curriculum. Some teachers today continue to guide little girls into the doll corner, and little boys away. Most teachers, however, claim to treat boys and girls the same way, and assert that sex typing seen in their classrooms is learned outside, or from peers, or is the result of 'natural' (that is, genetic) sex differences in interests and behaviour.

In an observational study of fifteen pre-school classrooms (Serbin, O'Leary, Kent and Tonick, 1973) teacher response to sex-typed social behaviours, including aggression and proximity-seeking, by 3- and 4-year-old boys and girls was examined. Controlling for sex differences in the occurrence of these behaviours, teachers did respond differently to the behaviour of boys and girls. Responses to boys' aggression were more frequent (82 per cent of all recorded incidents of boys' aggression received a teacher reaction – 23 per cent of the girls' did), and included a higher proportion of loud reprimands, audible to the entire group. Such patterns of response, intended as punishment, have been repeatedly demonstrated to reinforce aggression and other forms of disruptive behaviour (Brown and Elliot 1965; O'Leary et al., 1970; Pinkston et al., 1973). Thus teachers seemed to be reinforcing boys for behaviours they wished to decrease, behaviours which may prove to be increasingly disruptive to the classroom. This type of reinforcement history may be a factor in the higher rates of aggressive and disruptive behaviour reported for boys, and in the high referral rates of boys for such problems.

Towards proximity-seeking (staying within arm's reach of the teacher during lesson and play periods), which was higher in girls, a very different pattern emerged. Teachers gave little girls more attention when they were working or playing immediately beside them, than when they were farther away. For boys, a fairly constant level of attention was maintained as long as the child was in the vicinity – no differential attention was given to boys immediately beside the teacher compared with boys somewhat farther away. This pattern of differential attention for proximal play received by girls would be expected to reinforce proximity-seeking in girls.

The effects of spending a large amount of time in the teacher's vicinity may be considerable. The specific activities in which the child engages will be determined largely by the teacher's activities, and the child will be exposed to a considerable amount of verbal stimulation. Opportunities for exploration, for play in areas not often frequented by teachers such as block and truck corners, and for independent play and problem-solving may be more limited for girls than for boys. Such differential experiences, then, may have considerable long-term effects on boys' and girls' social and cognitive development.

For many boys the problem, as we have noted above, in the elementary grades is poor academic performance, often related to low attentiveness and/or disruptive classroom behaviour. Are boys less attentive than girls? At least at the pre-school level, the answer seems to be no (Maccoby and Jacklin, 1974). However, they do spend more time away from the teacher when given the opportunity during play periods, and as they develop the cognitive concept of gender constancy (that is, as their understanding of gender concepts increases) they attend increasingly to male adults, in preference to females. Girls do not show a comparable differential attention pattern (Slaby and Frey, 1975). Combined with sex stereotyping of reading and intellectual and academic pursuits as feminine in North America (Dwyer, 1973), this attention pattern may present problems for boys when they are taught reading by conventional methods, and primarily by female teachers. It is not clear, however, that introducing male teachers at earlier levels would solve the problem of boys learning to read. Male teachers also appear to react differentially to sex-typed behaviours (Lee and Wolinsky, 1973; Etaugh and Harlow, 1975; Fagot, 1977b; Perdue and Connor, 1978). Rather, the process whereby boys become increasingly less attentive may have to be dealt with directly by classroom reinforcement programmes and/or changes in cultural values labelling reading and other academic pursuits as 'unmasculine'.

## Changing the behaviour of teachers

Reluctance to modify behaviour related to sex-role learning in children is understandable. The fact that 'masculine' and 'feminine' sex roles are culturally defined as normal in boys and girls raises serious ethical issues for any attempt at change. However, many behaviours which have been identified as sex-role-related are positively or negatively valued in pre-school or school-aged children (for example, problem behaviours such as physical aggression or persistent dependency on adults are negatively valued, while activities such as play with blocks, crayons or dolls, and academic activities such as reading are considered constructive). Attempts to modify specific positively or negatively valued social and play behaviours, which comprise a large part of the prescribed sex roles for males and females, are frequently unobjectionable to parents and teachers.

Studies on the modification in the classroom of various sex-typed social behaviours have been carried out in the laboratory school at the State University of New York at Binghamton. Care is taken that the goals of each study (for example, decreasing proximity-seeking towards the teacher during free-play periods, decreasing physical aggression, increasing cooperative play with children of both sexes, broadening activity choices and experience with a variety of play materials) are consistent with the goals of the educational pre-school programme, and are understood by the parents of the children enrolled in the programme. In addition, certain limitations are placed on research designs (no reinforcement of sex-role-reversed behaviour, or of *any* negatively valued sex-role behaviour, such as aggression, is ever carried out). Rather all experimental studies focus on reducing specific aspects of sex-role-related problem behaviours, or on increasing behavioural variety and flexibility in social and play situations, by children of both sexes.

In the following sections, a series of experimental studies carried out by the sex-roles research group at the State University of New York at Binghamton on the effects of specific environmental factors on children's sex-typed social and play behaviours in the classroom is described.

## Classroom modification of dependent and independent behaviours

This study (Serbin, Connor and Citron, 1978) examined experimentally the effects of specific patterns of teacher behaviour, which had been observed in previous studies to correspond with high rates of dependent behaviour in children (Serbin, O'Leary, Kent and Tonick, 1973). As described above, in this initial observation study of fifteen classrooms, a high rate of proximity-seeking by girls was observed to correlate with sex-differentiated patterns of teacher attention. When girls were immediately proximal to the teacher, they received more attention than when they were working or playing at a greater distance. For boys, no such pattern was observed. Teachers interacted with boys at approximately the same rate whether they were immediately beside the teacher or elsewhere in the room. The pattern of differential attention received by girls would be expected to reinforce proximity-seeking, and higher rates of proximity-seeking in girls were found in this study, as in many other observational studies of pre-schoolers.

The purpose of the next study was to examine experimentally the hypothesis that teachers' attention patterns control the degree of proximity-seeking, a 'dependent' or feminine sex-typed behaviour, and also of more independent types of classroom play, including task persistence, exploration of new activities, and reduced solicitation of teacher assistance and attention. The study was conducted at the Department of Psychology laboratory pre-school, and involved two classes of pre-school (3- and 4-year-old) children. Children were ranked on levels of dependent behaviour, and assigned randomly within ranks to experimental or attention control conditions. In the experimental ('training') condition, teachers reversed their usual patterns of attention, using prompting and contingent social reinforcement to encourage independent task persistence and exploration of new activities, and to reduce proximity-seeking and solicitation of teacher attention. The results indicated that dependent and independent behaviours in the pre-school classroom are under strong environmental control. Children seemed to be immediately aware of and responsive to contingencies for teacher attention. No sex difference in responsiveness was found. Both boys and girls responded to treatment with increased independent and decreased dependent behaviour. Because no generalization of treatment effects to other play periods during the day, or beyond the training period, was found, independent and dependent behaviours were concluded to be under strong and immediate environmental control.

## Effects of teacher presence and modelling on sex typing of classroom activities

This research, spanning a two-year period, was carried out in two separate studies (Serbin and Connor, 1976; Serbin, Connor and Citron, 1977). Each involved four classes of pre-schoolers, again at the Department of Psychology laboratory pre-school. The goal of these studies was to examine experimentally the effects of teacher presence and modelling of specific toys on the sex typing of play activities. The first study employed one female teacher; the second involved four female and four male teachers. Since girls typically remain more proximal to the teacher in the classroom, and teachers typically focus most of their attention on children engaged in female-preferred activities (Fagot and Patterson, 1969; Etaugh, Collins and Gerson, 1975), it seemed likely that changing teacher attention patterns, by having the teacher located near and/or modelling different activities, might control directly the rates of play in these activities by girls and boys.

Results indicated teacher presence was a powerful influence on the play behaviour of both boys and girls. Children of both sexes increased their rates of play in both male-preferred activities (trucks, blocks) and female-preferred activities (dolls, kitchen play, drawing) when a teacher was involved in these activities. However, girls responded twice as strongly to the effect of teacher presence as boys did. The results support the hypothesis that teacher location and attention patterns are important determinants of sex typing of classroom play. Boys' response to teacher presence and modelling was influenced by the sex typing of the activity (they responded more to modelling of 'sex-appropriate' activities – truck and block play – than to modelling of 'sex-inappropriate' activities). Girls responded to teacher presence and modelling without regard to the 'sex appropriateness' of the activity. In sum, sex differences in rates of play in male-preferred activities, including block and truck play, seem to be largely due to the fact that teachers do not focus much attention on these activities during the free-play period. When they do engage in these activities, girls are as likely to participate as boys are. Other important findings were that boys' play was more controlled by cultural sex typing than girls' play, and that boys did respond significantly to teacher presence and modelling of culturally 'feminine' sex-typed activities, although not as strongly as they responded to modelling of traditionally 'masculine' toys. Thus the physical location of the teacher in the classroom and the activities in which he/she engages seems to be a powerful determinant of sex preferences for specific activities and forms of play behaviour.

## Effects of labelling activities as sex-appropriate or inappropriate on classroom play

In this study (Serbin, Connor and Iler, 1979), a naturalistic observation procedure was developed and employed in nine classrooms in two different pre-school settings (both private, non-profit community schools). Teacher procedures for introducing and demonstrating three toys: a fishing kit, a sewing kit and a number puzzle (a non-sex-preferred toy), were observed. Teachers were found to respond directly to the cultural sex typing of the toy in their introductions and in their selection of children to demonstrate or try out the toys. Both of the sex-typed toys (the fishing and sewing kits) caused the teachers to differentially involve boys or girls, respectively, in the introductions.

These patterns of differential teacher introduction of sex-typed toys were examined experimentally using a controlled, repeated measures design, at the SUNY-Binghampton Department of Psychology's laboratory pre-school. Fifty-six 3- and 4-year-old children participated in this study, in which two female sex-typed and two male sets were introduced, either using a sex-typed introduction calling on only children of the 'appropriate' sex to 'try out the toy and show us how it works', or calling on children of both sexes, with non-sex-biased introduction. Rates of play with toys were observed in a subsequent free-play period. When sex-typed instructions, of the kind observed in the classrooms described above, were used, boys and girls proceeded to avoid opposite-sex-typed toys. However, when non-sex-typed introductions were given, boys and girls did not exhibit significantly different rates of play with the dolls and trucks. It was concluded that teachers generally communicate the culturally 'appropriate' sex typing of play activities when presenting or introducing them to children; that the way in which toys are introduced has a direct effect on children's play patterns; and that cultural sex typing of toys such as dolls and trucks does not necessarily control children's rates of play with these toys. Teachers can override these cultural labels by using non-sex-typed introductions, explicitly demonstrating toys to both sexes, and calling on children of both sexes to try out the toys.

In this study, the interaction of cultural sex typing and immediate environmental events in controlling sex typing of play behaviour is evident. Typically, children's play in the classroom will conform to sex-typed labels, which are either previously acquired (virtually all 3- and 4-year-olds 'know' that dolls are for girls and trucks are for boys), or which are supplied by the teacher. Teacher behaviour can, however, if incongruent with cultural stereotypes, significantly increase children's play with toys which are culturally stereotyped as appropriate for the opposite sex.

## Peer influences

The effects of peers on sex-role behaviours have frequently been discussed. Peers and siblings are readily available as sex-role models in the home, play group, day-care or school setting. Few direct observational studies on peer interactions regarding sex-role behaviour in these settings are available, however. Several observational studies of peers as reinforcing or punishing agents for sex-typed behaviours in the pre-school classroom have been performed by Beverly Fagot and her colleagues. These reveal that 'inappropriate' activities are ignored, or actively punished by negative comments or by more violent means. Peers seem to interact positively primarily during sex-role appropriate activities (Fagot and Patterson, 1969; Fagot, 1977a). The influence of peers as agents of differential reinforcement may thus be considerable.

A recent study in our laboratory demonstrates the influence of peers on sex typing of play very dramatically. In this study, children were taken individually to a playroom containing a variety of male and female stereotyped toys (Serbin, Connor, Burchardt and Citron,

1979). Initially the children were very stereotyped in their toy selection choices. When we left them for a little while, they started to explore. A boy would play with the dishes and the doll; a girl would throw aeroplanes around the room. However, this relaxation of stereotypes did not happen when another child was in the room, and it especially did not happen when the other child was of the opposite sex. A little boy sitting colouring a picture at a desk in the room was enough to keep little girls with their dishes and dolls. We found the same effect in reverse for boys. A little girl colouring a picture in the room was enough to keep them with their trucks and planes. We concluded that just the presence of a peer, especially an opposite-sex peer, is likely to make a child conform to sex-role stereotypes. In a classroom, it is easy to see that children may avoid certain activities and play areas they have learned are sex-role inappropriate if other children, especially of the opposite sex, are nearby.

Rates of cooperative play between boys and girls are typically much lower than between same sex children. This may also keep children from exploring particular toys and activities. In other words, if boys and girls primarily play separately rather than together in the classroom, it is likely that boys will continue being involved primarily in male-typed activities and girls in female-typed activities. Fortunately, we found that this pattern is not difficult to reverse (Serbin, Tonick, and Sternglanz, 1977). When teachers indicate that they expect and approve of cross-sex, cooperative play, by simply commenting on it when it occurs, boys and girls do begin to interact and play more with each other. Comments such as 'John and Cathy are working hard together on their project' effectively convey to children that working with someone of the opposite sex is not disapproved of (a message they are likely to have received previously from sex-stereotyping indoctrination both outside and within the classroom).

## Freeing children from sex-role stereotypes

Children come into the classroom heavily 'programmed'. They have already learned that different characteristics, activities and behaviours are expected of males and females. They will conform to these sex roles in the classroom unless the teacher makes an active effort to communicate different expectations and values. If children are to be freed from stereotyping, they must be treated as individuals, rather than as members of a classified group. Teachers will have to make special efforts to introduce all toys to all the children. They will have to encourage children to take turns at all the activities, to explore new activities, and to engage in cooperative play with both boys and girls. We have shown that these things can be done effectively, but teachers will have to offset powerful home, peer and media influences. It is certainly a long-term project – it can't be expected to happen in a morning or in two weeks.

The process of freeing children from stereotypes will have to counter children's own tendencies to stereotype. For example, one day the children in our nursery school were running around the track at our university. They love to do this and to 'time' themselves, to see how fast they are. After all the children had run and had been timed, Michele was acclaimed the fastest in the class, and all the children took a final sprint around the track with their teacher. While they were running, they were passed by a female student who was running on the track. One of the boys looked up at the teacher with a very puzzled look on his face. He said, 'What's she doing here? Girls can't run!' Chucky was running next to his teacher, who was also running and was a female, and Chucky had just acknowledged that the fastest child in his class, Michele, was a girl.

Children do seem to filter out information that runs counter to their expectations or to their stereotypes. To change these, children will have to be taught that specific behaviours, specific roles, and specific interests are not part of 'being a boy' or 'being a girl'. Being a girl does not mean that one has to be passive and not able to run very fast. Children have to learn, have to be taught, that specific activities and specific roles are not exclusively assigned to one sex or the other.

## Conclusion

To summarize the findings I have reported, we discovered that teachers reinforce sex-role stereotypes in many subtle ways of which they are frequently not aware. We also found, however, that teachers can reverse these patterns effectively when they become aware of them. We demonstrated that increased independence, cooperative play between boys and girls, and exploration of all classroom activities by children of both sexes can be accomplished, if a teacher wishes to do so.

Will this mean a great deal of artificial programming or coercion? I do not think so. After all, teachers, like the rest of society, are already heavily 'programmed' to train and enforce traditional sex roles, which place arbitrary limits on the direction and extent of each child's individual development. If this programming can be reduced, I see the role of the teacher as a powerful force to combat some of the pervasive stereotyping that children receive during their early school years. As psychologists and educators have long been aware, this is the period when sex roles are learned. Thus learning during this period may also be a key to introducing children to more flexible, rather than sex-role determined, patterns of behaviour. This may, in fact, be a critical time for prevention of the cognitive and emotional handicaps that can result from conformity to rigid sex roles. From our data, it is clear that teachers will have to do more than 'not enforce' traditional sex-role stereotypes in their classrooms if they wish children to be free to develop as individuals. They will have to play a most active part in the process. The methods I have described involve little that could be labelled 'coercive' or 'manipulative'. Teachers simply introduced toys to all the children, or 'modelled' a greater variety of activities, or stopped responding differentially to passivity and aggression by boys and girls. These methods do, however, require an active awareness and involvement. Teachers will have to be involved enough and concerned enough to analyse their own behaviour and if necessary, make some changes.

# References

Austin, D.E., Clark, V.E. and Fitchett, G.W. (1971). *Reading Rights for Boys*. New York: Appleton-Century-Crofts.

Barclay, Lisa K. (1974). 'The emergence of vocational expectations in preschool children'. *Journal of Vocational Behavior*, vol. 4, pp. 1–14.

Beck, A.T. (1967). *Depression: Clinical, Experimental and Theoretical Aspects*. New York: Harper and Row.

Bem, S.L. and Bem, D.J. (1973). 'On liberating the female student'. *School Psychology Digest*, vol. 2, pp. 10–18.

Bentzen, F. (1963). 'Sex ratios in learning and behavior disorders'. *American Journal of Orthopsychiatry*, vol. 33, pp. 92–8.

Biber, H., Miller, L.B. and Dyer, J.L. (1972). 'Feminization in preschool'. *Developmental Psychology*, vol. 7, p. 86.

Bock, R.D. and Kolakowski, D. (1973). 'Further evidence of sex-linked major-gene influence on human spatial visualizing ability'. *American Journal of Human Genetics*, vol. 25, pp. 1–14.

Broverman, D.M., Klaiber, E.L., Kobayashi, Y. and Vogel, W. (1968). 'Roles of activation and inhibition in sex differences in cognitive abilities'. *Psychological Review*, vol. 75, pp. 23–50.

Broverman, I.K., Vogel, S.R., Broverman, D.M., Clarkson, F.E. and Rosenkrantz, P.S. (1972). 'Sex-role stereotypes: a current appraisal'. *Journal of Social Issues*, vol. 28, no. 2, pp. 59–78.

Brown, P. and Elliot, R. (1965). 'Control of aggression in a nursery school class'. *Journal of Experimental Child Psychology*, vol. 2, pp. 103–107.

Buffery, A.W.H. and Gray, J.A. (1972). 'Sex differences in the development of perceptual and linguistic skills', in C. Ounsted and D.C. Taylor (eds). *Gender Differences: their Ontogeny and Significance*. Baltimore: Williams & Wilkins.

Burchardt, C.J. and Serbin, L.A. (1982) 'Psychological androgyny and personality adjustment in college and psychiatric populations'. *Sex Roles*, vol. 8, pp. 835–51.

Carey, G.L. (1958). 'Sex differences in problem-solving performances as a function of attitude differences'. *Journal of Abnormal and Social Psychology*, vol. 56, pp. 256–60.

Child, I., Potter, E. and Levine, E. (1946). 'Children's textbooks and personality development: an exploration in the social psychology of education'. *Psychology Monographs* vol. 60, no. 3.

Clarizio, H.F. and McCoy, G.F. (1976). *Behavior Disorders in Children*, 2nd ed. New York: Crowell.

Coates, S.W. (1972). *Preschool Embedded Figures Test*. Palo Alto, California: Consulting Psychologists Press.

Connor, J.M. and Serbin, L.A. (1977). 'Behaviorally-based masculine and feminine activity preference scales for preschoolers: correlates with other classroom behaviors and cognitive tests'. *Child Development*, vol. 48, pp. 1411–16.

—— and Serbin, L.A. (1978). 'Children's responses to stories with male and female characters'. *Sex Roles*, vol. 4, pp. 637–45.

———, Serbin, L.A. and Ender, R.A. (1978). 'Responses of boys and girls to aggressive, assertive, and passive behaviors of male and female characters'. *The Journal of Genetic Psychology*, vol. 133, pp. 59-69.

———, Serbin, L.A. and Schackman, M. (1977). 'Sex differences on children's response to training on a visual-spatial test'. *Developmental Psychology*, vol. 13, pp. 293-4.

———, Schackman, M. and Serbin, L.A. (1978). 'Sex-related differences in response to practice on a visual-spatial test and generalization to a related test'. *Child Development*, vol. 49, pp. 24-9.

Doherty, E.G. and Culver, C. (1976). 'Sex-role identification, ability and achievement among high school girls'. *Sociology of Education*, vol. 49, pp. 1-3.

Dohrenwend, B. and Dohrenwend, B. (1976). 'Sex differences and psychiatric disorders'. *American Journal of Sociology*, vol. 81, pp. 1447-54.

Dwyer, C.A. (1973). 'Sex differences in reading: an evaluation and a critique of current methods'. *Review of Educational Research*, vol. 43, pp. 455-61.

Edelsky, C. (1976). 'The acquisition of communicative competence: recognition of linguistic correlates of sex roles'. *Merrill-Palmer Quarterly*, vol. 22, no. 1, pp. 47-59.

Ernest, J. (1976). 'Mathematics and sex'. *American Mathematics Monthly*, vol. 83, pp. 595-614.

Etaugh, C., Collins, G. and Gerson, A. (1975). 'Reinforcement of sex-typed behaviors of two-year-old children in a nursery school setting'. *Developmental Psychology*, vol. 11, p. 255.

——— and Harlow, H. (1975). 'Behaviors of male and female preschool teachers as related to behaviors and attitudes of elementary school children'. *Journal of Genetic Psychology*, vol. 127, pp. 163-70.

Fagot, B. (1977a). 'Consequences of moderate cross-gender behavior in preschool children'. *Child Development*, vol. 48, pp. 902-907.

——— (1977b). 'Preschool sex stereotyping: effect of sex of teacher vs. training'. Paper presented at the Annual Meeting of the Society for Research in Child Development, New Orleans.

——— (1978). 'Reinforcing contingencies for sex-role behaviors: effect of experience with children'. *Child Development*, vol. 49, pp. 30-6.

——— and Littman, I. (1976). 'Relation of preschool sex-typing to intellectual performance in elementary school'. *Psychology Reports*, vol. 39, pp. 699-704.

——— and Patterson, G.R. (1969). 'An in vivo analysis of reinforcing contingencies for sex-role behaviors in the preschool child'. *Developmental Psychology*, vol. 1, pp. 563-8.

Fain, P.R. (1976). 'Major gene analysis: an alternative approach to the study of the genetics of human behavior'. Boulder: University of Colorado. Unpublished doctoral dissertation.

Fennema, E. (1976) *Influences of Selected Cognitive, Affective, and Educational Variables in Sex-related Differences in Mathematics Learning and Studying*. Madison: Department of Curriculum and Instruction, University of Wisconsin.

——— and Sherman, J. (1977). 'Sex-related differences in mathematics achievement, spatial visualization and affective factors'. *American Educational Research Journal*, Winter, vol. 14, no. 1, pp. 51-71.

Flerx, V.C., Fidler, D.S., and Rogers, R.W. (1976). 'Sex role stereotypes: developmental aspects and early intervention'. *Child Development*, vol. 47, pp. 998-1007.

Fodor, I.E. (1974). 'Sex role conflict and symptom formation in women: can behavior therapy help?' *Psychotherapy: Theory, Research and Practice*, vol. 11, pp. 22-9.

Fox, L.H. (1975). 'Mathematically precocious: male or female?', in E. Fennema (ed). *Mathematics Learning: What Research Says about Sex Differences*. Columbia: ERIC Center for Science, Mathematics and Environmental Education, College of Education, Ohio State University.

Garai, J.E. and Scheinfeld, A. (1968). 'Sex differences in mental and behavioral traits'. *Genetic Psychological Monographs*, vol. 77, pp. 169-299.

Garrett, C.S., Ein, P.L. and Tremaine, L. (1977). 'The development of gender stereotyping of adult occupations in elementary school children'. *Child Development*, vol. 48, pp. 507-12.

Gayton, W.F., Haru, G., Barnes, S., Ozman, K.L., and Bassett, J.S. (1978). 'Psychological androgyny and fear of success'. *Psychological Reports*, vol. 42, pp. 757–8.

Gove, W. and Tudor, J. (1973). 'Adult sex roles and mental illness'. *American Journal of Sociology*, vol. 78, no. 4, pp. 812–35.

Graf, R.G. and Riddell, J.C. (1972). 'Sex differences in problem solving as a function of problem context'. *Journal of Educational Research*, vol. 65, pp. 451–2.

Guttentag, M. and Bray, H. (1976). *Undoing Sex Stereotypes*. New York: McGraw-Hill.

—— and Salasin, S. (1977). 'Women, men and mental health', in L.A. Carter, A.F. Scott and W. Martyna (eds). *Women and Men: Changing Roles, Relationships, and Perceptions*. New York: Praeger.

Hammen, C.L. and Padesky, C.A. (1977). 'Sex differences in the expression of depressive responses on the Beck Depression Inventory'. *Journal of Abnormal Psychology*, vol. 86, pp. 609–14.

Hanson, E.H. (1959). 'Do boys get a square deal in school?' *Education*, vol. 79, pp. 597–8.

Hartlage, L.C. (1970). 'Sex-linked inheritance of spatial ability'. *Perceptual and Motor Skills*, vol. 31, p. 610.

Heilbrun, A.B., Kleemeier, C. and Piccola, G. (1974). 'Developmental and situational correlates of achievement behaviour in college females'. *Journal of Personality*, vol. 42, pp. 420–36.

Hill, C.E., Hubbs, M.A. and Verble, C. (1974). 'A developmental analysis of the sex-role identification of school-related objects'. *Journal of Educational Research*, vol. 67, no. 5, pp. 205–206.

Hjelle, L.A. and Butterfield, R. (1974). 'Self-actualization and women's attitudes towards their roles in contemporary society'. *Journal of Psychology*, vol. 87, pp. 225–30.

Hutt, C. (1972). *Males and Females*. Harmondsworth: Penguin Books.

Jennings, S.A. (1975). 'Effects of sex typing in children's stories on preferences and recall'. *Child Development*, vol. 46, pp. 220–3.

Johnson, D.D. (1973–74). 'Sex differences in reading across cultures'. *Reading Research Quarterly*, vol. 9, pp. 67–86.

Koblinsky, S.G., Cruse, D.F. and Sugawara, A.I. (1978). 'Sex role stereotypes and children's memory for story content'. *Child Development*, vol. 49, pp. 452–8.

Krasner, L. and Ullman, L.P. (1973). *Behaviour Influence and Personality*. New York: Holt, Rhinehart & Winston.

Kuhn, D., Nash, S. and Brucken, L. (1978). 'Sex role concepts of two- and three- year olds'. *Child Development*, vol. 49, no. 2, pp. 445–51.

Landau, B. (1973a). 'This column is about women: emotional disturbances in childhood'. *Ontario Psychologists*, vol. 5, pp. 46–9.

—— (1973b). 'Women and mental illness'. *Ontario Psychologists*, vol. 5, pp. 51–7.

Lee, P.C. (1973). 'Male and female teachers in elementary schools: an ecological analysis'. *Teachers College Record*, vol. 75, pp. 79–98.

Lee, P.C. and Wolinsky, A.L. (1973). 'Male teachers of young children: a preliminary empirical study'. *Young Children*, vol. 28, pp. 342–52.

Levitin, T.E. and Chananie, J.D. (1972). 'Responses of female primary school teachers to sex-typed behaviours in male and female children'. *Child Development*, vol. 43, pp. 1309–16.

Looft, W.R. (1971). 'Sex differences in the expression of vocational aspirations by elementary school children.' *Developmental Psychology*, vol. 3, p. 366.

Maccoby, E.E. (ed.) (1966). *The Development of Sex Differences*. Stanford: Stanford University Press.

—— and Jacklin, C.N. (1974). *The Psychology of Sex Differences*. Stanford: Standford University Press.

Marantz, S.A. and Mansfield, A.F. (1977). 'Maternal employment and the development of sex-role stereotyping in five- to eleven-year-old girls'. *Child Development*, vol. 48, pp. 668–73.

Masters, J.C. and Wilkinson, A. (1976). 'Consensual and discriminative stereotyping of sex-type judgments by parents and children'. *Child Development*, vol. 47, pp. 208–17.

McNeil, J.D. (1964). 'Programmed instruction vs. usual classroom procedures in teaching boys to read'. *American Educational Research Journal*, vol. 1, pp. 113–19.

Nadelman, L. (1974). 'Sex identity in American children: memory, knowledge, and preference tests'. *Developmental Psychology*, vol. 10, pp. 413–17.

O'Leary, K.D., Kaufman, D., Kass, R. and Drabman, R. (1970). 'The effects of loud and soft reprimands on behaviour of disruptive students'. *Exceptional Children*, vol. 37, pp. 145–55.

Papalia, D. and Tennent, S. (1975). 'Vocational aspirations in preschoolers: manifestations of early sex stereotyping'. *Sex Roles*, vol. 1, pp. 197–9.

Parten, M.B. (1933). 'Social play among preschool children'. *Journal of Abnormal and Social Psychology*, vol. 28, pp. 136–47.

Pederson, D.M., Shihedling, M.M. and Johnson, D.L. (1975). 'Effects of sex examiner and subject on children's quantitative test performance', in R.K. Unger and F.L. Denmark (eds). *Woman: Dependent or Independent Variable*. New York: Psychological Dimensions.

Perdue, V.P. and Connor, J.M. (1978). 'Patterns of touching between preschool children and male and female teachers'. *Child Development*, vol. 49, pp. 1258–62

Pinkston, E.M., Reese, N.M., LeBlanc, J.M. and Baer, D.M. (1973). 'Independent control of aggression and peer interaction by contingent teacher attention'. *Journal of Applied Behaviour Analysis*, vol. 6, pp. 115–24.

Powell, B. and Reznikoff, M. (1976). 'Role conflict and symptoms of psychological distress in college-educated women'. *Journal of Consulting and Clinical Psychology*, vol. 44, pp. 473–9.

Quay, H.C. and Werry, J.S. (1974). *Psychopathological Disorders of Childhood*. New York: John Wiley.

Radloff, L. (1975). 'Sex differences in depression: effects of occupations and marital status'. *Sex Roles*, vol. 1, no. 3, pp. 249–65.

—— (1978) 'Sex differences in helplessness with implications for depression', in L.S. Hansen and R.S. Rapoza (eds). *Career Development and Counselling of Women*.

Ricks, F.A. and Pyke, S.W. (1973). 'Teacher perceptions and attitudes that foster or maintain sex role differences'. *Interchange*, vol. 4, pp. 26–33.

Saario, T.N., Jacklin, C.N. and Tittle, C.K. (1973). 'Sex role stereotyping in the public schools'. *Harvard Educational Review*, vol. 43, pp. 386–416.

Seligman, M.E.P. (1975). *Helplessness. On Depression, Development and Death*. San Francisco: W.H. Freeman.

Sells, Lucy W. (1973). 'High school mathematics as the critical fitter in the job market. Developing opportunities for minorities in Graduate Education, 47–59.' Proceedings of the Conference on Minority Graduate Education at the University of California, Berkeley, May 1973.

Serbin, L.A. (1972). 'Sex differences in the preschool classroom; patterns of social reinforcement'. Doctoral Dissertation, State University of New York at Stony Brook.

——, Citron, C.C., and Connor, J.M. Children's attention and recall of sex-typed and reversed sex-typed stories. Concordia University. Unpublished MS.

—— and Connor, J (1976). 'An experimental analysis of sex-stereotyped play behaviour: effects of teacher presence and modeling'. Paper presented to the Association for the Advancement of Behaviour Therapy, New York.

—— and Connor, J.M. (1979). 'Sex-typing of children's play preferences and patterns of cognitive performance'. *Journal of Genetic Psychology*, vol. 134, pp. 315–16.

—— Connor, J.M., Burchardt, C.J. and Citron, C.C. (1979). 'Effects of peer presence on sex-typing of children's play behaviour'. *Journal of Experimental Child Psychology*, vol. 27, pp. 303–309.

——, Connor, J.M. and Citron, C.C. (1977). 'Sex-stereotyped play behaviour in the preschool classroom: effects of teacher presence and modeling'. Paper presented at the annual meeting of the Society for Research in Child Development, New Orleans, March 1977.

——, Connor, J.M. and Citron, C.C. (1978). 'Environmental control of independent and dependent behaviour in preschool girls and boys'. *Sex Roles*, vol. 4, pp. 867–75.

——, Connor, J.M., and Iler, I. (1979). 'Sex-stereotyped and nonstereotyped introductions of new toys in the preschool classroom: an observational study of teacher behaviour and its effects.' *Psychology of Women Quarterly*, vol. 4, pp. 261–5.

——, O'Leary, K.D., Kent, R.N., and Tonick, I.J. (1973). 'A comparison of teacher response to the preacademic and problem behaviour of boys and girls'. *Child Development*, vol. 44, pp. 796–804.

——, Tonick, I.J. and Sternglanz, S.H. (1977). 'Shaping cooperative cross-sex play'. *Child Development*, vol. 48, pp. 924–9

Sexton, P.C. (1969). *The Feminized Male: Classrooms, White Collars and the Decline of Manliness*. New York: Random House.

Sherman, J.A. (1967). 'Problem of sex differences in space perception and aspects of psychological functioning'. *Psychological Review*, vol. 74, pp. 290–9.

Slaby, R.G. and Frey, K.S. (1975). 'Development of gender constancy and selective attention to same-sex models'. *Child Development*, vol. 46, pp. 849–56.

Stafford, R.E. (1961). 'Sex differences in spatial visualization as evidence of sex-linked inheritance'. *Perceptual and Motor Skills*, vol. 13, p. 428.

Stone, F.B. and Rowley, V.M. (1964). 'Educational disability in emotionally disturbed children'. *Exceptional Children*, vol. 30, pp. 426–32.

Thompson, S.K. (1975). 'Gender labels and early sex role development'. *Child Development*, vol. 46, pp. 339–47.

Tobias, S. and Donady, B. (1976). 'Counselling the math anxious'. Unpublished MS. Wesleyan University.

Todd, J. and Nakamura, C.Y. (1970). 'Interactive effect of informational and affective components of social and nonsocial reinforcer or independent and dependent children'. *Child Development*, vol. 41, pp. 365–76.

Urberg, K.A. and Labouvie-Vief, G. (1976). 'Conceptualizations of sex roles: a life span developmental study'. *Developmental Psychology*, vol. 12, no. 1, pp. 15–23.

Vener, A.M. and Snyder, C.A. (1966). 'The preschool child's awareness and anticipation of adult sex roles'. *Sociometry*, vol. 29, pp. 159–68.

Vondracek, S.I. and Kirchner, E.P. (1974). 'Vocational development in early childhood: examination of young children's expressions of vocational aspirations'. *Journal of Vocational Behaviour*, vol. 5, pp. 251–60.

Waterhouse, M.J. and Waterhouse, H.B. (1973). 'Primate ethology and human social behavior', in R.P. Michael and J.H. Crook (eds). *Comparative Ecology and the Behaviour of Primates*. London: Academic Press.

Wechsler, D. (1967). *Manual for the Wechsler Preschool and Primary Scale of Intelligence*. New York: Psychological Corporation.

Wender, P.H. (1971). *Minimal Brain Dysfunction in Children*. New York: John Wiley.

Williams, J.E., Bennet, S.M. and Best, D.L. (1975). 'Awareness and expression of sex stereotypes in young children'. *Development Psychology*, vol. 11, pp. 635–42.

Witkin, H.A., Ottman, P.K., Raskin, E., and Karp, S.A. (1971). *A Manual for the Embedded Figures Tests*. Palo Alto: Consulting Psychologists Press.

Wittig, M.A. (1976). 'Sex differences in intellectual functioning: how much difference do genes make?' *Sex Roles*, vol. 2, pp. 63–74.

Women on Words and Images. (1976). *Dick and Jane as Victims*. P.O. Box 2163, Princeton, New Jersey. Rev. edn.

Woody, R.H. (1969). *Behaviour Problems of Children in the Schools*. New York: Appleton-Century-Crofts.

# 4  Staffing for Sexism: educational leadership and role models*

*Michael Marland*

## Introduction

A schooling system that claims to offer its pupils the opportunities to develop their talents and help towards self-determination in their adult lives might be expected to itself have a career structure that demonstrated these virtues, one in which there was equality of the sexes in positions of influence and leadership, and no sex stereotyping of roles. Apart from the fairness and consistency of that expectation, it is reasonable to expect the pattern of adult employment in schools, that is all the staff including those who do not teach, to contribute powerfully to the lessons of the hidden curriculum: if there is a clear sexual division by function and seniority, a powerful message is being daily enacted for the pupils.

Most studies of the organization and management of schools put in the standard he/she disclaimer, and then outline the points to be made as if there was no gender pattern in school management. (Although the manuscript of one book on leadership in the primary school was submitted ingeniously with a note that 'throughout "he" will be used for the headteachers and "she" for the class teacher'!) In the growing literature on school organization insufficient attention has been given to the politics of power and the stereotyping of role resulting from the male/female inheritance we have in school management. An obvious

---

*A few sections of this chapter are derived from a paper I produced for the British Educational Management and Administration Society, 'The micro-politics of school improvement'.

exception to this gap is the compelling analysis of the changing role of the Senior Mistress at Nailsea School, Bristol, by Elizabeth Richardson (Richardson, 1973, pp. 227–332). She shows how in the development of that grammar school into a comprehensive school the perception of the role of 'senior mistress' was one of the blocks to the school's growth. I myself criticized 'the fallacy of the senior mistress' in an analysis of roles and responsibilities in pastoral care (Marland, 1974, pp. 94–8), claiming that in the larger complex school the introduction of 'intermediate pastoral heads' (heads of house or heads of year) 'often forces the senior mistress out on a limb, having literally no "place" in the hierarchical pattern . . . the senior mistress feels, and indeed actually is, out of the main stream' (ibid, p. 97). It has been left to the more avowedly feminist writers to study the balance of the sexes in school staffing.

For instance, Rosemary Deem has an interesting chapter on 'Women as teachers' (Deem, 1978, pp. 108–26) in which she clearly charts the relationship between the structure of capitalist society and the career reality. As she says 'teaching has promised more to the women entering it than it has actually given them, in terms of status, financial rewards, and career prospects . . . Women who enter teaching have been no less strongly socialized into accepting the existing sexual division of labour than have other women' (p. 109).

In the United States there have been studies by Lyon and Saario (1973), Taylor (1973), Clement (1975), and Gross and Trask (1976). Australia has also had some significant studies. Important as these analyses have been, many of them have focused almost entirely on the unfairness for women teachers and have not been discussed mainly from the point of view of the organization and curriculum of the school. There has thus been a gap between the organization studies and the feminist critiques. This chapter is planned to meet that need.

## Differential promotion

Although school teaching is one of the traditionally accepted female professions, and in the days of more single-sexed schools there were almost as many senior posts for women as for men, the ratio of men to women increases steeply the more senior the posts, especially in secondary schools. The following proportions of all the teachers in secondary schools in the UK on each scale were found by the HMI secondary survey to be women:

| Positions | Percentages |
| --- | --- |
| Probationers | 51 |
| Scale 1 | 58 |
| Scale 2 | 48 |
| Scale 3 | 34 |
| Scale 4 | 22 |
| Senior teachers | 20 |

From the balanced intake of probationers, what has happened to those women who do not go up the scales? Some stay on Scale 1 and many become part-time: 84 per cent of all part-time teachers in UK secondary schools are women (HMI, 1979, p. 47).

Looked at the other way round, the proportion of women and men who reach the different scale levels is significantly different. The 1978 National Union of Teachers figures in Table 4:1 combine primary and secondary schools.

**Table 4:1   Women and men teachers on different scale levels**

| | Percentage of all women and men teachers | |
| Scale | Women | Men |
|---|---|---|
| Senior teacher | 0·4 | 2·6 |
| 4 | 2·3 | 11·7 |
| 3 | 9·8 | 20·4 |
| 2 | 37·7 | 27·3 |
| 1 | 38·9 | 20·3 |

Source:  National Union of Teachers and Equal Opportunities Commission (1980), p. 55.

Similar figures are found in English and Welsh further education colleges, with 59·1 per cent of women in the lowest lecturer grade and tiny proportions in the highest grades (Table 4:2).

**Table 4:2   National statistics showing the sex of teachers in FE occupying each grade in 1975 ( % ) (excluding evening institutes and colleges of education)**

| Grade | Men | Women |
|---|---|---|
| Principal | 1·2 | ·2 |
| Vice-principal* | ·9 | ·1 |
| Other head of department | 4·7 | 2·0 |
| Principal lecturer | 6·3 | 1·7 |
| Senior lecturer | 19·1 | 8·8 |
| Lecturer grade II | 34·2 | 28·2 |
| Lecturer grade I | 33·7 | 59·1 |
| N = | 51 540 | 11 040 |

*Including vice-principals who were also heads of department (DES *Statistics of Education*, 1975, vol. 4, *Teachers*)
Source:  Bradley and Silverleaf (1979), p. 17.

These particular investigators did the revealing calculation of predicting the number of women who would reach each grade after standardizing for length of service, but presuming sex had no effect on promotion prospects. Table 4:3 shows the difference between predicted and actual.

Table 4:3  Relationship between actual and predicted numbers
of women teachers at each grade

|  | Actual numbers (A) | Predicted Numbers (P) | A/P |
|---|---|---|---|
| Vice-principal | 2 | 8 | ·25 |
| Head of department | 13 | 34 | ·38 |
| Principal lecturer | 22 | 47 | ·47 |
| Senior lecturer | 90 | 143 | ·63 |
| Lecturer grade II | 166 | 202 | ·82 |

Source: Bradley and Silverleaf (1979).

It will be seen that there is a fair chance of initial promotion, but that chance falls rapidly, so that the likelihood of a woman becoming a principal lecturer is less than half that of her male colleagues.

In the United Kingdom's largest education authority, the Inner London Education Authority, there is actually a higher proportion of women teachers in secondary schools than nationally (Table 4:4).

Table 4:4  Proportion of women secondary school teachers
nationally and in ILEA

| Women | National (%) | ILEA (%) |
|---|---|---|
| Proportion of full-time | 43 | 49·7 |
| Proportion of part-time | 80 | 69 |

Source: Mortimore (1981).

(Possibly the fact that the teaching force is younger accounts for these figures.) Nevertheless, the promotion differential is striking. The figures of women's leadership positions in the ILEA in 1981, shown in Table 4.5, might well be better than in many local education authorities, but the pattern is striking confirmation of the effects of differential promotion. In ILEA primary schools the differential can be even more sharply seen, for although 80 per cent of ILEA primary teachers are women, only 54 per cent are headteachers. Indeed the proportion of 80 per cent overall is distributed from 90 per cent in Scale 1, 83 per cent in Scale 2, 71 per cent in Scale 3, 62 per cent as deputy heads, and drops to 54 per cent as heads (ILEA, 1982).

There is, of course, a similar sexual balance in the inspectors/advisors, in LEA administrators, and in governing bodies. All these groups are very influential, and both symbolically and practically (in terms of attitudes towards appointments) the present balance is

Table 4:5    The percentage of women occupying posts within various senior categories in the Inner London Education Authority compared with the total of staff in those posts

|  |  | % |
| --- | --- | --- |
| (a) | primary-school headteachers | 55 |
| (b) | special-school headteachers | |
| | (i ) day | 48 |
| | (ii) boarding | 9 |
| (c) | boys' secondary headteachers | — |
| (d) | girls' secondary headteachers | 98 |
| (e) | mixed secondary headteachers | 22 |
| (f) | principals of colleges of further and higher education | 4 |
| (g) | principals of adult education institutes | 10 |
| (h) | staff, divisional and district inspectors | 28 |
| (i) | senior administrative officers | 23 |
| (j) | senior specialist posts | 19 |

Source:  Inner London Education Authority (1981).

unfortunate. There is little research that I know of which documents this sexual balance, but one study is particularly fascinating in its demonstration of the mis-match between those who govern and control and those who are the educational clients. In a study of Community Colleges in Leicestershire, institutions devoted to bridging the school/after-school gap and encouraging local control by users, M. T. Whiteside has shown the differences between governors, the colleges' management committee, and the college council:

> Despite the female predominance in college usage it was found that only one quarter of all governors were female. Questionnaire data showed that, on governing bodies, the few women were likely to represent parents. Membership of management committees, however, showed a marked shift towards representation of females, who made up nearly forty per cent of its total. On management committees, women were more likely than men to represent evening classes, and had above average representation from affiliated organisations and from teachers. However, women were considerably less likely to represent college council on the governing bodies. Thus, in terms of sex, college councils tended to elect representatives onto the governing body who were more like other governors than they were like other members of college council. (Whiteside et al., 1981, p. 41)

In this breakdown there is a clear demonstration of the differential representation displayed elsewhere – but on this occasion in a county and a type of institution specifically committed to representative accountability and control.

These examples of what can be called 'vertical segregation' (Hakim,

1979, p. 43) are consistent with trends in other kinds of British occupations, but appear to be amongst the worst. Catherine Hakim finds that over occupations as a whole 'the data also suggests a trend towards greater vertical segregation within broad categories of work'.

We do not have precisely comparable figures internationally, but the pattern revealed elsewhere is equally striking.

In the USA, for example, it is startling how few women become principals. The proportion decreased by 16 per cent from 1958 to 1968 (Clement, 1975, p. 7) and by 1971 only 6·5 per cent of all public secondary-school principals and vice-principals were women (even though the schools were all mixed) (Gross and Trask, 1976, p. 9).

Similar figures can be seen in other countries. For instance, in New South Wales, Australia, the figures are even bleaker (Table 4:6). Despite the much larger proportion of women teachers in primary schools, the pattern is the same as in secondary schools.

**Table 4:6    Proportion of women teachers in senior posts in schools in New South Wales**

*Secondary schools, New South Wales*

|  | Male | Female | Total | % Woman |
|---|---|---|---|---|
| Total teachers | 12 020 | 9 959 | 21 979 | 45·3 |
| Subject master/mistress | 1 698 | 288 | 1 986 | 14·5 |
| Deputy principals | 322 | 24 | 346 | 6·9 |
| Principals | 276 | 37 | 313 | 11·8 |

*Primary schools, New South Wales*

|  | Male | Female | Total | % Woman |
|---|---|---|---|---|
| Total teachers | 6 744 | 15 728 | 22 472 | 70·0 |
| Deputy principals | 703 | 167 | 870 | 19·2 |
| Principals | 1 286 | 113 | 1 399 | 8·0 |

Source: Derived from Jozefa Sobski (1979), pp. 21–2.

In these New South Wales primary schools young children would perceive the authority structure clearly in terms of 'who's in charge?' Despite the fact that in 1976 69 per cent of the primary teachers were women, only 10 per cent had authority (Arbib, 1978, p. 8), combining principals, teachers in charge of class 4 schools, and deputy and assistant principals.

The schools inspectors in New South Wales are another example. The ratio of women to men at the top levels has worsened, from 1:11 to 1:42, (Sexism in Education Committee, 1977, p. 64).

In 1978, women were also only 8% of school inspectors and tended to cluster in traditionally 'feminine' subject areas. Almost no women are represented in the upper echelons of the Department of Education, particularly at policy level. They have no say in decisions which profoundly affect them. (Anti-Discrimination Board, 1979)

As in the USA, the balance has not improved over the years. For instance, New South Wales analysed the proportion of male and female holders of 'promotion positions' between 1961 and 1976. Table 4:7 gives the findings.

**Table 4:7   Proportion of male and female teachers holding promotion positions in New South Wales in 1961 and 1976**

|      | Primary | | Secondary | |
| --- | --- | --- | --- | --- |
|      | *Male %* | *Female %* | *Male %* | *Female %* |
| 1961 | 60·7 | 39·3 | 76·3 | 23·7 |
| 1976 | 60·2 | 39·8 | 81·0 | 19·0 |

Source:  Sexism in Education Committee (1977), p. 58.

In the United States the old male dominance of Oxbridge is astoundingly replicated in the influential *Phi Delta Kappa*, described in its own words as 'a professional and honour society for men in education with chapters in many countries. It is the largest professional fraternity in the world. This membership is comprised of top leadership and outstanding professionals throughout the state.' It is, however, male.

The sheer numerical difference between women and men has powerful effects on the way schools are run, the message given to pupils, and the chances for young teachers.

## Career characteristics

Less frequently commented on, even by the most searching of the feminist writers, is the effect that this differential has on the characteristics of those who are promoted.

Because of the pressures that operate on career aspirations and opportunities and of the undoubted prejudice of the appointers, women holding senior posts frequently have more experience than men of the same level. In universities, Blackstone and Fulton found that in both the USA and the UK:

> There are practically no combinations of publication rate and age in which as many women hold senior ranks as do men; . . . in other words, even when they run twice as hard they [women] do not quite reach the same spot. (Blackstone and Fulton, 1975, p. 268)

In the USA, Gross and Trask found that women elementary school principals differed hugely in their length of teaching experience. The mean years of elementary teaching experience for women before they become principals was 14·7, compared with 4·6 for men! (Gross and Trask, 1976, p. 46). Indeed, in the USA all women teachers are more experienced than men: the averagewoman teacher has 13·1 years as compared with 9·0 for men (1966 figures, Clement, 1975, p. 7). As far as I know, there are no comparable figures for the UK, but, with its usual thoroughness, ILEA has analysed and published the figures showing the relationship between experience and promotion in its schools. In primary schools, even 'when length of service was taken into account, there was still an imbalance between men and women, with men being represented in the more senior posts and women in the less senior posts. For example, even among teachers with less than five years experience, more than fifty per cent of men had attained posts of Scale 2 or above, compared with just over thirty per cent of women' (ILEA, 1982, p. 2). Although the average length of service of all full-time women secondary teachers is less than that of men, similar figures to those of the USA are found amongst those women who do stay in the profession: 'men have a greater probability of early advancement in their careers' (ibid, p. 4).

# Role differentiation

The results of the vertical segregation and the differential experiences for those women who do manage to reach high positions is a sexist role differentiation. The kinds of responsibility tasks in which women in senior schools end up tend to have clear characteristics. It is easier for women to get promotion in the three stereotyped 'women's' fields: the young child; 'girls' subjects' (even in mixed schools); and pastoral care.

'Women's fields' are a crude reflection of the broader stereotypes about occupations. Secondary-school teaching subjects can be located on a continuum for the perceived suitability of women to teach them and be heads of departments. This continuum parallels the pattern for girls' entry to and success in school examination subjects. Craft, design, and technology, science and mathematics are the male end, home economics and business studies, the women's end. In the middle art, languages, English and the humanities can go to a woman if there is not a strong enough man.

A similar pattern is found throughout the world of developed schooling. For instance, a study in Western Australia found 'industrial arts' taught only by men, home economics only by women, and only one man in the entire state teaching commercial studies (Western Australia Committee appointed to enquire into the incidence of sex-based discrimination (1976), pp. 34–5).

Although 'the care' (as the phrase often is) of young children is usually thought of as being especially suitable for women, and many of the promoted posts gained by women are in the primary schools, headships of junior schools often go to men and infant schools to women. The actual proportion of the teachers in various kinds of schools in the UK makes this stereotyping clear. In Table 4.8 I have extracted the figures of men and women in each type of school, shown the percentage of full-time teachers who are women, and arranged the list of types of schools in rank order according to the proportion of women teachers:

**Table 4:8    Proportion of women and men teachers in different types of schools**

| | Full-time teachers | | |
| Type of school | Number women | Number men | % who are women |
| --- | --- | --- | --- |
| Nursery | 1 465 | 6 | 99·6 |
| Infant | 36 374 | 511 | 98·6 |
| First | 17 010 | 2 313 | 88·0 |
| JM and I | 59 272 | 21 028 | 73·8 |
| First and middle | 3 230 | 1 161 | 73·6 |
| Junior | 32 894 | 18 002 | 64·6 |
| Middle deemed primary | 5 854 | 3 237 | 64·3 |
| Special | 8 499 | 4 971 | 63·1 |
| Middle deemed secondary | 5 522 | 4 819 | 53·4 |
| Modern | 14 356 | 17 320 | 45·3 |
| Technical | 370 | 447 | 45·3 |
| Sixth-form college | 1 436 | 1 951 | 42·1 |
| Comprehensive | 65 903 | 90 634 | 42·1 |
| Grammar | 7 148 | 9 869 | 42·0 |

Source:  Derived from Department of Education and Science (1976).

So the message is that women are concerned with the very young (notice the difference between the first two types and the second two; and between 'Middle deemed primary' and 'Middle deemed secondary') or the Special, but in sixth-form colleges, comprehensive schools and grammar schools men are required for most positions. The list is virtually the same as the rank order according to the prestige of schools in the public mind. When in the secondary school women do reach senior positions, there is often a hidden catch: the post is limited to girls, or a mere rag-bag of chores, or limited to pastoral care.

Eileen Byrne rightly castigates the sexual divisions of senior staff in typical mixed schools:

> Twenty years of staffing schools has taught me that senior masters, apart from occasionally caning boys, typically deal with school organisation, curricular reconstruction, major administration, CSE examinations, and resource allocation, while senior mistresses typically deal with social functions, pregnant schoolgirls, difficult parents, coffee for and entertaining of visitors (in my experience), and school attendance. Equal is not held to mean the same here. (Byrne, 1978, p. 233)

The linking of women with the senior pastoral care posts in United Kingdom schools is particularly limiting. It springs from both a limited idea of the function of pastoral care (see Marland, 1974 and Best et al., 1980) and from a stereotypical view of women's 'special strengths'. The fatuous pairing of women with 'caring' is well documented:

> Two posts were advertised, one for the pastoral care of girls and one for curriculum development. I was interested in a curriculum development post. Men and women were interviewed on separate days and *I was only asked about pastoral care.* (NUT and EOC, 1980, p. 38. My italics.)

This is bad for women, pastoral care, curriculum development, and the political balance of the school.

Often the expectations are less formally embodied in the job specifications and structure, but are powerfully evident in the informal aspects of role given as an unstated gloss to the actual task. In writing about the declining role of the Senior Mistress at Nailsea School, Elizabeth Richardson quotes the post-holder, Joan Bradbury, as having 'a feeling that the staff wanted to keep her in the role of a kind of "school mum" ' (Richardson, 1973, p. 228). Richardson goes on to note that even though Joan Bradbury had important timetabling and administrative tasks, there was a 'reluctance of staff to recognise this side of her work'. In a particular political moment in staff discussions, Joan Bradbury declared that nobody listened to her: 'Nobody takes any notice until it comes out from a different face'. Richardson comments:

> Her feeling of having been unheard or ignored or forgotten was very strong; and it appeared to me that it was carrying something more than her own sense of frustration in the committee – something about the shared experience of women in general in a staff group like this, something about a sense of left-outing, of being considered of little account, of having to leave the major decisions to men, of denying their own capacity to take executive leadership even in a school in which girls had consistently outnumbered boys throughout its eleven years of existence. (Richardson, 1973, p. 230)

What seems to happen too often is that those with responsibility posts, men and women, get caught by a combination of external social attitudes and internal influences such as I have described to act out roles, and even to wish others to act out roles. The men create the roles for the women, who then in return create roles for the men which involve this prejudice. I have heard senior male teachers at governors' appointment meetings, staff discussion meetings and small-group discussions, almost goad women into acting the part. I have noticed when organizing residential in-service training courses that the ratio of women to men is startlingly different between courses on departmental management and ones on pastoral care. Perhaps most powerful is the range of concerns and reactions expressed by men and women in staff discussion and planning: I suspect that a typology of contributions to staff discussion would show a clear sex bias (though I also suspect it is declining).

Definite differences were also found in reactions to the task of leadership among women principals in the USA study. They appeared to have lower aspirations for professional advancement, tended to worry less about their work, and in the elementary school placed greater emphasis on three criteria for evaluating a school: 'its concern with individual differences among its pupils, the social and emotional development of its pupils and its efforts to help "deviant" pupils'. The study found that 'the professional performance of teachers and pupils' learning were higher on the average in the schools administered by women than by men' (Gross and Trask, 1976, pp. 218–19).

There would nowadays be much disagreement in the UK about the 'lower aspirations' for advancement, and indeed the NUT survey finds the opposite (NUT and EOC, 1980, p. 51). Also Bradley and Silverleaf do not find it except as influenced by lack of geographical mobility (Bradley and Silverleaf, 1979, p. 18). However, it probably was true not so long ago, probably is true among older or less well qualified women, and certainly is true of the mythology of schools.

Senior women teachers, then, have often had different promotional experience, greater difficulty in promotion, and are associated with a narrower range of tasks judged to be suitable for them. Having arrived, they are in a minority, may have developed differences of attitude and approach, and have to work in a climate that clearly does not expect senior women, except in a few traditional preserves. A combination of these factors often leads to a definite and strongly felt political situation in which there are pressures on attitudes, role tasks, discussions, arguments, and the very people themselves – both women and men. It is not, therefore, merely a numerical difference: the way up and the positions available are to a considerable extent different (and I suspect this is especially marked in certain areas in the country). This colours who applies, when they apply, and what they apply for. It also, again, teaches the young of both sexes.

With Gross and Trask, then, I must conclude that 'sex, indeed, does make a difference in the operation and management of schools' (Gross and Trask, 1976, p. 227). A school hoping to use its strengths most effectively in improving its work will need to face the powerful but not much analysed relationship between sex stereotypes, leadership roles and the in-school planning process. Again, the action needs to be part psychological, in that we all need to analyse ourselves and face what we find, and part structural, in that the school needs to monitor the male/female staff balance, ensure the roles and the structure are not warped by sex stereotyping, and encourage proper career development for women.

The picture revealed by all these figures seems to me to be even worse than one might have felt it to be from participation or casual observation. Furthermore it is a picture set against the pattern of ancillary staffing in schools which sharply demonstrates society's stereotypes: office staff – women; caretakers – men; cleaners (who are

their subordinates) – women; cooks – women; 'dinner ladies' –
women; librarians (if schools have them!) – women; and in the ILEA,
media resources officers – men.

There can be little doubt that such occupational differentiation
affects pupils' perceptions and creates what Catherine Hakim in a
Department of Employment study of occupational segregation calls
'prisons of the mind' (Hakim, 1979, p. 50).

## Reasons for the differential

Schools reflect and work by the biases of society, and that is in a way
a sufficient statement to explain the pattern, but it is worth concentrating on the main elements concerning education, for in such a
concentration lies the possibility of intervention. The most powerful
factor holding women back is probably the very stereotype that attracts
them into teaching. Catherine Hakim has analysed the (pre-sex-
discrimination legislation) concentration of two million women
workers in occupations in which over 90 per cent of all the employees
were women. She comments:

> With the possible exception of secretarial work, these are all occupations
> which offer paid employment for types of work carried out on an unpaid
> basis in the home by women . . . Thus a great many of the occupations in
> which women are over-represented are typically feminine in the sense that
> they draw on skills exercised on an unpaid and non-specialist basis within
> the home. (Hakim, 1979, p. 31)

In a sense the same is true of teaching. Katherine Clarnicoates'
research into primary-school teachers (in Spender and Sarah, 1980,
pp. 69–80) leads her to comment: 'Teaching . . . was seen not as contradiction but as something complementary to their "usual" and
"natural" role of wife and mother.' (p. 70)

To the extent that many women teachers, most particularly in
primary schools, are responding to the socialization of social prejudices
that suggest that women should have, indeed the prejudice is sometimes so naive that it suggests they simply *do* have, a so-called natural
feeling for the care and upbringing of small children, there will be little
or no attraction to promotion to managerial or administrative posts.
Especially in the USA where such posts are actually called 'Administrators', there can be a feeling not merely that such aspirations are 'not
for me', but even that such posts are antipathetic to the very motives
that brought such women into teaching.

The stereotyping I have described is powerful because it is so widespread and in a way self-fulfilling. It prevents many women even
contemplating certain posts. When they do apply, however, they
frequently hit definite discrimination. This is well documented in the
National Union of Teachers/Equal Opportunities survey, (NUT/
EOC, 1980, pp. 51–4):

Of all people, women teachers should realise the importance of devoting oneself to one's children while they are small.

Men with junior experience are capable of organising infant departments, but women teachers are not presumed to be capable of organising junior departments.

Lou Buchan has given the fullest chronicle that I know of a woman's struggle through procedural and attitudinal prejudice (Spender and Sarah, 1980, pp. 81–9). Her graphic account of the 'sophisticated and pernicious mechanisms for disqualifying women' includes the full gamut of stereotypes, including the jibe on achieving promotion that the inspector 'must have liked your legs'.

There is a very definite sex differential in satisfaction with pay, with women reporting higher levels of satisfaction with pay than men, even though their earnings distribution is lower. For instance, 1978 data showed that women earning £4000 per annum expressed a similar level of satisfaction to that of men earning £6000 (Hakim, 1979, p. 51). One reason would seem to be the socialization of women to *expect* less than men, and another that people tend to compare their salaries with their own sex. Either way, these facts support the idea that for the majority of women there is less salary dissatisfaction and therefore less drive to promotion. In view of the distribution of earnings in teaching that is not surprising. Turnbull and Williams (1974) have shown the sex differentials in the form of a simple earnings order:

1  Male graduate in secondary school
2  Male graduate in primary school
3  Female graduate in secondary school
4  Male non-graduate in secondary school
5  Male non-graduate in primary school
6  Female graduate in primary school
7  Female non-graduate in secondary school
8  Female non-graduate in primary school.

There are a number of factors which come simply from the still more common expectation that the male career will dominate. Thus in the Bradley and Silverleaf further education survey only 2·1 per cent of women had moved home three times or more to gain promotion, whereas the comparable figure for men was 6·3 per cent. They also showed, as must be true of schools also:

> The prospects of becoming a senior lecturer were almost doubled for the geographically mobile, while the chances of reaching head of department status and above were even greater. The relative lack of mobility among women must therefore be seen as a definite disadvantage in terms of promotion. (Bradley and Silverleaf, 1979, p. 17)

A stronger force in inhibiting even applications from women for promotion is the widespread expectation by both women and men that the responsibilities for the house and more particularly the children are especially female. Thus time and again the women primary teachers interviewed by Katherine Clarnicoates expressed things like:

> I really dread getting the flu or something that forces me to stay at home. My husband really does help me a lot but . . . if I ever get poorly . . . you know you can see the house literally coming down about your ears. The pattern . . . the routine you've built up to keep one step ahead of everything just falls apart. I've always believed that no one is indispensable but sometimes I wonder . . . and he can't understand why I get so 'het up'. All he says is 'Leave it until *you* get better'. I know it sounds ridiculous but I just can't afford to be ill. (in Spender and Sarah, 1980, p. 78)

Whereas even the man concerned with the balance of home and school put it only like this:

> It's quite a conflict really to sort out time given to teaching and time given to my family . . . you know you've only a few hours in which to teach . . . it's hard to decide – well – how many hours can I give to school and how much time do I give to the family. (ibid., p. 79)

There seems no doubt that for many women 'emancipation' has meant merely the freedom to do two jobs and bear a double load, and that many men married to teachers, especially primary teachers, consider that teaching leaves their women with time and energy to take much more than a half share of the house. No wonder such women do not consider adding to their tension, burden and guilt by applying for promotion. The ILEA figures bear this out: an analysis of all applications for secondary posts of Scale 3 and above in 1981 showed that only 39·6 per cent of applicants were women (ILEA, 1982, p. 5). (In mixed and boys' schools the rate of success was about the same; overall, including girls' schools, women did proportionately better.)

In some school systems there are procedures for promotion that clearly make it especially hard, indeed virtually impossible, for women to gain promotion. The following extract from a report by the New South Wales Anti-Discrimination Board on the Secondary Teaching Service makes clear that the system *requires* movement to achieve the necessary 'seniority', and that 'seniority' is a formal requirement, lost if there is a career break for child-rearing:

> There is no true equal opportunity in the New South Wales Secondary Teaching Service because women cannot comply successfully with the promotion rules, regardless of their merit and suitability for leadership roles.
>
> The main reason for women's inability to compete in what is not essentially a seniority system is that they cannot move home and family about the State in order to take up vacancies, as many men do. Another impediment is loss of accreditation on re-entry to the Service after periods of child-raising.
>
> Barriers to permanency (a pre-requisite for promotion) include medical requirements, compulsory superannuation membership and the demand for Statewide mobility. These requirements take no account of women's typical life patterns.
>
> Perhaps the most significant barrier results from lateral transfer of

promoted teachers. This is due to a leap in seniority which a promoted teacher gains. Men typically take up a country promotion and then, after a qualifying period, transfer to a more desirable location. Wave after wave of younger men repeatedly overtake capable women who are anchored to a particular district and consequently remain at the junior level. Before 1961 women were not even permitted promotion in co-educational schools.

The result of this direct and indirect discrimination, which has been structured into the system, is that women are disappearing from the top positions in schools. For example:

|  | 1961 | 1979 |
|---|---|---|
| Female Principals | 44 (22%) | 34 (10%) |
| Female Deputies | 38 (20%) | 23 ( 7%) |

In 1979, the Principals' Promotions (eligibility) List has 157 names on it, only 6 of whom are women who are mostly low in seniority order and are unlikely to be appointed as they may reach retiring age before their turn comes. Thus far in 1979, 33 new principals have appointed, *none* of whom are women.

Without a thorough overhaul of current rules and practices this decline in numbers will inevitably continue until there are virtually no female principals or deputies in New South Wales high schools. (Anti-Discrimination Board, 1979)

It is arguable that the Burnham system in the UK is less overtly discriminatory as formal seniority is not required, and application can be made from any scale position to any other – even though leaps are not very common. However, the legal impossibility of giving promoted posts to part-time teachers must severely affect women's careers. While there are obvious practical problems about carrying leadership responsibilities without teaching full-time, these are not insuperable. In fact, certain responsibilities, for example, for aspects of the curriculum, could equally well be done by a part-time teacher. Indeed, the HMI study of primary schools revealed that only a quarter of the present responsibility holders exercised an influence outside their own classrooms! (HMI, 1978). Such posts could be thought of as visiting consultants, with a reduced teaching load.

## A programme for professional equality

Can schools be so different from society that the vertical segregation of most occupations can be avoided? Probably not completely, but I am convinced that the present shocking discrepancies could be substantially improved. For this to be done the central deficiency in the teaching profession from the point of view of career development has to be faced. This itself is not entirely a problem of sex differentiation and careers, but one of very poor procedures for career guidance and development for teachers. Women have the disadvantages of facing prejudice, having reduced geographical mobility, often mid-career breaks, and possibly possessing self-images and concepts of teaching which are less amenable to seeking responsibility posts. It is inevitable that they will be the main losers from the poor career development help for teachers. The best evidence in the UK comes the the ILEA's studies of its teachers' promotion applications and success. This shows clearly that the problem is much less bias at the appointing stage and much more the effect of the pressures I have described in keeping women from applying:

> The monitoring of recent applications has shown that women have at least as good a chance as men of being appointed to the senior posts to which they apply. However, since more men apply for these posts, more men are still being appointed to all senior posts, except Scale 3, in the Authority's secondary schools, thus maintaining the present imbalance. One implication of these analyses is that the imbalance would be reduced if more women could be encouraged to apply for senior teaching posts. (ILEA, 1982, p. 9)

If these unfortunate difficulties are to be alleviated, considerable efforts are required by government, system, school, in-service providers and professional counsellors. My word 'alleviate' may seem insufficiently optimistic, but I am mindful of how serious the situation is, and how difficult it will be to work against what two USA writers have called: 'the effects of years of massive, systematic, and perhaps unthinking injustice' (Lyon and Saario, 1973, p. 123).

The following suggestions for action make what I hope is a coherent, complementary package, approaching the problem from a number of different directions:

1 Local education authorities should actively seek women for consideration for promotion to senior positions

2 Figures of male and female holders of all promoted positions in schools and LEAs should be regularly gathered and published, and governing bodies should consider those for their school annually

3 Appointing boards should be so composed and briefed that the existing biases against women are modified

4 Job specifications of senior posts should be scrutinized to ensure there are no essentially sexist roles

5 DES, colleges and departments of education, and LEAs should increase and make more practical in-service training for middle and senior management

6 Heads, principals, heads of departments, and other team leaders should ensure that proper career counselling and a programme of career development is available for all staff, and that women teachers are given help appropriate to their needs

7 Schools with women working part-time for a period but hoping to return to full-time work later should have a deliberate programme:

(a) to keep the part-timers fully in touch (it is common for schools to exclude part-timers from full communication and involvement)

(b) to endeavour to give them some specific if modest responsibility beyond their own timetable to keep their hand in and to prepare for later formal responsibility

(c) to ensure they have a full programme of career development,

including monitoring of their work (see Stokes, 1981), evaluation discussions, and career counselling.

8 Despite the poor employment prospects in the mid-1980s, LEAs
should provide courses to assist the re-entry of mature women to
full-time teaching, and these courses should include specific training for holding responsibility

9 There should be a review of the salary structure and formal promotion system to ensure there are no covert sex discriminatory
procedures.

## Conclusion

The triple reasons for removing the sex differentiation in the staffing of
education are overwhelmingly convincing:

1 Equality for professionals to advance to the levels and types of work
for which they have the qualities and experience

2 Opportunity for schools to be led, planned, managed, and evaluated by both women and men for the good of the curriculum,
organization and leadership

3 Models for boys and girls to observe adults of both sexes taking the
full range of positions and levels of responsibility.

The facts show that we are as far away from attaining these goals as
ever: we need to start the programme at once.

## References

Anti-Discrimination Board (New South Wales) (1979). *Report on a Practice in the New
South Wales Secondary Teaching Service*. Anti-Discrimination Board, New South Wales.
Arbib, Patricia (1978). *Sexism and Schools*. New South Wales: NSW Department of
Education.
Best, Ron, Jarvis, Colin and Ribbins, Peter (1980). *Perspectives on Pastoral Care*.
Heinemann Educational Books.
Blackstone, Tessa and Fulton, Oliver (1975). 'Sex discrimination among university
teachers: a British-American comparison'. *The British Journal of Sociology*, vol. XXVI,
no. 3, pp. 261–75.
Bradley, Judy, and Silverleaf, Jane (1979). 'Women teachers in further education'.
*Educational Research*, vol. XXII, no. 1, pp. 15–21.
Byrne, Eileen M. (1978). *Women and Education*. Tavistock Publications.
Clement, Jacqueline Parker (1975). *Sex Bias in School Leadership*. Evanston, Illinois:
Integrated Education Associates.
Dale, R.R. (1969) *Mixed or Single-sex School*, 3 vols. Routledge & Kegan Paul.
Deem, Rosemary (1978). *Women and Schooling*. Routledge & Kegan Paul.
Department of Education and Science (1975, 1976). *Statistics of Education*. HMSO.
Gross, Neal and Trask, Anne E (1976). *The Sex Factor and the Management of Schools*.
John Wiley.
Hakim, Catherine (1979). *Occupational Segregation*. A comparative study of the
degree and pattern of the differentiation between men and women's work.
Department of Employment.
HMI Inspectorate (1978). *Primary Education in England*. HMSO.
——— (1979). *Aspects of Secondary Education*. HMSO.

Inner London Education Authority (1981). *Education Committee Minutes*. ILEA.
—— (1982). *Secondary Schools Staffing Survey*. Report by the Education Officer, 22 July, 1982, ILEA.
Lyon, Catherine Dillon, and Saario, Terry Tinson (1973). 'Women in public education: sexual discrimination in promotions'. *Phi Beta Kappa*, vol. LV, no. 2, pp. 120–3.
Marland, Michael (1974). *Pastoral Care*. Heinemann Educational Books.
Mortimore, Peter (1981). 'Characteristics of secondary school teachers: implications for in-service planners'. *British Journal of In-Service Education*, vol. 7, no. 3, pp. 187–92.
Musgrove, Frank (1971). *Patterns of Power and Authority in English Education*. Methuen.
National Union of Teachers and Equal Opportunities Commission (1980). *Promotion and the Woman Teacher*. NUT and EOC.
Partington, G. (1976). *Women Teachers in the Twentieth Century*. Windsor: NFER Publications.
Richardson, Elizabeth (1973). *The Teacher, the School, and the Task of Management*. Heinemann Educational Books.
—— (1975). *Authority and Organisation in the Secondary School*. Schools Council Research Studies. Basingstoke: Macmillan Education.
Sexism in Education Committee, New South Wales Ministry of Education (1977). *Report of the Committee on Sexism in Education*.
Sobski, Jozefa (1979). *Submission to the Teacher Education Inquiry, with Particular Reference to the Position of Women and Girls in Education*. The Social Development Unit, New South Wales Ministry of Education.
Spender, Dale and Sarah, Elizabeth (eds) (1980). *Learning to Lose, Sexism and Education*. The Women's Press.
Stokes, Peter (1981). 'Monitoring the work of teachers', in Michael Marland and Syd Hill. *Departmental Management*. Heinemann Educational Books.
Taylor, Suzanne A. (1973). 'Educational leadership: a male domain?'. *Phi Delta Kappa*, vol. LV, no. 2. pp. 124–8.
Turnbull, P., and Williams, G. (1974). 'Sex differentials in teachers' pay'. *Journal of the Royal Statistical Society*, Series A. vol. 137, no. 2, pp. 245–58.
Western Australia Committee appointed to inquire into the incidence of sex-based discrimination (1976). *Males and Females in the State Education System of Western Australia*. A Report to the Minister for Education, July 1976.
Whiteside, M.T., Tann, C.S., and Gann, N. (1981). *The Three New Community Colleges*. Final report of the research project based at Leicester University School of Education. Social Science Research Council. Available from the British Lending Library.

# 5 Anxiety, Aspirations and the Curriculum

*Margaret B. Sutherland*

Women are more anxious than men, girls are more anxious than boys. This has been repeatedly established, in a variety of investigations. And while it could be said, unkindly, that in a world where the conduct of affairs and policy decisions are in the hands of men, the anxiety of the female half of the population is self-explanatory, on a serious level it is important to consider this difference in anxiety. It is also important to note that the explanation I have just mentioned would be a sweeping generalization. In discussing differences between the sexes it is essential not to assume that these differences are absolute; though there may be differences on average, there is always considerable overlap – and this is true about anxiety levels as it is true about other observed average differences.

But we have to pay serious attention to this matter of anxiety on the part of females, for although we may do much, by changes in legislation and by the provision of education, to produce more equal opportunities for both males and females, these changes and improvements are going to be ineffectual unless we manage to change the feelings of females about making use of these opportunities. If anxiety remains characteristic of many girls and women, we are simply going to retain the *status quo*. Access to higher education has been open to women for many years now, but we have by no means achieved equality in representation of the sexes there. While there is a great variety of causes for this, one apparent cause is the anxiety which leads many girls to decide that they would not do well in such studies and so to opt out of them. Even more strikingly, we have had equal political rights for many years now but the number of women MPs remains astoundingly low. Yet if women think 'I'd feel I was making a fool of myself, making speeches in public' or 'How could I know what the right policy was?' or 'No one would vote for me!', it is not surprising that the number of female Members of Parliament remains small. Unless we can do something about the level of anxiety in girls, their aspirations will be self-protectively low, and any attempts to increase equality of opportunity will be frustrated. Anxiety prevents females from taking advantage of opportunities open to them.

So there are various questions to be answered about anxiety. First, what is it? Secondly, is it really a good or bad characteristic? Thirdly, what can we do about it?

## Definitions of anxiety

I should make it clear that I am talking about anxiety in the everyday sense of that word. It is a word used also to describe a pathological state of illness – and women are also more likely than men to suffer from it (though there is some evidence (Leighton, 1967) to suggest that the incidence of such illnesses may be socially conditioned). But if we take the ordinary meaning, we find that a distinction has been made between state anxiety and trait anxiety:

> Anxiety states (A-states) are characterized by subjective, consciously perceived feelings of apprehension and tension, accompanied by or associated with activation or arousal of the autonomic nervous system. Anxiety as a personality trait (A-trait) would seem to imply a native or acquired behavioural disposition that predisposes an individual to perceive a wide range of objectively non-dangerous circumstances as threatening and to respond to these with A-state reactions disproportionate in intensity to the magnitude of the objective danger. (Spielberger, 1966)

It is useful to be reminded of the physiological components of anxiety but what mainly concerns us is the anxiety trait – the continuing tendency to feel that certain situations may be too much for us to cope with; that in certain circumstances we may be made to look foolish and our self-esteem consequently reduced. It is not simply a matter of avoiding physical dangers or being worried about them; it is especially the tendency to foresee the possibility of failure and loss of self-respect, the uncertainty about a possibly damaging outcome of a situation. But we may differ in our reactions to the anxiety: Cronbach and Snow (1977) note that: 'We conceive of the anxious person as alert to threats. He may have a ready coping style that handles a particular threat effectively (e.g. conformity, dependency) or he may become emotionally disorganised.'

This matter of 'coping style' deserves more attention than it has had so far in educational research. All too often, research tries to find out if people are 'anxious', then studies relationships between the trait and other traits or performances; but as educators we should be more concerned as to what people do when feeling anxious. Do they conform, avoid the situation – or work to ensure that the foreseen unpleasant result does *not* take place? It is the 'coping strategy' which determines whether anxiety is debilitating or facilitating.

## Assessment of anxiety

How in fact do we know if people are anxious? The assessment of anxiety has mainly been by questionnaires, asking such questions as: 'Do you feel nervous if people watch you working?'; 'Are you frequently afraid you may make a fool of yourself?'; 'Do you worry very much that something bad is going to happen?'; 'When you are taking a test does the hand you write with shake a little?' (see Phillips, 1978). But of course such questionnaires are open to criticism. We may not all mean the same thing by the words used and there may be social conventions about the anxieties we think we can admit to. Sarason (1960) suggested that his discovery of greater apparent anxiety in girls than in boys might be due to the fact that it is socially more acceptable for females than for males to admit to such reactions. But there is also the problem of knowing whether different tests of anxiety measure the same thing – or whether tests apparently measuring different things are in fact measuring the same common characteristic. Certainly there seems to be much in common in the questions asked and the characteristic measured by tests of anxiety, stress or introversion and neuroticism as investigated by Eysenck (1969). It has indeed been said (Cronbach and Snow, 1977) that 'American Anxiety is British Neuroticism and Introversion'.

If we do not rely on questionnaires for assessment, we can try to judge by the individual's own spontaneous statements, or even by individual actions; but obviously much depends on the willingness of the individual to admit to anxious reactions – and again, on the coping style of the individual. Alternatively we can ask peer groups or other observers, for example, teachers, to assess those they know for anxiety characteristics. Peer groups may give some useful information here. Teachers are not always very good at making assessments which correspond to the individual's own assessments or to those of the peer group; but since many individuals think they conceal their anxiety well from the rest of the world, and since many do try to conceal this trait, it is perhaps not altogether astonishing that teachers are not always well able to assess the true state of affairs. (Presumably it is more difficult to 'cover up' with peers.)

## Causes of anxiety

Causes have also not been clearly defined. It may well be that a multiplicity of causes is present, some in the individual, some in the environment and experiences. The amount of uncertainty as to the outcome of a situation seems to be important – which of course depends partly on the individual's estimate of ability to cope with the situation. Pavlovian experiments long ago showed the possibility of producing nervous breakdown by making it increasingly impossible for the (non-human) subject to judge the precise nature of a stimulus and, consequently, to predict the right response to make. But individual capacity to endure uncertainty may also depend on characteristics of the central nervous system or biochemical reactions within the individual. Or, in other cases, the physical developments of adolescence may make the individual unsure of ability to control events. So, apart from cases where the environment subjects some individuals to conditions of danger and unusual stress, there are many circumstances which can lead to anxiety states and anxiety traits. It has to be noted, however, that in girls anxiety develops well before adolescence (Sarason, 1960; Barker-Lunn, 1972; Bennett, 1976). It is interesting to speculate whether the observed tendency of girls in childhood to attend to adult approval, while boys tend to concentrate on peer-group reactions, could mean a greater uncertainty about approval, leading to greater anxiety about performance on the girls' part.

## Is anxiety good or bad?

Initially I suggested that anxiety is a damaging characteristic since it can prevent women and girls from using the opportunities that are open to them. But perhaps that is to dismiss anxiety too readily: it can, as suggested earlier, also be facilitating. For in common experience, people sometimes find that some degree of anxiety is helpful. They may indeed worry that they are not worrying enough about some project. Certainly, from the teaching point of view, we may feel that it is time some pupils were anxious about the results of their lack of application. One of the most interesting cases of possibly helpful anxiety is the case of stage fright or 'first night nerves', for we are assured by many highly successful performers that it is normal for them to feel nervous, highly anxious, before going on stage to perform. This is associated with very good, successful performances whereas the performance given when this feeling of preliminary anxiety has been lacking is often less satisfactory, not at the individual's best level. (Though we must also note that not all performers have this reaction; and some highly nervous people can also give a thoroughly bad performance.) Inevitably we come back to the pattern illustrated by the Yerkes-Dodson work of 1908, a curvilinear relationship between amount of arousal and performance. A certain amount of anxiety seems to correlate with the best performance; too much or too little anxiety means a performance which is less good. This finding has been replicated in a number of researches dealing with a variety of learning or skill situations (Cronbach and Snow, 1977), though some investigations have not found the expected 'arch' relationship.

What complicates research results and causes problems in the teaching situation is the variety of other factors which affect the relationship between anxiety and performance. One is the difficulty level of the task. For simple tasks, anxiety level is best low; and for very difficult tasks, again, it is desirable for it to be low. But the feedback which is received or not received during the performance can be important. Uncertainty about whether the individual can cope may be reduced, progressively, by the assurance of doing well (for example, feeling the audience responding, getting the answers right); negative feedback can increase anxiety; and absence of feedback leaves the anxiety and uncertainty unaltered.

But feedback also depends on how well the individual is actually performing; and this in turn depends on the ability level of the individual. So that in a learning or performance situation we may have the four types of interaction: individuals who are high in ability and high in anxiety; those who are low in ability and high in anxiety; or those who are high in ability and low in anxiety or low in both ability and anxiety. Teachers frequently recognize such types: pupils who can be infuriating because they have the ability to perform well but do not bother to give a really first-class performance; or the able pupil who on occasion does not do herself justice because of 'nerves' or 'trying too hard'; and the occasional unfortunate who does try but without successful outcomes, or who goes completely 'to pieces', so that what might have been a just passable performance fails dismally. Then there are those who seem to have little ability but little concern about this situation – should they be regarded as blessed and left to take life easily?

Looking at these interactions and the indications that anxiety – in just the right amount – is valuable, we might conclude that the role of the teacher is to decrease the anxiety of those who have too much and to induce anxiety in those who have too little so as to ensure optimal performance all round. But – apart from the delicate problem of judging what is too much and too little in these circumstances – we cannot leave it at that. For what is important is how the individual decides to cope with an anxiety-causing situation. In many of the researches cited, and in many school situations, the individual *has* to face the anxiety-causing problem and to cope with it, effectively or ineffectively. But there is another very popular strategy for coping with an anxiety-causing situation – avoidance.

## Avoidance of anxiety

After all, from the individual's point of view this seems an ideal solution. If there is a danger of loss of self-esteem in a certain situation, and if that situation can be avoided, then the obvious action to take is to evade the situation, walk away from it, do something else. While this might seem to some moralists an unworthy response, that view is not likely to be taken by the average child or even the average adult – the more so as the avoidance may have no undesirable consequences for other people. Indeed the individual taking evasive action may instead do something which other people rather like or approve of. Any loss or damage may be to the individual alone – a loss of enjoyment, a missed opportunity to make progress and to enhance the individual's self-esteem, a failure to develop a potential ability which, in the long run, would have benefited others as well as the individual. But such losses and damages are hypothetical; the escape from the anxiety-causing situation is real.

In the case of girls and women society positively encourages such avoidance reactions. It is – by popular tradition – charmingly feminine not to state political opinions in public, not to seek positions of responsibility and authority. It is good to cultivate domestic science skills; it is right for a woman to think of marriage as more important than a career. So if girls have anxieties about their ability to do mathematics or science, then they take advantage of our permissive school system and opt out – possibly choosing domestic science instead of physical science. If they are uncertain about their academic ability, they do not have to face the expected rigours of university courses – they can opt for colleges of education instead. If they have worried about their first degree achievements, then they do not need to try for a higher degree. And no one forces them to stand for election within organizations or for Parliament or to seek promotion at work. So females quietly and with social approval take avoiding action.

I should not like it to be thought that I suggest these other occupations and situations are without anxiety-causing components. Indeed, the field of human relationships is one in which uncertainty and anxiety can abound. But the failures and successes are perhaps less publicly marked and less clearly defined there; and human relationships are unavoidable. I would not suggest either that the alternative studies do not demand rigorous standards of achievement; but these hazards are less clearly foreseen; and assessment and feedback may differ. One could say that in domestic science, for example, there is often a positive satisfaction from practical activities which may be lacking in more abstract subjects. Cake-making may offer a positive feedback which is lacking in the composition of French prose. And of course there are other, perfectly good, reasons for choosing such subjects and courses of study.

## Aspirations

Consequently, one way of dealing with anxiety is to set one's level of aspiration so that one feels reasonably confident about reaching it (though in research situation tasks the highly anxious tend to set unrealistically high or low goals for themselves). Girls and women are at times commended for the 'realism' of their vocational aspirations. Barker-Lunn (1970) found that at the 11 + level girls' career choices were more down to earth than those of boys – they were ready to opt for such occupations as nurse, secretary. But is there something to be said for setting the sights higher – for test pilot or star? And Kelsall (1970) found women students more ready than men to adjust their future plans in the light of their success or otherwise during university years. But should women have enough confidence to ignore possibly temporary setbacks and stick to the higher aspirations they once set themselves? All too often we find that girls and young women do not expect to earn as high salaries, or reach as eminent positions in their chosen occupation. Is this excessive realism?

Certainly the statistics of entries for external examinations show the extent to which girls avoid the subjects in which females are thought to be less likely to succeed than males. The drop-out from mathematics and science has been amply documented and discussed. But in avoiding these subjects, girls are renouncing a very great range of occupations. They are deliberately excluding important work possibilities, even if, at the moment of decision, not all girls are clear as to the future consequences of avoiding certain subjects (my colleague Jackie Bould effectively demonstrates this point – see Chapter 9).

Society readily accepts the modest aspirations of girls. Moreover, when girls do aspire to uncharacteristic careers or subjects, there are social reactions which seem calculated to reinforce anxiety: 'You won't have much chance of getting a job in that area'; 'Won't you feel odd as the only girl in a group of men?'; 'A PhD is rather a toss-up for a woman'; 'Aren't you making rather an exhibition of yourself?'

Again, one recognizes that there may be other reasons for limiting one's aspirations. Some people may simply prefer an easy-going life. But when the tendency of girls is so markedly towards aiming at work and positions which are at a level well below that to which their abilities could bring them, it does seem probable that the avoidance of anxiety is influential in at least some cases. And when one finds the very ready acceptance of a limited choice of subjects, the enthusiasm for avoiding subjects which are traditionally (and actually) found difficult by girls, then it seems that girls are indeed taking the easy way out. They are avoiding situations in which they expect to fail or in which, at best, they feel highly uncertain of success.

## Adapting the curriculum

In these circumstances of self-limited ambitions and avoidance of certain subjects of study and the careers they lead to, what can schools do to try to reduce the bad effects of girls' anxiety?

### Methods

It seems probable that greater care in the choice of methods used in teaching especially the 'problem' subjects might serve to reduce the uncertainty which girls feel in these areas. Unhappily, research results do not show consistently satisfactory results for a given method. Once again various other factors come into the reckoning here – the method that suits able pupils may be unsatisfactory with slower pupils; the conviction with which a teacher uses a given method may have some effect on the response of the class; the general atmosphere of the classroom and of the school may contribute to helping or hindering pupils' progress. Here, too, pupils of different personality types will respond differently to permissive or formal methods, as Bennett's research (1976) and that of others has indicated. Nevertheless, it is likely that some methods would be more beneficial than others for the anxious learner. When feedback reassures the learner, anxiety may be lessened; and here, obviously, programmed learning would appear valuable – though research with this technique has shown that we must also maintain the reassurance of a personal interest in the pupil's progress (and for the less anxious pupils it may be necessary to adjust the programme to prevent too leisurely an approach to learning).

Similarly, there is some research evidence, though not as yet fully conclusive, to suggest that girls respond less happily than boys to discovery methods. The more anxious learners prefer to know whether they are doing the right thing; and they like to have the situation clearly defined for them. Once again, it is important for them to have feedback as to the correctness of their progress. So while the curriculum must eventually develop the self-confidence to explore ideas and situations for oneself, it is probable that structured lessons and courses, at least in the earlier stages of study, are going to be helpful to girls who are uncertain of their own competence in a subject area. There is indeed a general value in clear presentation of what is expected of the learner; the purpose set before classes should be explicit as should the standards by which work will be assessed.

## Modelling

One of the more reassuring experiences for the anxious female learner seems to be to see someone of the same sex successfully carrying out the task which is to be learned. The influence of the mother's example in girls' decisions to stay at school beyond the statutory leaving age, to seek higher education, to combine marriage with a career, has been noted in various investigations (for example, Rauta and Hunt, 1975). This consideration makes us look thoughtfully at the relative advantages of single-sex and coed schools, so far as they provide or fail to provide reassurance for girls with anxiety about their ability, as females, to succeed in various subjects and in positions of authority. It must be admitted that in the girls' school the pupils are more likely to perceive that women can hold positions of authority, can organize, can speak in public, can teach and study the whole range of school subjects. There is also no problem about girls finding themselves a minority group in a class if they opt for a subject normally thought of as a 'boys' subject'. There are of course many factors to be considered in the coed versus single-sex schools debate, but in view of the evidence which has been produced about the reinforcement of sex bias in choice of subjects in coed schools, the recent almost universal moves towards coeducation suggest that – as so often happens in these educational 'reforms' – changes have been made without careful consideration by administrators of their possible effects.

But we must also recognize that the female teacher is not always considered an appropriate 'model' by the teenage girl. The teacher's competence may seem to the girl something remote from her own abilities. Hence it is useful to consider the extent to which schools could use the influence of rather older girl pupils to reassure anxious learners of their competence in such areas as mathematics and science. Some work reported by Keating (1976) and Casserly (1978) indicates that this influence of older girl pupils has, in some groups, increased the confidence of the younger girls, reduced their desire to drop out of these subjects, and even reduced their anxiety about being thought 'less feminine' if they like such studies.

Increased attention is, fortunately, being given to the less direct kind of modelling which occurs when illustrations in textbooks and other materials show – or fail to show – people with whom the learner can identify as an expert in the subject area. (But as schools too often are condemned to go on using old books – especially in these times of shortage of resources – the effect of biased illustrations still has to be guarded against.)

## A compulsory curriculum

One way of preventing the avoidance by girls of anxiety-producing subjects would, of course, be to make all subjects compulsory, at least to the end of the compulsory period of education. One would hope that in such a situation the known compliance of girls would triumph and they would find themselves learning successfully the subjects which, otherwise, they would have discarded; and presumably they would then, as they found themselves succeeding, lose their anxiety about these subjects. Here there is a certain amount of evidence about the possible results of such a policy if one looks at the experience of other countries which have set a compulsory curriculum before their pupils. In Sweden one has to admit that after a nine-year basic comprehensive-school curriculum in which only a very limited amount of time is given to options, massive sex bias is evident in the subjects chosen for study in the upper secondary stage (Nordic Council of Ministers, 1979). Yet in the Soviet countries where, similarly, a common curriculum is studied by both boys and girls during the basic comprehensive school period, there is a greater proportion of girls entering first degree studies in higher education in the science and applied science areas (even if, in the latter case, some sex bias is still evident); and occupations entered by girls in East Germany, for example, do show much greater numbers of females taking up work formerly regarded as the province of males (Staatliche Zentralverwaltung für Statistik, 1975). Admittedly the effects here depend not only on the school policy but on the labour market and employment policy. Nevertheless, at least girls leaving school in these countries have studied science and mathematics to a more advanced level than most of those in systems where they can opt out of these areas. So possibly there is something to be said for the compulsory curriculum – and the relatively modest recent regulation of the Department of Education and Science that all future teachers shall at least have a qualification equivalent to O-level mathematics.

## Counselling

If we are nonetheless going to continue with a school system which allows considerable freedom to the pupil to decide which subjects are to be avoided, then we must take steps to see that pupils are better advised as to their choice of subjects. In particular, it is important to make it clear to girls how many career opportunities they may be renouncing by what seems an easy choice of a subject which will give them, they think, less trouble and worry. Counselling is a skilled occupation. Teachers who undertake it must also be clear about the effects of subject choices and about the motivations which may underlie the apparently innocuous and conventional choice of courses by girl pupils.

Counselling also is important at another level, in giving help and guidance to those pupils in whom anxiety is at a greater than average level – those pupils whose lives really are made miserable by their apprehensions of failure and loss of self-esteem. This type of anxiety should be diagnosed early; and whatever is possible done to reduce it, using specialist resources where necessary.

## Parents

It must be recognized that all too often parents can be causes of anxiety. Parents naturally transmit their expectations of their children, and the children, according to the realism of the standards set and according to their own personalities and abilities, live up to these expectations, or avoid situations in which their inability or unwillingness to fulfil the expectations will be evident. Again, the anxieties of parents play their part in this interaction and this is an aspect of home life which has received insufficient attention, though some work has been done on it (Entwisle and Hayduk, 1978). Schools then must be in touch with parents and must try to avoid the situation where the patient work of the school in reducing a girl's anxiety about her general ability, career prospects or success in certain subjects is counteracted by parents who are full of traditional prejudices and expectations about girls' abilities.

## To stimulate or reduce anxiety?

In this discussion of curriculum development, we have been assuming that anxiety is to be reduced; yet, as we have noted, on occasion anxiety appears to be valuable. Can we afford to dispense with it altogether? Is there a danger that, if we do so, we shall produce a situation where people produce performances which are not as good as they could be? Might girls, in particular, become less hard-working and less satisfactory pupils?

It all comes back to the question of motivation. Somehow the school has to give those experiences of successful performance which enhance self-esteem and which encourage individuals to enjoy further such enhancement by better performance. It also has to give experience of the enjoyment which results from working to optimum capacity. (These prescriptions are admittedly easier to write than to follow.)

Possibly, in discussions arising in social or moral education classes, some assistance could be given towards developing effective anxiety-reducing strategies by illustrating the processes of (a) becoming clearly aware of what the problem is; (b) thinking what, if anything, can be done to solve the problem and ensure a good outcome; (c) taking appropriate action; (d) having taken this action, refraining from further speculation as to a bad outcome. But this is a highly rational process, difficult to teach and difficult to apply. It seems that the experiential approaches earlier indicated in the discussion of curriculum adaptation might be more effective – and they would certainly be easier to follow.

Teachers thus have, in this area of their work, a particularly difficult task. They must be aware of the effects that anxiety may be having on the work and aspirations of a variety of individual pupils (boys as well as girls). They must try to judge where stimulation is required and where reassurance is essential. They must be skilled in diagnosing the motivation of pupils and in developing the better kinds of motivation. And of course they must meanwhile cope with their own anxiety and aspiration levels – and teaching is probably one of the most anxiety-stimulating occupations.

Nevertheless it is essential that the school system should act to reduce the effects of debilitating anxiety experienced especially by the female population, and discourage the fatally easy strategy of avoiding the problem situation. Without such improvements, other improvements in the educational and social circumstances of girls are likely to be nullified.

## References

Barker-Lunn, J.C. (1970). *Streaming in the Primary School*. Windsor: NFER Publishing.
——(1972). 'The influence of sex, achievement level and social class on junior school

children's abilities', *British Journal of Educational Psychology*, vol. 42, no. 1, pp. 70-4.

Bennett, N., (1976). *Teaching Styles and Pupil Progress*. Open Books.

Casserly, P.L., reported in *ETS Developments*, New Jersey, vol. XXV, no. 3 (1978).

Cronbach, L.J. and Snow, R.E. (1977). *Aptitudes and Instructional Methods*. New York: John Wiley.

Entwisle, D.P. and Hayduk, L.A. (1978). *Too Great Expectations*. Baltimore and London: Johns Hopkins University Press.

Eysenck, H.J. and Eysenck, S.B., (1969). *Personality Structure and Measurement*. Routledge & Kegan Paul.

Keating, D.P. (ed.) (1976). *Intellectual Talent: Research and Development*. Baltimore and London: Johns Hopkins University Press.

Kelsall, R.K., Poole, A. and Kuhn, A. (1970). *Six Years After*. Sheffield: Higher Education Research Unit, University of Sheffield.

Leighton, A.H. (1967). 'Some observations on the prevalence of mental illness in contrasting communities' in R. Platt, and A.S. Parkes (eds) (1967). *Social and Genetic Influences on Life and Death*. Edinburgh and London: Oliver & Boyd.

Nordic Council of Ministers (1979). *Sex Roles and Education*. Secretariat for Nordic Cultural Co-operation, Denmark.

Phillips, B.N. (1978). *School Stress and Anxiety*. New York and London: Human Sciences Press.

Rauta, I. and Hunt, A. (1975). *Fifth Form Girls: their Hopes for the Future*. HMSO.

Sarason, S.B. et al. (1960). *Anxiety in Elementary School Children*. New York: John Wiley.

Spielberger, C.D. (1966). *Anxiety and Behaviour*. Academic Press.

Staatliche Zentralverwaltung für Statistik (1975). *Die Frau in der DDR*. Dresden: Verlag Zeit im Bild.

Yerkes, R.M. and Dodson, J.D. (1908). 'The relations of strength of stimulus to rapidity of habit-formation'. *Journal of Comparative Neurological Psychology*, vol. 18, pp. 459-82.

# 6 Sex Differences in Achievement Orientations: consequences for academic choices and attainments

*Barbara G. Licht and*
*Carol S. Dweck*

A large body of recent literature has examined children's beliefs about their performance in situations of intellectual achievement. One of the most intriguing findings is that girls, relative to boys, have less confidence in their ability to succeed in challenging intellectual tasks. This pattern emerges during the pre-school and early school years despite the fact that girls consistently perform as well as, if not better than, boys during these years across a variety of achievement domains. Girls' lower level of confidence is of great interest not only because it seems unrealistic, but because it appears to have a detrimental effect in the long run on girls' intellectual accomplishments. In this chapter we examine children's achievement-related beliefs which seem to affect their intellectual performance; the nature and origins of sex differences in these beliefs; and the ways in which an understanding of these variables can help us explain some known patterns of sex differences in achievement that emerge in the later school years (for example, boys' greater achievements in mathematical areas and girls' greater achievements in verbal areas). We then report our own recent research designed to examine directly the beliefs that may underlie sex differences in mathematics and verbal achievement. We also explore some new avenues of research which suggest that it may be the brightest girls who show the most maladaptive beliefs, and conclude by presenting some preliminary suggestions for altering the self-limiting tendencies that girls are likely to develop.

## Sex differences in achievement-related beliefs and behaviours

A number of studies have examined how children view the causes of the difficulties* they experience in achievement situations (ie., causal attributions for failures). It has been found that children's causal attributions are among the best predictors of how they will perform in the face of failure. When confronted with difficulty, children who attribute their failures to variable or controllable factors (in particular, insufficient effort) are more likely than other children to maintain high expectations for future successes (Diener and Dweck, 1980; McMahan, 1973; Nicholls, 1975; Weiner et al., 1971; Weiner et al., 1976; Jackaway, 1975). They are more likely to respond with increased effort and, consequently, they may be prompted to show higher levels of problem-solving as a result of confronting failure (Diener and Dweck, 1978, 1980; Dweck, 1975; Dweck and Bush, 1976; Dweck and Reppucci, 1973; Weiner, 1972, 1974; Weiner et al., 1971; Licht and Dweck, 1982). In contrast, children who attribute their failures to factors that are stable and beyond their control (particularly insufficient ability) tend, in the face of difficulty, to lower their expectations for future successes; and they are less likely than other children to increase their efforts in order to meet such challenges. In fact, they may respond with a deterioration of effort and performance so marked that they are unable to solve virtually the same problems they had solved with ease prior to confronting difficulty. These children have been called 'learned helpless' since their causal attributions imply that the termination of failure is beyond their control (see Dweck and Reppucci, 1973, cf. Seligman and Maier, 1967). The term 'helpless' in this context, however, does not imply that these children are actually facing an uncontrollable failure, but rather that they appear to believe they are.

Several investigators have tried to alter the way that helpless children respond to failure by altering their causal attributions for failure. They have directly taught children to attribute their failures to insufficient effort in order to determine whether the children would then maintain or even increase their efforts when confronted with

---

*The terms 'difficulty', 'failure', 'obstacles', 'challenges' are frequently used interchangeably in this chapter. They generally refer to difficulties of the magnitude that children frequently encounter in school (for example, a series of difficult problems). These terms are not meant to imply a *major* academic setback (for example, failing a subject or grade level).

difficulty. The success of these procedures (Andrews and Debus, 1978; Chapin and Dyck, 1976; Dweck, 1975; Fowler and Peterson, 1981; Schunk, 1982) is important, not only because of its clinical/educational implications, but also because it demonstrates that children's beliefs about their achievements are more than just predictors or reflections of their achievement behaviours – they can actually be among the *causes*.

When one considers the logical implications of children's causal attributions, it becomes clear why they have the effects they do. Since one's abilities are generally viewed as relatively stable, the belief that one's difficulties are caused by insufficient ability implies that failure may well continue despite one's efforts (Weiner, 1972; 1974; Weiner et al., 1971). Thus a lowering of expectations and effort should follow. A lessening of one's efforts should, in turn, further lessen one's chances for success. Thus the child's beliefs about his/her abilities are likely to be confirmed regardless of the validity of these beliefs. In contrast, attributing a failure to insufficient effort implies that an increase in effort or alteration of strategy should result in a successful outcome. Thus, it is not surprising that these children maintain high expectations of future success even in the face of difficulty. Furthermore, increased effort should be the logical consequence of such an attribution. Since in many situations, increases in effort will indeed pay off with improved task performance (even if one's abilities are not particularly high), this attribution is likely to be reinforced. Thus, children's attributions not only have implications for the behaviour that immediately follows failure, but the consequences of these attributions make them self-perpetuating, regardless of how accurate or inaccurate these beliefs may be.

A similar logic is applicable to the attributions that children make for their successes. Children who attribute their successes to variable factors such as luck should not maintain stable, high expectations, even if they have experienced considerable success in the past. Since one's luck can change at any minute, so too can one's successes if they are due primarily to luck. In contrast, children who view success as an indication that they possess the necessary abilities should, after experiencing success, possess high expectations of future success on this and similar tasks. Indeed, attributions of success to ability are associated with high levels of confidence following success, while success attributions to luck are not (Diener and Dweck, 1980; Nicholls, 1975).

Not only are children's attributions related to their expectations, achievement efforts, and subsequent level of performance, but some research is emerging which suggests that one's attributions may also affect one's emotional reaction to achievement situations (Covington et al., 1980; Nicholls, 1975, 1976a, 1976b; Sohn, 1977; Weiner, 1974; Weiner et al., 1979). While failure is generally associated with a negative affective response and success with a positive affective response, one's emotional reaction is also a function of the attribution one makes for the particular outcome. For example, when faced with failure, attributing it to insufficient ability is associated with the greatest amount of negative affect. While the view that one's failures resulted from not trying hard enough may elicit some feelings of guilt, this does not appear to be as distressing (Covington et al., 1980; Nicholls, 1975; 1976b). In light of the literature which shows that negative emotional arousal can interfere with cognitive functioning (see Paul and Bernstein, 1973), it is likely that the debilitating effects of failure on the performance of helpless children are partly mediated by the negative emotional reaction elicited by the attributions they make for their failures. In a similar vein, attributing one's successes to ability is associated with the greatest positive affect, while attributions of success to luck give rise to comparatively little satisfaction (Nicholls, 1975; 1976a; 1976b).

As suggested at the outset, girls are more likely than boys to show the helpless pattern of achievement-related beliefs and behaviours. Girls are more likely than boys to attribute their failures to ability, while boys are more likely to view their difficulties as stemming from insufficient effort (Dweck and Bush, 1976; Dweck and Reppucci, 1973; Nicholls, 1975; Licht and Shapiro, 1982; Nicholls, 1978a). Boys are also more likely than girls to blame the evaluator (for example, the teacher's unfairness or fussiness) for their difficulties (Dweck and Bush, 1976; Licht and Shapiro, 1982). While this attribution may result in lower expectations and efforts in the current situation (as long as that teacher or evaluator is in charge), it still allows a boy to maintain confidence in his intellectual abilities. Thus, when the evaluator is no longer present, the child should respond with renewed hope of success (Dweck, Goetz and Strauss, 1980).

While girls are more likely than boys to use ability as an explanation for failure, they are less likely than boys to use ability as an explanation for their successes. They show instead a stronger tendency than boys to view their successes as due to factors such as luck, which imply some uncertainty about their ability to succeed in the future – particularly if the tasks are expected to become more difficult (Nicholls, 1975; 1976b; Licht and Shapiro, 1982; Nicholls, 1978a).

Consistent sex differences also emerge when investigators ask children to indicate how well they expect to do on novel achievement tasks that the children are about to undertake. In this setting, girls tend to underestimate their chances for success – given their level of past achievements and given the performances that they subsequently display. In contrast, the expectations of boys are inclined to be overestimates (Crandall, 1969; Montanelli and Hill, 1969; Parsons et al., 1976; Jackaway, 1975; see also Lenney, 1977 and Maccoby and Jacklin, 1974 for reviews). This sex difference can also be found when children are asked to predict future academic performances (Battle, 1966; Crandall, 1969; Dweck et al., 1980; Heller and Parsons, 1981; Parsons et al., 1982), despite girls' history of superior grades during elementary school (Dweck et al., 1980; McCandless et al., 1972; see also Maccoby and Jacklin, 1974 for review).

Not only do girls hold lower expectations of success for themselves when they enter a new situation than do boys, but girls' expectancies are also more likely to deteriorate when encountering difficulty or heightened evaluative pressure (Dweck, Goetz and Strauss, 1980; Dweck and Gilliard, 1975; Nicholls, 1975); and girls' expectations are less likely to recover again even when the situation changes substantially. Dweck et al. (1980) found that after encountering failure (which lowered the expectations of both sexes), a change in the evaluator resulted in a greater recovery of expectations for boys than for girls (predicted on the basis of boys' greater tendency to blame the evaluator); and a change in both the task and the evaluator resulted in a return of boys' expectations to their pre-failure levels. Girls, however, failed to show such a complete recovery. As the authors suggested, it may be that when girls blame their ability for their failures, the ability that they condemn is not specific to any one task. Rather they may be blaming a more general ability which would lead them to view a failure on a particular task as an indication that they will encounter difficulty across a variety of achievement situations.

It is not only the case that girls and boys may provide different explanations and draw different implications from their successes and failures, but there is also some data to suggest that the sexes may differ in how they evaluate their performance in the first place. Parsons et al. (1976), for example, report a study where girls rated their performance on a concept identification task more poorly than boys did, despite the fact that the girls had actually performed better.*

In view of these sex differences in children's achievement-related beliefs, it is not surprising to find sex differences in the tasks children seek and in how they respond to the challenges they confront in intellectual achievement situations. Boys are more likely than girls to choose difficult tasks over easy ones both in the laboratory and in a naturalistic free-play setting (Butterfield, 1965; Crandall and Rabson, 1960; Molnar and Weisz, 1981; Nicholls, 1978b; Veroff, 1969); and once they have chosen to begin a difficult task, they are more likely than girls to persist until it is successfully completed (Molnar and

---

*It is worthwhile to underscore an issue that, while suggested at several earlier points, could easily get lost. That is, girls do not demonstrate lower levels of confidence in their abilities to succeed on all tasks in all achievement situations. Rather, as others (Crandall, 1969; Dweck et al., 1980; Dweck and Licht, 1980; Lenney, 1977; Parsons et al., in press) have noted, the characteristic pattern of sex differences is most likely to emerge when there is some uncertainty of success. The expectations of both sexes are more in line with 'reality' when the tasks are highly familiar and/or perceived as easy; when children have received unambiguous feedback reflecting on the likelihood that they will succeed or fail; and when children are prompted to attend carefully to the relevant data from their past performance or feedback. The confidence of the two sexes diverges, however, when the tasks are novel and/or difficult – in other words, when children are confronted with challenges.

Weisz, 1981). Girls, in contrast, are more likely to avoid those situations that hold the threat of failure. Furthermore, in situations where children do not have the option of choosing the tasks they wish to work on, boys are more likely to meet difficult tasks and evaluative pressures with an escalation of effort, while girls sometimes show lower achievement efforts in difficult and evaluative situations than in situations where success is more assured (Dweck and Bush, 1976; Dweck and Gilliard, 1975; Harter, 1975; Nicholls, 1975).*

While girls' response to failure and evaluative pressure may seem unreasonable given the evidence of their ability (high grades, etc.), it is quite consonant with their causal attributions. However, given the evidence of girls' actual ability, it is reasonable to ask how they come to attribute failures to low ability.

# The origins of sex differences in children's achievement-related beliefs and behaviours

As suggested earlier, sex differences among children in the confidence with which they approach challenging situations of intellectual achievement is particularly intriguing since it emerges at an age when girls and boys do not seem to differ in terms of their relevant reinforcement histories. If anything, girls should come to expect greater academic achievements, since in the primary years they receive consistently higher grades. A number of explanations have been offered to account for this apparent irrationality.

It has been suggested that the sex difference in children's confidence may not be 'real' at all, and that it may reflect no more than the attempts of both sexes to present themselves in a socially desirable light (Hill and Sarason, 1966; Sarason et al., 1960; see also Crandall (1969) and Lenney (1977) for discussion). That is, girls may be responding in a way that makes them appear modest because modesty is in line with society's stereotype of what females should be. Boys, in turn, may be responding in a highly confident manner because self-confidence is consistent with society's masculine stereotype (see Bem (1974) for description of stereotypes).

While there may be some truth in this argument, it cannot adequately account for the large body of research that demonstrates girls' lesser confidence in their intellectual abilities. First, as Lenney (1977) points out, in several studies, assessments of expectations and

---

*It should be noted that it is not all girls who show the helpless pattern of beliefs and behaviours nor is it the case that all boys are mastery-oriented. Within each sex, one is bound to find almost the entire range of helpless and mastery-oriented patterns. Nevertheless, sex differences in these patterns do emerge in a large number of studies; and they can be of sufficient magnitude to cause concern. An understanding of the mechanisms that underlie sex differences in achievement-orientations will undoubtedly help us explain individual differences within each sex.

other achievement-related beliefs were solicited with procedures that provided anonymity to the respondents. Thus, there should have been little motivation for those subjects to present themselves in a socially desirable fashion (that is, in accordance with sex-role stereotypes). Crandall (1969) also examined the plausibility of the social desirability hypothesis. She reasoned that if socially desirable responding were an important influence in these studies, then children who were most strongly motivated to present themselves in a socially desirable light should also be the most likely to state expectations in the manner that was 'appropriate' for their own sex. She found, however, no relationship within either sex between the tendency to present oneself in a socially desirable light and the degree to which one responded in a sex-appropriate manner. Thus, the sex differences outlined above appear to be quite 'real'.

Many of those who accept girls' lower level of confidence as a 'real' phenomenon also invoke sex-role stereotyping explanations. It has been proposed, for example, that the parents of girls generally reinforce dependency and insecurity while parents generally reinforce their sons for being independent and self-confident (Hoffman, 1972). However, there has been little positive support for such differential treatment of young boys and girls (see Maccoby and Jacklin, 1974 for review). Furthermore, even if this differential upbringing does occur to some degree, it cannot fully account for the particular pattern of sex differences that occurs. Specifically, Dweck and Bush (1976) found that the sex difference in helplessness varied as a function of who was evaluating the children's performances. Girls showed the helpless pattern of attributions and performance primarily when the evaluator was an adult female. In fact, when the evaluator was perceived to be a peer – particularly one of the same sex – the pattern of sex differences was actually reversed. That is, boys showed greater helplessness than girls. If boys were generally socialized to be confident about certain abilities and girls were generally socialized to be insecure about theirs, girls should have responded more helplessly than boys regardless of who was providing the evaluation. That this was clearly not the case suggests instead that if one wishes to understand why girls respond in a 'helpless' fashion to situations of intellectual achievement with adult female evaluators, the most fruitful approach would be to examine the kinds of interactions children have had in that very situation. In the elementary school years, most evaluations for intellectual performances are given by the teacher, who in most cases will be female.

It has been suggested that the differential expectations that teachers hold for boys and girls may have an impact on their differential levels of confidence (Fox, 1976a). While research supports the view that teachers' expectations can have an impact on children's performances (see Brophy and Good (1974) for review), it has not been demonstrated that elementary-school teachers hold lower expectations for girls. In fact, in the elementary school years, teachers often hold girls in higher esteem. They rate girls more highly than boys on almost every conceivable dimension, including their effectiveness as learners (Coopersmith, 1967; Digman, 1963; Stevenson et al., 1968). Furthermore, children of both sexes accurately perceive the teachers' more favourable view of girls (Dweck and Goetz, 1977). It is unlikely therefore that elementary-school teachers foster lower levels of confidence in girls by directly communicating lower expectations for them. Further support for this argument is provided by a study reported in Parsons et al. (1976) where children were asked to give their expectations of their future performances on a series of tasks as well as their perceptions of how other people – their teacher, parents, and best friend – would expect them to perform. There were no differences between girls and boys in their perceptions of what significant others would expect from them. Girls and boys differed markedly, however, in how their own expectations corresponded to their perceptions of what others would expect. For boys, there was a very strong correspondence between these two sets of expectations. For girls, their own expectations were related only to the expectations they felt their teachers would hold for them, and even here this relationship was considerably weaker for girls than it was for boys (for boys, $r = \cdot 90$; for girls $r = \cdot 53$). It is clear that, at least in the elementary-school years, girls and boys do not develop different expectations because they believe that significant others have different expectations of them. Rather, girls and boys appear to differ in how they interpret or incorporate the expectations that others may have for them.*

Another explanation for the sex differences described above was proposed by Crandall (1969). In view of the fact that girls do not receive more negative evaluations of their abilities, she suggested that girls were more *sensitive* to the negative feedback they did receive, while boys were more sensitive to the positive. Indeed the attributions children make for their successes and failures (at least when it is delivered by adult female evaluators) are clearly in line with this. As discussed above, girls are inclined to see their failures as indicative of their abilities; therefore, it is their failures that will be viewed as predictive of future outcomes. Since girls are less likely to view their successes as predictive of future performances, they should pay less attention to their successes than to their failures. For boys, the situation is reversed – it is their successes that are viewed as informative.

In order to examine some of the factors that might lead girls to see their failures as indicative of ability and boys to view their successes as

---

*The expectations that parents hold for the intellectual accomplishments of their daughters also fall short of accounting for the lower confidence of girls. Parents, like teachers, do not appear to develop differential expectations for the two sexes until adolescence (see Maccoby and Jacklin (1974) for review) – long after girls begin to doubt their own abilities. It may be the beliefs that children hold concerning their own abilities that shape the expectations parents develop for their children.

indicative of theirs, Dweck et al. (1978) examined teacher–student interactions in fourth- and fifth-grade classrooms. The observers coded every instance of evaluative feedback in terms of the sex of the child receiving the feedback, whether the feedback was positive or negative, and to what the feedback referred. Feedback could either refer to the child's school work or to the child's conduct (for example, get back to your seat; you're sitting so nicely and quietly). Work-related feedback was further categorized into feedback that referred to the intellectual quality of the child's work (for example, your answer is wrong; your ideas are good) versus feedback that referred to non-intellectual aspects of the child's work (for example, you didn't skip lines; your paper was neat).

Several aspects of the teachers' evaluations were expected to affect the way in which children would interpret this feedback; and the Dweck et al. (1978) investigation examined whether the evaluations given to boys versus girls differed along these dimensions. It was predicted that the overall positive or negative quality of the teacher–student interaction would affect the child's interpretation of negative evaluations. That is, if a teacher were generally critical of certain children, these children might, over time, come to attribute their low marks to the teacher's overall negative attitude toward them rather than to the actual quality of their work (cf. Enzle et al., 1975; see Kelley, 1971). It was also expected that children would be less likely to view negative evaluations (for example, a low grade) as indications of intellectual inadequacies if the negative feedback they received in class referred largely to non-intellectual aspects of their school work (cf. Cairns, 1970; Eisenberger et al., 1974; Warren and Cairns, 1972). In contrast, a negative evaluation would more readily be viewed as an indication of low ability if in the past the criticisms received referred exclusively to the intellectual quality of the child's work. Finally, children's causal attributions should be affected by any explicit attributions that the teachers made for the children's failures.

Parallel predictions could be made regarding how children come to interpret success feedback. If a teacher has been generally positive toward certain children and has in the past praised them for non-intellectual matters, then a high grade may be attributed to factors that do not reflect on the children's intellectual competence (for example, favourable attitude of the teacher, one's neatness). In contrast, when a child receives a positive evaluation from a teacher who has in the past been generally negative and who has given little praise for non-intellectual matters, the positive evaluation is more likely to be viewed as a reflection of the intellectual quality of the child's work.

Thus, boys' tendency to discount their failures as indications of their abilities and girls' tendency to discount their successes would be understandable if (1) teachers were generally more negative towards boys (see also Brophy and Good, 1974); (2) a substantial proportion of the criticisms directed toward boys, but not toward girls, referred to conduct and non-intellectual aspects of their work; and (3) the teacher explicitly attributed boys' failures to factors other than ability (for example, lack of effort). This is indeed what was found. While the amount of positive and negative feedback that was directed at the *intellectual* quality of the children's work was virtually equivalent for the two sexes, there were striking differences in the receipt of negative feedback for non-intellectual matters. Boys received far more criticism than girls for their conduct and for the non-intellectual aspects of their work. In fact, of all the negative feedback boys received in the classroom, nearly two-thirds was directed at non-intellectual matters. Even if one looks only at the feedback directed towards the children's work, nearly half (45 per cent) of the work-related criticism boys received referred to aspects of their performance that could not reflect on their intellect (for example, neatness). The girls, however, received relatively little criticism for non-intellectual matters. Thus, the proportion of all negative evaluation that was related to the intellectual quality of their work was extremely high (nearly 90 per cent). Further, while teachers only infrequently made explicit attributions for children's failures, they were eight times more likely to attribute a boy's failure to insufficient effort than they were a girl's. The sex differences in the positive evaluations that the teachers gave were also in the predicted direction, although the results were not as striking as they were for the negative evaluations.

Thus it appears that when boys receive a negative evaluation, their history of classroom feedback can provide many plausible and readily available interpretations other than insufficient ability. They can more easily than girls see a negative evaluation as a reflection of the teachers' overall attitude toward them, or they can view it as a reflection of the non-intellectual aspects of their school work. Finally, even if boys view a negative evaluation as resulting from inadequacies in the intellectual quality of their work, the teachers' explicit attributions make it more likely that they will attribute their errors to a lack of motivation.

One may wonder at this point whether this differential treatment of boys and girls in the classroom actually causes the interpretations that boys and girls give for their successes and failures. It is important to note that the issue here is not whether the behaviour of girls and boys warrants this differential treatment, but whether such feedback will influence the interpretations they give to subsequent evaluations. To investigate this, Dweck et al. (1978) simulated the two reinforcement histories characteristic of what happened to girls and boys in the classroom. Children performed on a task which could be evaluated both in terms of the intellectual quality of their performance (correctness of the solution) as well as its non-intellectual aspects (for example, how neatly they printed their answers); and the task was arranged so that all children would succeed on some trials and fail on others.

Children in one group (half of whom were males and half females) were given a reinforcement history similar to what boys receive in the classroom. That is, the negative feedback given by the evaluator referred sometimes to the intellectual quality of their work and sometimes to non-intellectual aspects. Children in another group (also half male and half female) were given a reinforcement history more characteristic of what girls experience in the classroom. That is, the evaluator's criticisms referred exclusively to the incorrectness of the child's solution. The children then all performed on a second task on which they received failure feedback that did not have a clearly specified referent, and the children were asked to give an explanation for the negative evaluation they received. In accordance with prediction, children of both sexes who received the feedback that boys typically receive gave the attribution more characteristic of boys. Most of them attributed their negative evaluation to insufficient effort. In contrast, children of both sexes who received the feedback girls receive in the classroom overwhelmingly attributed their negative evaluation to their abilities. This research clearly demonstrates that the differential treatment of boys and girls that Dweck et al. (1978) observed in the classroom can indeed have an impact on the subsequent interpretations that children make for the outcomes they experience in achievement situations.

There is an interesting irony in how girls come to develop the pattern of achievement-related beliefs that seems to hinder them when they confront intellectual challenges. They seem to develop this maladaptive pattern as a consequence of their *more* favoured treatment by teachers – for example, less criticism and fewer complaints about their not trying hard enough. While this differential treatment may reflect, in part, differential responses to boys and girls for the same behaviours, it also appears to be the case that the behaviour of the two sexes warrants such differential treatment (Serbin et al., 1973; Etaugh and Harlow, 1973). That is, it is likely that girls actually are neater, better behaved, and more likely to work hard in order to do well and please the teacher. In other words, it appears to be girls' greater compliance to the demands of elementary school that results in their more favoured treatment by teachers, which in turn contributes to girls' failure to develop the achievement orientations necessary to succeed later on in the really challenging areas. It is also likely that girls' greater compliance to the demands of elementary school will affect their achievement orientations in more direct ways as well. When a child generally does try hard to do well and please the teacher, not only should the teacher be less inclined to attribute the child's difficulties to insufficient effort, but independent of any teacher feedback, the child herself/himself should be less inclined to attribute difficulties to insufficient effort. Unfortunately, this should result in a greater inclination to attribute one's difficulties to insufficient ability – even when the most realistic and adaptive attribution in a given situation may be that a little more effort than usual and/or an alteration of strategies was needed.

There is further irony in the logical implications that follow from the Dweck et al. (1978) investigation. One might reason that in order to help girls develop more adaptive achievement orientations, one should give girls the classroom feedback that boys typically receive. However, to do so would mean criticizing girls in areas (for example, neatness, conduct, effort) where criticisms may be wholly unwarranted. What may seem to be an immediate and logical extension of the Dweck et al. (1978) findings is clearly not included in the practical recommendations we would make on the basis of the analysis presented here. Later we explore some possible ways to alter children's achievement-orientations as well as influence their development in the first place. But first, we explore the implications that different achievement orientations have for children's performance in specific academic areas.

## Implications of sex differences in achievement orientations for performance in specific academic areas

As indicated earlier, there are striking sex differences in children's achievement-orientations. Girls tend to enter novel situations of intellectual achievement with lower expectations of success; and when success is achieved, girls are less likely than boys to interpret it as a reflection of their ability. When children confront difficulty in situations of intellectual achievement, girls are more likely to interpret it as an indication of insufficient ability; and consequently are more likely than boys to show disruptions of effort and performance following failure. Additionally, the debilitating effects of failure are more likely to generalize to future achievement situations for girls than for boys. Girls are more likely to avoid the tasks on which they have previously experienced difficulties, and their expectations of future success are less likely than boys' expectations to recover following failure.

At first glance, the picture we have painted for girls appears rather grim; and one might predict that girls would come to expect certain doom in any situation of intellectual achievement, and that they would avoid them all. Yet we know this is not the case. As we have proposed elsewhere (Dweck and Licht, 1980), academic tasks vary in the degree to which they possess the characteristics that are most debilitating to girls. Indeed, certain academic tasks and certain academic areas in general may possess characteristics that are compatible with girls' achievement orientations and that should facilitate their performance. Similarly, boys' achievement orientations may make them well-suited for certain academic pursuits, but ill suited for other academic areas. *

---

*This is not intended as justification for the status quo (that is, sex segregation into 'sex-appropriate' fields), but rather as a potential explanation for the status quo and why

As an example of how this analysis may help explain commonly observed achievement differences between the sexes, we have argued (Dweck and Licht, 1980) that mathematics appears to be an area that in general possesses the characteristics that fit best with boys' achievement orientations, while the verbal areas seem to possess those qualities that fit best with the achievement orientations of girls. In other words, we proposed that an analysis of sex differences in achievement-orientations may help explain their differential choice of mathematical versus verbal areas and their differential performance in these areas.

The performance differences to which we refer are among the best-documented sex differences reported in the literature. In verbal areas, females perform as well as or better than males throughout the school years (Anastasi, 1958; Maccoby, 1966; Maccoby and Jacklin, 1974; Donlon et al., 1976). While girls' mathematical achievement is equivalent to that of boys' during most of the elementary-school years, girls begin to fall behind around the start of junior high; and the male–female discrepancy in mathematics becomes more pronounced over the years (Fennema and Sherman, 1977; Flanagan et al., 1964; Fox, 1976b; Hilton and Berglund, 1974; Maccoby and Jacklin, 1974; Donlon et al., 1976; Ekstrom et al., 1976).

It is important to note that some of the most recent data we have collected also show some sex differences in mathematics achievement. This is despite society's changing views of mathematics as a male 'domain' (Sherman and Fennema, 1977; Farley, 1969). This is not to suggest that sex-role stereotyping explanations of sex differences in achievement (for example, girls perceive mathematics as a male domain and lower their expectations of success as a result) are not important. Nor for that matter do we wish to discount the possible contribution of biological factors. However, our analysis is intended to demonstrate that there are other critical factors that must be considered in attempting to explain sex differences in mathematics versus verbal achievement. These factors are children's achievement orientations that arise in the early elementary-school years and may render girls and boys most willing or best able to cope with the demands of different kinds of intellectual pursuits. As we discuss below, it is later, at the end of elementary school or beginning of junior high that the mathematical and verbal areas become noticeably discrepant in terms of those characteristics that would favour the achievement orientations of one sex over the other. In the next section we contrast the mathematical and verbal areas in terms of those characteristics that seem most likely to interact with children's achievement orientations.

it is so difficult to modify. Our intention is to provide a refined analysis that will allow us to predict more precisely when debilitation versus facilitation will occur for each sex. This can then serve as the basis for appropriate interventions designed to alleviate debilitation.

Following this, we present findings from our recent research designed to test this analysis.

## Analysis of mathematical and verbal areas: factors in debilitation and facilitation

### Probability of failure

In view of girls' responses to failure, one would expect them to be most debilitated in areas where they must confront difficulty on a regular basis. Beginning in the late elementary school years, mathematics appears to be an area where, regardless of one's aptitude, one is likely to confront novel and confusing material quite often. This seems less likely to be the case in verbal areas. Once the basic verbal skills (reading, writing, spelling, vocabulary) have been acquired, increments in difficulty tend to be gradual. When a child is confronted with reading, defining or spelling a new word, he/she can usually succeed by carefully applying the same rules and skills that were used in the past. In most cases children are not likely to be confronted in verbal areas with a large set of new tasks that require them to grapple with completely novel concepts.

In mathematics, however, new units often begin with a totally new set of concepts to be mastered; and this may require the child to think in very novel ways, ways that he/she has not confronted in earlier units or in other aspects of his/her life (for example, conceptualizing an imaginary number or solving simultaneous equations in algebra). A careful application of old skills and modes of thinking, though perhaps necessary, will not be sufficient. Thus to enjoy mathematics and perform up to one's abilities, one must be able to maintain one's confidence and one's concentration in the face of novelty and in the face of failure, since it is a rare individual who can grasp such new concepts without experiencing a fair degree of confusion. This is precisely the kind of situation that is poorly matched to the achievement orientations girls are likely to hold. In contrast, given boys' tendency to view a novel task with a moderate risk of failure as challenging, this characteristic of mathematics may serve to make it attractive to them, and to facilitate their performance.

The differential responses of males and females may be exacerbated further by the fact that each new unit in mathematics begins with a new name (for example, algebra, geometry, calculus, etc.). This may serve as a reminder that a whole new set of skills must be mastered – a suggestion that may be attractive to males but cause concern to females who already have a tendency to discount previous successes as predictive of future success.

### Salience of failure

As Dweck and Licht (1980) have pointed out, it is not the commission of an error *per se* that should trigger girls' maladaptive attributions;

rather it is the *realization* that their performance has been deficient in some way. Factors that serve to increase the visibility of one's errors should be troublesome for girls, but less so for boys.

The factor that seems most likely to contribute to the visibility of one's performance deficiencies is the clarity of the correctness criteria. When responses can be easily judged as correct or wrong – that is, there is only *one* correct way to answer the question – then both the teacher and child will be more likely to notice any deficiencies in performance. In contrast, on tasks where the teacher must make subjective judgements to evaluate the child's performance, then teachers may be hesitant to correct what appears to be a minor deficiency, and the children will have no way of knowing themselves that their answers may have been somewhat off the mark.

In mathematics there is usually only one correct answer and the criterion of correctness is extremely objective, while in verbal areas the criterion is generally more ambiguous. This is not to say that there are no verbal tasks for which answers are either clearly right or wrong (for example, spelling), but they are far less frequent than in mathematics. This is particularly true in the later school years where there is less emphasis on tasks like spelling and more emphasis on tasks like interpreting the meaning of what was read and expressing one's ideas.

One may be tempted to argue at this point that the greater clarity of the correctness criterion in mathematics should also serve to make girls' successes more salient to them, thus compensating for the salience of failures. However, increasing the visibility of girls' successes would not be expected to help girls since they are less likely to view their successes as reflecting on their intellectual ability. In fact, it is the boys who should benefit from the increased visibility of their successes since they are more likely to see their successes as reflecting on their intellect.

### Interpretation of failure feedback

While girls show a general tendency to view failure feedback as reflecting on their intellectual ability, feedback varies in terms of how readily it may elicit this interpretation. Girls should be most debilitated in areas where the failure feedback is most easily interpreted in this manner. In contrast, given boys' greater confidence in their intellectual ability and lesser confidence in how much the teacher likes them, boys should feel more helpless (that is, less able to control their outcomes) in areas where evaluations are seen as potentially influenced by teachers' personal bias.

As discussed in Dweck and Licht, one of the factors that should influence the relative plausibility of these two interpretations is, again, the clarity of the correctness criterion. The more ambiguous the criterion of correctness, the more readily the feedback can be seen as reflecting the influence of the teacher's personal bias. As indicated above, in mathematics more than in verbal areas, there is an objective criterion of correctness. In fact, in mathematics children often do not even have to rely on the teacher at all to know how they have done. They can often simply check their answers against those given in their books. And when answers are correct, the teacher must recognize this, regardless of his/her feelings about the child. Thus, there appears to be another mechanism through which the clarity of the correctness criterion in mathematics should make that area attractive and facilitative to boys but not to girls.

A second characteristic that should affect the likelihood that failure feedback will be seen as reflecting on one's intellect is the degree to which skills of a non-intellectual nature are involved in successful execution of a task. The more that performance of non-intellectual skills is required, the more readily can failure feedback be attributed to non-intellectual factors. In contrast, if executing the task successfully relies minimally on non-intellectual skills, then a low grade should more readily be seen as reflecting on one's intellect (Dweck et al., 1978).

In general, non-intellectual skills seem to play a more central role in verbal than in mathematical tasks. For example, when writing a composition, it is not only the quality of one's ideas that are likely to be evaluated, but one's handwriting, the format, and so on. In a similar vein, consider a child's presentation of a book report to the class, which is likely to be viewed, at least in part, as practice in public speaking. Since clear communication depends not only on the content, but on the manner of presentation as well, it is not unlikely that the teacher will give the child feedback on the latter. This greater emphasis on non-intellectual factors in verbal areas should make the feedback less readily seen as reflecting on one's intellect and, therefore, less threatening. While this should make the verbal areas more compatible than mathematics with girls' achievement orientations, it should make verbal areas less desirable for boys since they attach less value to, and show poorer performance in, the kinds of non-intellectual skill areas that contribute to verbal performances.

## Compensation for perceived inadequacies

Since girls are generally more likely than boys to foster suspicions of intellectual inadequacies, girls should feel more secure in areas where avenues are available to compensate for their perceived weaknesses. This opportunity appears to be more readily available in verbal than in mathematical tasks.

In the later school years, verbal tasks tend to include several components of a diverse nature. For example, when writing an essay, it is not only the quality of ideas that contributes to the overall quality of the product, but the clarity of one's expression, the precision of one's grammar, and perhaps spelling as well. Also, as indicated earlier, there are several components of a non-intellectual nature (for example, handwriting) that will affect the overall quality of the product. If a girl perceives herself as being weak in a particular intellectual area, she may find consolation in the fact that she can probably compensate by excelling in some other component(s) of the task. In mathematics this option is less available. One either knows or does not know how to solve the problem, and it is difficult to compensate for or to camouflage a lack of knowledge.

In summary, given the characteristics of mathematics and verbal areas, confusion and failure should occur with greater frequency and be more noticeable in mathematics; and failure feedback should be more likely to be seen as a reflection of intellectual ability in mathematics than in most verbal areas. In contrast, the likelihood that failure feedback will be viewed as reflecting the teacher's negative bias will be greater in verbal than in mathematics tasks. These factors should all act together to make mathematics more compatible with the achievement orientations of boys, and verbal areas more compatible with the achievement orientations of girls.

## Empirical support for the analysis

An important question in evaluating our analysis is whether the children themselves perceive mathematics and verbal areas as differing in the way we have proposed. To address this issue, two hundred sixth-grade children were asked a number of questions designed to tap their perceptions of mathematics, reading and language arts. The perceptions of both sexes were remarkably similar and generally corroborated our analysis.

One of the most important components of our analysis involves the objectivity of the correctness criterion in mathematics since it has important implications for the likelihood that a deficiency in performance will be noticed and the likelihood that failure will be viewed as reflecting teacher bias. Children were therefore asked to choose the area where there was 'only *one right* way to answer the questions'. In accordance with our analysis, children showed a strong and significant tendency to choose mathematics over reading and language arts. Another component of the model involved the degree to which non-intellectual factors contributed to the children's performance. Children were asked about the importance of neatness and handwriting in the three subject areas. While children acknowledged that neatness, in general, was important in both mathematics and verbal areas, there was a clear and significant consensus that one's handwriting (a non-intellectual domain in which girls excel) was relevant to one's performance only on verbal assignments.

Perhaps most important and most striking were the children's responses when asked directly about how one's grades in these subject areas reflect on one's intellect. Mathematics was overwhelmingly chosen as the subject where a person '*must* be *smart* in order to do well'; and reading was the overwhelming choice when children were asked for the subject where someone could do well 'even if they *weren't* smart'. Thus, children in late elementary school are more likely to perceive mathematics in such a way that makes it forbidding to those who hold the achievement orientations that girls often do; but more attractive than verbal areas if one holds the achievement orientations that boys are likely to hold.

Another important aspect of the model that has received empirical support since we originally proposed it relates to perhaps the most important issue outlined above – the impact of confronting novel and confusing material at the start of new units. It was our prediction that when children with a 'helpless' achievement orientation confront these confusing new concepts, their acquisition of new academic material will be impaired – they will learn less than they are actually capable of learning and are motivated to learn. This was not expected to be the case with 'mastery-oriented' children. In other words, we hypothesized that children's achievement orientations (helpless versus mastery-oriented) would interact with the demands of new academic material (presence versus absence of confusing concepts in the initial stages of learning) to determine how much children would actually learn. Further, since our central issue is the impact of children's achievement orientations on their academic performance, it was particularly important to examine this hypothesis in an actual classroom setting. This is exactly what we have done (Licht and Dweck, 1982).

Fifth-grade children were classified as helpless or mastery-oriented on the basis of their causal attributions for failure. Children within each attribution group were randomly assigned to one of two learning conditions. One involved the programming of confusion during the initial phases of learning new material in the classroom. The other condition involved learning the *identical* material without the programmed confusion in the initial phases. Thus, the design was a 2 (helpless versus mastery-oriented) × 2 (learning conditions: confusion versus no-confusion) × 2 (sex) design. The confusion and no-confusion conditions may be seen as simulations of how learning proceeds in two different subject areas that differ in terms of the likelihood that new units will begin with novel and confusing concepts. While this is a distinction that seems to apply well to mathematical versus verbal areas, the implications of this research can be extended to any two subject areas or units that differ along this dimension.

In this study, children in all groups were presented with some new academic material to learn during a one-hour classroom session. The material, which was presented in a booklet, explained the basic principles of instrumental learning (for example, 'Suppose something good happened because of the way you acted. Then you'd probably want to act that way again. Now what if something bad happened because of the way you acted. Then you wouldn't want to act that way again. Here are some examples . . .'). Both groups had an equal opportunity to learn this material which was presented *identically* for both groups. What differentiated the confusion and no-confusion groups were the two sections of the booklet that preceded the presentation of the material on instrumental learning. For children in the no-confusion condition, these two preceding sections presented some principles of imitation in a clear and straightforward manner. For children in the confusion condition, these two sections, also about imitation, were written so as to elude comprehension. The vocabulary was well within their level. However, the syntax, although largely correct, was convoluted (for example, 'How can one best describe the nature of the people who will most of all be that way which will make the imitating of others happen most often? Is it that these are the people we want to be like because they are fine or is it that these are the people we want to be liked by?'). For both the confusion and no-confusion groups, the imitation material was presented as part of the same subject area as the material on instrumental learning. However, the two sections on imitation were also designed so that an understanding of the imitation sections would in no way facilitate an understanding of the instrumental learning material that followed. Any differences between the confusion and no-confusion conditions could *not* be attributed to the no-confusion children having more relevant background information.

At the end of the booklet, there was a seven-question multiple-choice test that assessed the child's understanding of the material on instrumental learning only. As soon as a child finished the test it was graded. Whenever a child did not reach the criterion of 100 per cent correct, he/she was given a review booklet (which covered only the material on instrumental learning) and another test comparable to the first. This was repeated until the child reached the criterion or the session ended. Thus, children who did not fully understand the material the first time were given ample opportunity to do so. The dependent variable of interest was the proportion of children in each group who reached the criterion by the end of the session.

The predicted interaction between the confusion versus no-confusion manipulation and the children's achievement orientation was clearly obtained. In the confusion condition, the difference between helpless and mastery-oriented children was significant. While 71·88 per cent of the mastery-oriented reached the criterion, only 34·65 per cent of the helpless children did so. The poor performance of the helpless children, however, cannot be attributed to a lesser ability to learn the material since the helpless children performed at least as well as the mastery-oriented in the no-confusion condition where the *same* material was presented without the preceding confusion experience. Here, 68·36 per cent of the mastery-oriented reached the criterion and 76·57 per cent of the helpless children did so. These results show that when acquisition of new material involves dealing with novel and confusing concepts, the helpless children will perform more poorly than they are capable of doing while the mastery-oriented will perform at their best. The helpless children, however, will be likely to perform up to their abilities in academic areas where new units do not regularly begin with such confusion.

Although this particular study did not find sex differences in the children's achievement orientations, as indicated earlier, it is frequently the case that girls are more helpless than boys. Thus, taken together, the finding that girls are more helpless and our finding that helpless children are less able to deal with confusion, suggest that girls' achievement orientations may hinder them in their attempts to deal with the acquisition demands of challenging subjects like mathematics.

# New directions: are the brightest girls the most helpless?

The above analysis becomes even more intriguing (albeit more complex) when one considers together two sets of findings: (1) findings which suggest that among females it may be some of the brightest ones who possess the least adaptive achievement orientations (Crandall, 1969; Crandall et al., 1962; Stipek and Hoffman, 1980; Licht and Shapiro, 1982), and (2) findings which suggest that sex differences in mathematics achievement (favouring boys) are greatest at the top of the distribution. Investigations of the mathematically gifted (Astin, 1974; Benbow and Stanley, 1980; Fox, 1976b; Keating, 1976) have reported male–female discrepancies of a much greater magnitude for this select group than those typically reported for the whole distribution considered together.

Support for the notion that among females it may be the brightest ones who are the most likely to be helpless comes from research on children's expectations and attributions. Crandall et al. (1962) and Stipek and Hoffman (1980) found a surprising tendency for girls' expectations of success on novel intellectual tasks to be *negatively* related to their previous levels of academic achievement; and Crandall et al. (1962) found the same negative relationship between expectations and scores on standardized I.Q. tests. In contrast, for the boys in these studies, there was the predicted positive relationship between expectations and measures of intelligence and achievement. It appears that the less capable girls may be overestimating their chances of success while the most capable ones are underestimating theirs. To the degree that lower expectations will result in avoiding challenging tasks and lower levels of persistence in the face of difficulty (Battle, 1965; Diggory, 1966; Feather, 1966; Tyler, 1958), these data would suggest that it may be some of the brightest girls who will be the most likely to underachieve as a result of their achievement orientations.

Data on children's causal attributions also suggest that girls are not realistically processing their previous success and failure experiences.

Several studies (Crandall et al., 1962; Stipek and Hoffman, 1980; Licht and Dweck, 1982) have found the expected relationship between previous successes (measured by I.Q. or achievement scores) and causal attributions for males, but not for females. That is, the brightest and/or higher achieving males were more likely than unsuccessful males to attribute their failures to effort and less likely to blame their abilities when they failed. For the girls, however, the attributions they made were not related in this way to their previous level of achievement nor to their I.Q. scores.

Licht and Shapiro (1982) assessed directly sex differences in attributions within achievement levels. Children in the fifth and sixth grades were divided into four achievement levels according to their report card grades in mathematics. Mathematics was chosen since it was the most discriminating grade the teachers gave (that is, As and Bs were given more sparingly in mathematics than in reading or language arts); and it was desirable for the highest level to include a very capable group. Significant sex differences in attributions were indeed found, but only among the 'A' students. As expected, the high-achieving girls were more likely than the high-achieving boys to attribute their failures to insufficient ability; and they were less likely to attribute their successes to high ability – the attributional pattern that has been shown to be predictive of a maladaptive response to failure.

Why might it be that sex differences are strongest among the 'A' students? Perhaps the girls at the top of the distribution may hold such unrealistically high standards that they seldom view themselves as successful (for example, see Stouwie et al., 1970). Even though they may seem highly successful by most *objective* standards, they may be experiencing considerable failure when they judge themselves against their own criteria. Along these lines, it may be that the girls who show the most unrealistically low levels of confidence are the 'A' students who view themselves as doing poorly because they are not at the very top of the class (see also Crandall, 1969). Perhaps another possibility is that the high-achieving girls may view themselves as so motivated and well disciplined that they cannot entertain the possibility that they did poorly on an academic task because of insufficient effort. Since blaming the teacher would also be out of character, blaming their abilities when they confront difficulty may seem like the most reasonable option. Perhaps another factor is that the high-achieving girls may be the ones who are most likely to receive the pattern of teacher feedback that leads to the development of maladaptive attributions (that is, discriminant use of failure feedback to refer to the intellectual quality of the child's work). Some of these notions are currently under investigation.

In summary, the evidence suggests that girls' tendency to avoid mathematics, and to fall behind in mathematical achievement, may be related to a debilitating pattern of achievement beliefs. Furthermore, it is possible that this pattern is most prevalent among the brightest girls.

It would seem that any serious attempt to reduce the discrepancy must address these factors.

## Conclusion

What can be done to encourage the development of more facilitating achievement orientations in girls so that they are more likely to seek challenges and persist in the face of them? It should be noted that our goal here is not to encourage all girls to pursue mathematics as a career. Nor do we wish to imply that careers relying more exclusively on verbal skills are not as worthy of being pursued. Our goal instead is to increase the range of choices that girls consider and to encourage choices based on interests and values, not on fear of failure.

One possible strategy is to increase the degree of challenge children typically encounter in school. Findings from treatment (Attribution Retraining) studies support the notion that children do not develop stable high levels of confidence and high levels of persistence in the face of difficulty simply as a result of having experienced repeated successes (Chapin and Dyck, 1976; Dweck, 1975). (If they did, we would find a far lower incidence of maladaptive achievement orientations among the highest achieving girls.) The treatment strategies that seem to promote a tendency to persist in the face of difficulty instead involve experience with challenges and errors. It is not unlikely that bright girls encounter very few intellectual obstacles until the later school years; and by the time they encounter any notable difficulty or confusion, they have already developed a pattern of achievement-related beliefs that makes them poorly equipped to cope with it.

Research also supports the view that children can be directly taught to view the 'struggle' to master material not as a condemnation of their ability nor as a failure at all, but rather as a challenge to be overcome and as information that either prolonged concentration and/or an alteration of strategy may be necessary (Andrews and Debus, 1978; Brophy and Good, 1974; Chapin and Dyck, 1976; Dweck, 1975; Fowler and Peterson, 1981). Systematically arranging children's learning environments to support adaptive views is clearly not an easy task. However, if successful, the outcome should well be worth the effort.

## References

Anastasi, A. (1958). *Differential Psychology* (3rd edn). New York: Macmillan.
Andrews, G.R. and Debus, R.L. (1978). 'Persistence and the causal perception of failure: modifying cognitive attributions'. *Journal of Educational Psychology*, vol. 70, pp. 154–66.
Astin, H. (1974). 'Sex differences in scientific and mathematical precocity', in J.C. Stanley, D.P. Keating, and L.H. Fox (eds), *Mathematical Talent: Discovery, Description*

*and Development*. Baltimore, Md.: The Johns Hopkins University Press.

Battle, E.S. (1965). 'Motivational determinants of academic task persistence'. *Journal of Personality and Social Psychology*, vol. 2, pp. 209–18.

—— (1966). 'Motivational determinants of academic competence'. *Journal of Personality and Social Psychology*, vol. 4, pp. 634–42.

Bem, S.L. (1974). 'The measurement of psychological androgyny'. *Journal of Consulting and Clinical Psychology*, vol. 42, pp. 155–62.

Benbow, C.P., and Stanley, J.C. (1980). 'Sex differences in mathematical ability: fact or artifact?' *Science*, vol. 210, pp. 1262–4.

Brophy, J.E., and Good, T.L. (1974). *Teacher–Student Relationships*. New York: Holt.

Butterfield, E.C. (1965). 'The role of competence motivation in interrupted task recall and repetition choice'. *Journal of Experimental Child Psychology*, vol. 2, pp. 354–70.

Cairns, R.B. (1970). 'Meaning and attention as determinants of social reinforcer effectiveness'. *Child Development*, vol. 41, pp. 1067–82.

Chapin, M. and Dyck, D.G. (1976). 'Persistence in children's reading behaviour as a function of N length and attribution retraining'. *Journal of Abnormal Psychology*, vol. 85, pp. 511–15.

Coopersmith, S. (1967). *The Antecedents of Self-esteem*. San Francisco: Freeman.

Covington, M.V., Spratt, M.F. and Omelich, C.L. (1980). 'Is effort enough, or does diligence count too? Student and teacher reactions to effort stability in failure'. *Journal of Educational Psychology*, vol. 72, pp. 717–29.

Crandall, V.C. (1969). 'Sex differences in expectancy of intellectual and academic reinforcement', in C.P. Smith (ed.), *Achievement-related Motives in Children*. New York: Russell Sage Foundation.

——, Katkovsky, W. and Preston, A. (1962). 'Motivational and ability determinants of young children's intellectual achievement behaviours'. *Child Development*, vol. 33, pp. 643–61.

—— and Rabson, A. (1960). 'Children's repetition choices in an intellectual achievement situation following success and failure'. *Journal of Genetic Psychology*, vol. 97, pp. 161–8.

Diener, C.I. and Dweck, C.S. (1978). 'An analysis of learned helplessness: continuous changes in performance, strategy and achievement cognitions following failure'. *Journal of Personality and Social Psychology*, vol. 36, pp. 451–62.

—— and Dweck, C.S. (1980). 'An analysis of learned helplessness: II. The processing of success'. *Journal of Personality and Social Psychology*, vol. 39, pp. 940–52.

Diggory, J. (1966). *Self-evaluation: Concepts and Studies*. New York: Wiley.

Digman, J.M. (1963). 'Principal dimensions of child personality as inferred from teachers' judgments'. *Child Development*, vol. 34, pp. 43–60.

Donlon, T., Ekstrom, R. and Lockheed, M. (1976). 'Comparing the sexes on achievement items of varying content'. Paper presented at the meeting of the American Psychological Association, Washington, D.C., September 1976.

Dweck, C.S. (1975). 'The role of expectations and attributions in the alleviation of learned helplessness'. *Journal of Personality and Social Psychology*, vol. 31, pp. 674–85.

—— and Bush, E.S. (1976). 'Sex differences in learned helplessness: I. Differential debilitation with peer and adult evaluators'. *Developmental Psychology*, vol. 12, pp. 147–56.

——, Davidson, W., Nelson, S. and Enna, B. (1978). 'Sex differences in learned helplessness: II. The contingencies of evaluative feedback in the classroom, and III. An experimental analysis'. *Developmental Psychology*, vol. 14, pp. 268–76.

—— and Gilliard, D. (1975). 'Expectancy statements as determinants of reactions to failure: sex differences in persistence and expectancy change'. *Journal of Personality and Social Psychology*, vol. 32, pp. 1077–84.

——, Goetz, T.E. and Strauss, N.L. (1980). 'Sex differences in learned helplessness: IV. An experimental and naturalistic study of failure generalization and its mediators'. *Journal of Personality and Social Psychology*, vol. 38, pp. 441–52.

—— and Goetz, T.E. (1977). Unpublished data.

—— and Licht, B.G. (1980). 'Learned helplessness and intellectual achievement', in

J. Garber and M. Seligman (eds), *Human Helplessness: Theory and Application*. New York: Academic Press.

—— and Reppucci, N.D. (1973). 'Learned helplessness and reinforcement responsibility in children'. *Journal of Personality and Social Psychology*, vol. 25, pp. 109–16.

Eisenberger, R., Kaplan, R.M. and Singer, R.D. (1974). 'Decremental and nondecremental effects of noncontingent social approval'. *Journal of Personality and Social Psychology*, vol. 30, pp. 716–2.

Ekstrom, R., Donlon, T. and Lockheed, M. (1976). 'The effect of sex-biased content in achievement test performance'. Paper presented at the meeting of the American Educational Research Association, San Francisco, California, 21 April 1976.

Enzle, M.E., Hansen, R.D. and Lowe, C.A. (1975). 'Causal attributions in the mixed-motive game: effects of facilitory and inhibitory environmental forces'. *Journal of Personality and Social Psychology*, vol. 31, pp. 50–54.

Etaugh, C. and Harlow, H. (1973). 'School attitudes and performance of elementary school children as related to teacher's sex and behaviour'. Paper presented at the meeting of the Society for Research in Child Development, Philadelphia, March 1973.

Farley, S.M.C. (1969). 'A study of the mathematical interests, attitude and achievement of tenth and eleventh grade students' (Doctoral dissertation, University of Michigan, 1968). *Dissertation Abstracts International*, vol. 29, 3039A. (University Microfilms No. 69–2312).

Feather, N.T. (1966). 'Effects of prior success and failure on expectations of success and subsequent performance'. *Journal of Personality and Social Psychology*, vol. 3, pp. 287–98.

Fennema, E. and Sherman, J. (1977). 'Sex-related differences in mathematics achievement, spacial visualization and affective factors'. *American Educational Research Journal*, vol. 14, pp. 51–71.

Flanagan, J., Davis, F., Dailey, J., Shaycoft, M., Orr, D., Goldberg, I and Neyman, C. (1964). *The American High-school Student*. Pittsburgh: University of Pittsburgh.

Fowler, J.W. and Peterson, P.L. (1981). 'Increasing reading persistence and altering attributional style of learned helpless children'. *Journal of Educational Psychology*, vol. 73, pp. 251–60.

Fox, L. (1976a). 'The effects of sex-role socialization on mathematical participation and achievement'. Paper prepared for Education and Work Group, Career Awareness Division of National Institute of Education, December 1976.

—— (1976b). 'Sex differences in mathematical precocity: bridging the gap', in D.P. Keating (ed.), *Intellectual Talent: Research and Development*. Baltimore, Md.: The Johns Hopkins University Press.

Harter, S. (1975). 'Mastery motivation and need for approval in older children and their relationship to social desirability response tendencies'. *Developmental Psychology*, vol. 11, pp. 186–96.

Heller, K.A. and Parsons, J.E. (1981). 'Sex differences in teachers' evaluative feedback and students' expectancies for success in mathematics'. *Child Development*, vol. 52, pp. 1015–19.

Hill, K.T. and Sarason, S.B. (1966). 'The relation of test anxiety and defensiveness to test and school performance over the elementary school years: a further longitudinal study'. *Monographs of the Society for Research in Child Development*. Serial No. 104, vol. 31 (Whole No. 2).

Hilton, T. and Berglund, G. (1974). 'Sex differences in mathematics achievement – a longitudinal study'. *Journal of Education Research*, vol. 67, pp. 231–7.

Hoffman, L.W. (1972). 'Early childhood experiences and women's achievement motives'. *Journal of Social Issues*, vol. 28, pp. 129–55.

Jackaway, R. (1975). 'Achievement attributions and the low expectation cycle in females'. Paper presented at convention of American Psychological Association, Chicago, 1975.

Keating, D. (ed.) (1976). *Intellectual Talent: Research and Development*. Baltimore, Md.: The Johns Hopkins University Press.

Kelley, H.H. (1971). *Attribution in Social Interaction*. Morristown, N.J.: General Learning Press.

Lenney, E. (1977). 'Women's self-confidence in achievement settings'. *Psychological Bulletin*, vol. 84, pp. 1–13.

Licht, B.G. and Dweck, C.S. (1982). 'Determinants of academic achievement: the interaction of children's achievement orientations with skill area'. *Developmental Psychology*, in press, 1984.

―――― and Shapiro, S.H. (1982). 'Sex differences in attributions among high achievers'. Paper presented at the meeting of the American Psychological Association, Washington, D.C., 1982.

Maccoby, E.E. (1966). *The Development of Sex Differences*. Stanford, California: Stanford University Press.

―――― and Jacklin, C.N. (1974). *The Psychology of Sex Differences*. Stanford, California: Stanford University Press.

McCandless, B., Roberts, A. and Starnes, T. (1972). 'Teachers' marks, achievement test scores, and aptitude relations with respect to social class, race, and sex'. *Journal of Educational Psychology*, vol. 63, pp. 153–9.

McMahan, I.D. (1973). 'Relationships between causal attributions and expectancy of success'. *Journal of Personality and Social Psychology*, vol. 28, pp. 108–14.

Molnar, J.M. and Weisz, J.R. (1981). 'The pursuit of mastery by preschool boys and girls: an observational study'. *Child Development*, vol. 52, pp. 724–7.

Montanelli, D.S. and Hill, K.T. (1969). 'Children's achievement expectations and performance as a function of two consecutive reinforcement experiences, sex of subject, and sex of experimenter'. *Journal of Personality and Social Psychology*, vol. 13, pp. 115–28.

Nicholls, J.G. (1975). 'Causal attributions and other achievement-related cognitions: effects of task outcome, attainment value, and sex'. *Journal of Personality and Social Psychology*, vol. 31, pp. 379–89.

―――― (1976a). 'Effort is virtuous, but it's better to have ability'. *Journal of Research in Personality*, vol. 10, pp. 306–15.

―――― (1976b). 'When a scale measures more than its name denotes: the case of the Test Anxiety Scale for Children'. *Journal of Consulting and Clinical Psychology*, vol. 44, pp. 976–85.

―――― (1978a). 'Sex differences in achievement behavior and causal attributions for success and failure in New Zealand children'. Paper presented at meeting of the American Educational Research Association, Toronto, 1978.

―――― (1978b). 'The development of the concepts of effort and ability, perception of academic attainment and the understanding that difficult tasks require more ability'. *Child Development*, vol. 49, pp. 800–14.

Parsons, J.E., Adler, T.F., Futterman, R., Goff, S.B., Kaczala, C.M., Meece, J.L. and Midgley, C. 'Expectancies, values, and academic behaviors', in J.T. Spence (ed.), *Perspectives on Achievement and Achievement Motivation*. San Francisco: Freeman, in press.

―――― Kaczala, C.M. and Meece, J.L. (1982). 'Socialization of achievement attitudes and beliefs: classroom influences'. *Child Development*, vol. 53, pp. 322–39.

――――, Ruble, D.N., Hodges, K.L. and Small, I. (1976). 'Cognitive-developmental factors in emerging sex differences in achievement-related expectancies'. *Journal of Social Issues*, vol. 32, pp. 47–61.

Paul, G.L. and Bernstein, D.A. (1973). *Anxiety and Clinical Problems: Systematic Desensitization and Related Techniques*. Morristown, N.J.: General Learning Press.

Sarason, S.B., Davidson, K.S., Lighthall, F.F., Waite, R.R. and Ruebush, B.K. (1960). *Anxiety in Elementary School Children: A Report of Research*. New York: Wiley.

Schunk, D.H. (1982). 'Effects of effort attributional feedback on children's perceived self-efficacy and achievement'. *Journal of Educational Psychology*, vol. 74, pp. 548–56.

Seligman, M.E.P. and Maier, S.F. (1967). 'Failure to escape traumatic shock'. *Journal of Experimental Psychology*, vol. 74, pp. 1–9.

Serbin, L.A., O'Leary, K.D., Kent, R.N. and Tonick, I.J. (1973). 'A comparison of teacher response to the pre-academic and problem behavior of boys and girls'. *Child Development*, vol. 44, pp. 796–804.

Sherman, J. and Fennema, E. (1977). 'The study of mathematics by high school girls and boys: related variables'. *American Educational Research Journal*, vol. 14, pp. 159–68.

Sohn, D. (1977). 'Affect-generating powers of effort and ability self attributions of academic success and failure'. *Journal of Educational Psychology*, vol. 69, pp. 500–505.

Stevenson, H.W., Hale, G.A., Klein, R.E. and Miller, L.K. (1968)). 'Interrelations and correlates in children's learning and problem solving'. *Monographs of the Society of Research in Child Development*, vol. 33, (7, Serial No. 123).

Stipek, D.J. and Hoffman, J.M. (1980). 'Children's achievement-related expectancies as a function of academic performance histories and sex'. *Journal of Educational Psychology*, vol. 72, pp. 861–5.

Stouwie, R.J., Hetherington, E.M. and Parke, R.D. (1970). 'Some determinants of children's self-reward criteria'. *Developmental Psychology*, vol. 3, pp. 313–19.

Tyler, B.B. (1958). 'Expectancy for eventual success as a factor in problem-solving behavior'. *Journal of Educational Psychology*, vol. 49, pp. 166–72.

Veroff, J. (1969). 'Social comparison and the development of achievement motivation', in C.P. Smith (ed.), *Achievement-related motives in children*. New York: Russell Sage.

Warren, V.L. and Cairns, R.B. (1972). 'Social reinforcement satiation: An outcome of frequency or ambiguity?' *Journal of Experimental Child Psychology*, vol. 13, pp. 249–60.

Weiner, B. (1972). *Theories of Motivation*. Chicago: Markham.

—— (1974). *Achievement Motivation and Attribution Theory*. Morristown, N.J.: General Learning Press.

——, Frieze, I., Kukla, A., Reed, L., Rest, S. and Rosenbaum, R. (1971). *Perceiving the Causes of Success and Failure*. New York: General Learning Press.

Weiner, B., Nierenberg, R. and Goldstein, M. (1976). 'Social learning (locus of control) versus attributional (causal stability) interpretations of expectancy of success'. *Journal of Personality*, vol. 44, pp. 52–68.

——, Russell, D. and Lerman, D. (1979). 'The cognition-emotion process in achievement-related contexts'. *Journal of Personality and Social Psychology*, vol. 37, pp. 1211–20.

# 7 'Telling How It Is': language and gender in the classroom

*Dale Spender*

In using the terms 'sex role stereotyping' – and even 'sex differentiation' – there is a need for caution, for one of the main dimensions of sexism tends to be blurred by such usage; it is the dimension of power. When we speak of sex roles we must remember that we are not speaking of two comparable entities, but of two groups, of different power, and two groups which are *treated differently in relation to that power*. Sex roles are not just a matter of conditioning; we cannot simply resocialize women and men and thereby eliminate sexism.

An analogy helps to illustrate this point. We would never, for example, speak of 'race roles'. We would not want to suggest, implicitly or explicitly, that blacks and whites enjoyed comparable status and that each group experienced comparable disadvantage by being conditioned to adopt a race role which could be readily changed by consciousness raising. We are aware that racism is more than a matter of prejudice, that it has a power dimension, and that one group derives advantage from racist practices while the other experiences disadvantage. We recognize that racism has a material base and that there is a need for significant social change on an international scale if we are to combat racism.

Sometimes I think this need for enormous change in our social organization tends to get lost when we are talking about sex roles or sex stereotyping. While it seems indisputable to me that both sexes are conditioned to perceive less than the full range of human qualities open and appropriate to them, and while this may be equally harsh – and equally wasteful – for both sexes, we must not forget that one sex is conditioned for power and the other for powerlessness; that one sex derives advantage from the arrangement and the other, disadvantage. And this is not just a matter of consciousness – although consciousness is a crucial factor – it is real power that males as a group have in our society and it is that real power that has to be confronted if we are to tackle the problem of sexism.

Under the rubric of 'sex role stereotyping' it is perfectly in order to talk of the oppression of men, but this is a qualitatively different state from the oppression of women. For the solution to male oppression lies in male hands. If they so choose, males can alter the power configurations of society so that it is no longer necessary for them to be seen as the superior sex, no longer mandatory for them to be in control. Then the whole process of conditioning males for positions of power (with its consequent divorce from nurture, support, cooperation, etc.) would be so inappropriate and dysfunctional that it is almost inevitable that a new male (and a new female) role would emerge. Such a choice is not open to women; and this is one of the fundamental assertions of feminism. Power is not in the hands of women; we do not control the social agencies and we cannot just choose to change the social organization. We are absent from the policy and decision-making areas of society (in education, for example, Eileen Byrne points out that 97 per cent of the policy- and decision-makers are male, Byrne, 1978, p. 15). For women to begin to change sex stereotyping it is necessary that we first confront male control, and this must be kept at the forefront of any analysis of sex differentiation and schooling.

Perhaps I can best elaborate on this point by reference to my own research in possible sex differences in language. To simply describe the manner in which females talk, and the manner in which males talk, and to conclude that both sexes labour under limitations and constraints, would be to omit a crucial dimension; and as a feminist it is a dimension which I have no intention of omitting. To me the fundamental question is not *how*, but *why*? I want to know the reasons for sex differences in language, I want to know the ends that they serve, and this necessitates going beyond description and developing a framework in which these differences can be interpreted.

I would claim that anyone can ascertain that in most mixed sex situations, men talk more, they interrupt more, they define the topic of conversation and women support them. This is not difficult to 'prove'. All that is required is a tape-recorder, a stop-watch and minimal numeracy. But to gather this readily available data is, for me, not the end point of research. I have numerous questions to ask, questions which are located in my own feminist frame of reference and which lead me to inquire what advantage men derive from talking more. For one thing feminism has helped me to understand is that it is usually males who derive advantage from difference.

That difference is usually interpreted in favour of males in a sexist society is a factor which has also emerged clearly in my own research area. There are some blatant sexist assumptions that have permeated language/gender research. It has generally been believed in our society – and it seems that researchers in language/gender are not outside such a belief – that the way men talk is the right way and that if there are any differences displayed by women, they are considered to be in the nature of 'deficiencies'. Language/gender research is not alone in operating on such sexist assumptions. Feminist critiques of many of the disciplines indicate that comparable assumptions have flourished in much research that we have accepted as unbiased and credible in the past.* But in language/gender research, the standard, desirable and positive way of using language has been epitomized by male usage, and women have been compared to this standard. This has resulted in (a) an almost obsessive search for female difference; and (b) wherever any difference can be found, the conclusion generally is that this difference constitutes a lesser form of language use. This is a manifestation of the power dimension of our society and it is a dimension which can never be ignored when analysing sex differentiation.

In terms of language use, perhaps males have got it right; perhaps their way of talking is the desirable form; perhaps women are deficient and inferior and we are actually measuring the properties of language, rather than the status of the sexes, when we produce such findings in language/gender research. This is a possibility and I am prepared to accept theoretically that the ideal form of language use (which females should aspire to) is one in which each individual talks a lot, monopolizes the conversation, interrupts and determines the topic. I remain open minded on this question because, unfortunately, virtually no research has been conducted on the efficacy, the desirability, the advantages of male verbal behaviour. Its 'superiority' is taken for granted, not tested. It is assumed (in a sexist society) that the male way is the right way; as Simone de Beauvoir has said, 'A man is in the right in being a man; it is the woman who is in the wrong.' (de Beauvoir, 1972, p. 15).

The assumption has been that male speech is the norm; female speech is deviant. Research has been conducted on this basis, and predictably it has almost always found in favour of men. What other conclusions could emerge? Where there have been so few systematic studies on how 'good' male language use is, there has been almost an undignified scramble to document how 'bad' female language use is. From the outset, research has been conducted not on the premise that there are two groups of equal status but on the premise that there is one group that is positive and one that is negative. With such premises being fed into the research process, the results that are 'fed out' help to reinforce and justify those initial premises. Research in the social sciences is so often a case of making one's own prejudices and beliefs 'come true'.

---

*See Dale Spender (ed.), *Men's Studies Modified: the Impact of Feminism on the Academic Disciplines* (Oxford: Pergamon Press, 1981), for a review of the sexist assumptions that have prevailed in most disciplines.

I can provide an example. Within language/gender research it has been frequently assumed that men's language is forceful, confident and masterful (the positive values) while women's language is hesitant, qualified and tentative (a distinct disadvantage in a competitive society), and a considerable amount of energy has been expended, not in testing this original assumption, but in finding the source of women's inadequacy. Study after study has been designed to find out where it is women go wrong (ostensibly within their language use). Robin Lakoff (1975) suggested that it was women's use of the *tag question* which rendered their language deficient and made it appear hesitant and qualified. A tag question is supposedly a question tagged onto the end of a statement* – a half-way structure – which allows the user to make a statement and at the same time to qualify it, as in 'Dinner will be ready at eight, okay?' or 'I won't be home tonight, all right?'

Many were convinced that this was the answer and studies were carried out to determine whether women used more tag questions than men. It was found that they did not. Betty Lou Dubois and Isabel Crouch (1975) found that men used more tag questions than women. I would like to suggest that if this were a society in which the sexes were of equal status, such a finding would have constituted a breakthrough. The initial assumption – that men have got it right and women have got it wrong – would have been called into question and it would have been hypothesized that there was something problematic about men's usage. But this is not a society where the two sexes enjoy parity and no such hypothesis emerged. When it was found that men used more tag questions than women, this did not give rise to the logical conclusion that (a) women's language was perfectly in order, or (b) that it was men's language that was hesitant and qualified. Finding that women were not wrong on this particular count did not challenge the belief that they were wrong in general. Few seem to have abandoned the search; they simply began to look elsewhere for the evidence.

Of course, such research is 'rigged'; the findings are a foregone conclusion – by definition, they will be in favour of males. One thousand, or one hundred thousand studies may be conducted to find the source of women's deficiency and nothing may be found (although, statistically, this is a remote possibility), but what will this prove? It will not prove that there is nothing wrong with women's language, but that researchers are 'looking in the wrong place'. Such research can continue indefinitely and while there may be absolutely no evidence that women's language is deficient, the belief that it *is* can continue unchallenged. Studies which do not locate the source of deficiency can be counted as 'failures' and go unreported, while those which do find

---

*As a grammatical construct, there is some difficulty with a tag question for there is no grammatical form which represents 'half way between a question and a statement'. There is also the problem that some tag questions are authoritative rather than questioning, as in 'You won't do that again, *will you*?'

differences, and which may be reported, are rarely attributed to statistical probability and are often seized upon as the 'truth' as Carol Jacklin (1980) has pointed out. We receive a biased account of women's and men's language. It is an account in which much of the research is 'irrelevant' for the conclusions are often little but the prejudices that the researchers started with, rather than findings which emerge from the investigation.

As a feminist I do not seek to replicate male mistakes and to aim for a reversal, finding only in favour of females. I will settle for the more modest, reasonable and equitable aim of finding in favour of females, 50 per cent of the time. But in our sexist society this constitutes a radical departure from the prevailing value system. It constitutes a challenge to the existing power relations to assume – and to conduct research on the assumption – that women are half right and men are half wrong. By adopting these premises I feed in very different assumptions and I obtain very different feedback; I construct very different findings which make the unequal status of the sexes problematic rather than ostensibly 'natural'.

It is because these considerations about power are fundamental to my research that I am wary of terms such as 'sex roles' and 'sex stereotyping'. Sex stereotyping suggests that men talk one way and women talk another, and the world would be a better place if they both talked the same; but in a sexist society this is usually construed to mean that women should learn to talk like men. From a feminist perspective I would rather suggest that it might be more advantageous if men were to learn to listen like women. In the classroom this would seem to be an educationally sound suggestion.

Little research has been done on language and gender in the classroom but this does not mean that we are starting with a blank sheet and with no myths to repudiate. There has been considerable research on language in education in the last decade, and the absence of gender as a variable is more likely to be explained by educationists' predilection for assuming that the standard student is a male, than by the absence of gender differentiation in classroom language.

To place current research on language in education in context it is necessary to review the contribution made by the language across the curriculum movement. This movement has been responsible for making links between language and learning and for extending linguistic considerations beyond the traditional confines of English. Those who are identified with this movement (Douglas Barnes, James Britton, Michael Marland and Harold Rosen, for example) have been instrumental in developing the thesis that language plays a crucial role in learning; indeed, Barnes (1972) went so far as to suggest that language and learning were virtually one and the same thing when he stated that 'the very act of verbalizing demands a reorganisation of ideas which merits the name learning' (p. 114).

This movement, which was spearheaded by English teachers, came at a time when English teachers were deprived of their traditional role and justification. When the efficacy of teaching grammar was called into question – as it undoubtedly should have been, being after all little but a residual practice from the days of a classical education – English teachers were in a sense purposeless, because it was no longer possible for them to claim that they taught children to read and write, or even talk, by drilling them in the principles of grammar. While grammar may be an interesting subject in its own right it could no longer be claimed to be directly related to one's own language use. For many English teachers there was an identity crisis – what were they to teach; what was their role? – but it was a crisis which was shortlived once language across the curriculum made its presence felt as an educational theory, for it reinstated English teachers at the centre of educational practice.

However, regardless of the timely nature of the emergence of this movement (and much research is generated by comparable considerations) it has been highly influential, and not just in Britain, but in many other countries as well. It has provided the basis for much current educational theory and practice, to the extent that in England, The Bullock Report (Department of Education and Science, 1975) recommended that all schools under its jurisdiction should formulate a language across the curriculum policy. Briefly, the primary contention of this movement has been that language – particularly in the form of talk – is necessary for learning, and Harold Rosen (1971) claimed that unimpeded talk was necessary if students were to think and to learn. 'Restrict the nature and the quality of that dialogue,' he says, referring to the enormous range of talking pursuits available, 'and ultimately you restrict thinking capacity' (p. 126).

Such statements, of course, aroused my interest. I was aware that in society in general there were impediments imposed on female language use that were not experienced by males and I saw no reason to suspect that the same patterns would not manifest themselves in educational institutions. If the patterns of language use were comparable (with males talking more, interrupting more and defining the parameters of the talk), and if talk were essential for learning, then perhaps females were being educationally disadvantaged. In quantitative, if not qualitative, terms females could be being penalized. Douglas Barnes (1976) had stated that 'Often when we meet a problem we want to talk it over' and that 'it is as if the talking enables us to rearrange the problem so that we can look at it differently' (p. 19), but if in mixed sex classrooms females did not have the opportunity to talk the problem over (and males in contrast *did* have the opportunity), then it could be that females were being deprived of the opportunity to learn, that they were being discriminated against.

Such issues, however, were not on the agenda of language and learning research. This was not the direction followed by investigators who, in their attempts to document the opportunities for talk, began to present data of a disconcerting nature. It was quickly recognized that students experienced little opportunity to talk in the classroom and the issue of language and power became a focus of attention. Not all those present in the classroom enjoyed equal prestige or power. There was an educational hierarchy of teacher/student and, as the authority figures, teachers had the power, and consequently were able to exercise control over talk. It was teachers (female and male) who talked more, interrupted more and prescribed the parameters of the talk. To the adherents of the language across the curriculum movement, this constituted a misuse of power, for rather than facilitating learning, it was argued, teachers actually retarded and inhibited it by their monopolization and control of talk. It was claimed that teachers talked too much and that they excluded the experience of their students. Harold Rosen (1971) refers to the 'Rule of Two-Thirds' and quotes Flanders (1962) when he states that 'In the average classroom someone is talking for two-thirds of the time, two-thirds of the talk is teacher talk, and two-thirds of the teacher talk is direct influence' (p. 120) – that is, teachers are constantly in the position of telling students 'how it really is'.

Such classroom findings are not dissimilar to feminist findings in language and gender, where it has been established that there is a social hierarchy in which men have power, and which they utilize to control talk, although it is not the 'Rule of Two Thirds' that has been put forward here but the maxim that a talkative female is one who talks half as often as a man (Kramer, 1975). Feminists have found that there is a qualitative as well as a quantitative difference, because it is not just that men talk more, but that they are more likely to define reality, to tell women 'how it really is' (see Kramarae, 1980 and Spender, 1980b). Feminists have claimed that these differences are not the result of sex but of power, and this claim seems to be substantiated by the evidence presented in the area of language and learning. Not that investigators in language and learning have been overly sensitive to the ramifications of power differences beyond the broad divisions of teacher/student.

The primary focus in language and learning has been on excessive teacher talk and the obstacle that this constitutes to learning for supposedly all students. If only a third of the available talking time in class is allocated to students, then it can hardly be argued that they are being encouraged to use their language for learning. But an issue which arises from this evidence and which has not been systematically pursued is that of the distribution of this one third talking time which students are allocated. Is it equitably distributed among the students? Do class, ethnic or gender factors play a role in the distribution? Such questions are difficult to answer, for by and large students have been classified as a homogeneous group, and in typical, and limited, social science manner, have been compared or contrasted with another ostensibly homogeneous group, that of teachers.

But it is not just the amount of teacher talk that has been of interest. That teachers talk more is a manifestation of their power (as well as a source of perpetuating that power). That same power is also manifested in other ways. Teachers have the power to determine the reality in their classrooms and to 'block' the learning of their students; they are the authority figures and they can decree 'how it really is'. They can define what counts as knowledge, what is significant, relevant and appropriate; they can use their experience as the yardstick against which their students are measured and often found wanting.

'Speech is not only a tool which each of us can use in making sense of the world,' states Douglas Barnes, *'but also a means of imposing our view of the world on others'* (Barnes, 1976, p. 116: my italics). Judging from the data which Barnes gathered it is clear that teachers frequently used their speech to impose their version of the world on their students; such practices often require the students to deny their own personal experience in order that they might adopt the teacher's schemata.

To many of us who have come to our understanding of the world via the feminist route these findings in language and learning should come as no surprise. Virtually since its inception the modern feminist movement has recognized the unfortunate outcomes of hierarchical divisions. When one group in society is accorded authority, dominance, supremacy, then that group also possesses the capacity – and it seems the propensity – to define reality, to insist on the validity of its own personal experience, to claim legitimacy for its world view as the only world view. In the event of contradiction those who are not members of the 'superior' group are more often than not required to repudiate their own experience. Whether the hierarchy is students and teachers or whether it is based on any other unequal divisions of race, class or sex, the results are much the same; wherever there is discontinuity between the dominant and the oppressed group it is resolved in favour of the dominant group. Teachers may think they know 'how it is' and may be only too willing to tell their students; and men may think they know 'how it is' and be only too willing to inform women.

To some extent this helps to explain why we have the research findings that we do in language and gender. Women may not experience their language use as deficient or inadequate, but women in a sexist society do not have the power to tell it 'how it is'; their version of experience is often discounted. (This applies to many other areas besides language and gender; women's version of experience from history to their mental and physical health often does not count either. See Mary Daly, 1979.)

There are many repercussions of having one group who is able to 'tell it how it is'. Douglas Barnes states that within the social institution of education, much 'depends upon generating an artificial dependency in the learners, so that they gain knowledge only by submitting to the teacher's view and not by thinking for themselves' (Barnes, 1976, p. 118), and one means of promoting this dependency is for teachers to be able to determine reality. Again, the parallels with feminist findings are quite clear. I am sure that many feminists would assert with the same certainty as Douglas Barnes that within a sexist society, much 'depends upon generating an artificial dependency in women so that they gain knowledge only by submitting to the man's view and not by thinking for themselves'.

There are many examples of the way teachers use their *power* to tell it 'how it is' and to construct the dependency and inferiority of their students (which of course, in turn, helps to justify their own authority and 'supremacy'). Douglas Barnes describes a geography lesson which he observed in a rural secondary school and in which the teacher 'distributed copies of an excellent aerial photograph of the area around the school'. Barnes says

> Most of the pupils came from farms in the area; the photograph reflected their world to them, the patterns of settlement, the distribution of cultivation and pasture. I expected a fine discussion, for the photograph would enable them to reflect upon their everyday knowledge and to see it more schematically. But the teacher wrote three words on the blackboard, 'shape', 'tone' and 'texture', and asked for definitions. (Barnes, 1976, p. 118)

There was no 'fine discussion'; instead there was silence. And it is a silence that can be conveniently interpreted as an indication of lack of ability on the part of the students. Barnes states of the teacher that 'By insisting that the pupils talk about the photograph *in his terms* he detached them from what they knew best, their everyday lives' (p. 118). The teacher divorced the students from their experience, he consigned their view of the world to the realm of *non data*, and to Barnes, this is inimical to learning. He argues, on educational grounds, that we must begin with our own experience in order to learn, that we must take our own lives as a starting-point if we are to become involved in active learning.

It is by talking things through from the basis of one's own personal experience that one is able to forge new meanings, make new connections, able to learn. When those who are participating in the talk enjoy equal power, when their experience is equally valid, then it is possible to explore how we come to know what we know and to change it. This is very different from being told 'how it is' for in one context we are autonomous and in the other we are dependent.

But to return to the geography lesson. Douglas Barnes is most explicit in his statement on the way in which the teacher pre-empts learning. The students could not join the discussion on the teacher's terms ('shape', 'tone' and 'texture') and the teacher prevented them from starting on their own terms. 'He was asking them to arrive without having travelled' states Barnes (p. 118) and this constitutes an impossible demand. But it is a demand which has a dividend from the teacher's point of view. It is relatively easy to make someone who enjoys less authority appear stupid and no doubt this teacher could have found sympathetic support from his colleagues if he had informed them that these kids could not even talk about their own homes and farms, that they simply did not know anything! Such conclusions, however, would not be based upon the students' ability, nor indeed upon their 'knowledge' but would be a measure of the teacher's power to define reality. Like the research process discussed earlier, the teacher's authority is being fed into the classroom, and that same authority is then fed back; the students, and what they know, their personal experience, can be quite irrelevant, for it is not their performance which is being measured.

But hierarchies are not confined to educational institutions. They abound in our society in general and they all afford the same opportunities as they do for authority figures in the classroom. In terms of sex it is relatively easy to observe the way in which men as the 'superior' beings define reality, and as a result are able to construct the dependency, the inferiority and the 'stupidity' of women, which of course in circular fashion helps to justify men's own claims for supremacy.

I would like to give you an illustration of this process in operation and describe the proceedings of a conference I attended where I was a member of a workshop on sexism and education.

For the participants, who were mostly women and mostly teachers, the topic encompassed their everyday existence – their invisibility on the educational hierarchy and in the curriculum, the discriminatory practices against them – and like Douglas Barnes I expected a 'fine discussion' from this context; I expected to be involved in a dynamic learning process.

But while we thirty-two women began to talk tentatively of our experience of sexism and education, one of the five men assumed control and informed us that we were there for a purpose and that we should 'get back to the point'; his point! 'It is sexism in the system we are here to talk about,' he declared, 'and not your individual experience'. Like the geography teacher whom Barnes describes, this man insisted that the group talk about sexism in his terms, which were very different from the terms of some of the women present. And like the students Barnes describes, we women became relatively silent. While we comprised 86 per cent of the group, we talked for only 45 per cent of the time (and the 14 per cent who were men talked for 55 per cent of the time), but perhaps more important than the amount of talk was the nature of the talk. More than one man present was keen to define sexism for the women, to tell us 'how it is', and I cannot help speculating on the later discussion of the men with some of their colleagues. Would they assert, in bemused and patronising tones, that we knew nothing of sexism, that we could not even begin to discuss it, that we were 'stupid'?

If all the members of that group had had equal power then it is possible that we could have become involved in negotiations that merit the name of learning. But one sex has more power than the other and in this instance members of that sex used that power to impose their own version of the world upon those of us who did not share it. We were 'blocked' by the men, who not only talked and interrupted more, but who, significantly, defined the topic of conversation and the form it should take.

I think it possible that Douglas Barnes and I have each described the same phenomenon – the effects on talk and on learning in a hierarchical context. We have each witnessed the construction of dependency, inferiority and 'stupidity' which can occur when an individual or a group is accorded the authority and the power to decree reality. But one factor which Douglas Barnes has overlooked (along with many other adherents of the language across the curriculum movement) is that educational stratification is not confined to teacher/student. There are other forms of stratification operating in the classroom, one of which is male and female. And this has educational implications.

Males talk more, interrupt more, and are more likely to decree what is 'real', and they do this both inside and outside educational institutions (Spender, 1980b; Spender and Sarah, 1980). While this may have repercussions for female teachers, it is also significant for female students. It is not just that they do not share the same access to talk – though this in itself could constitute a serious impediment for girls – it is also that any element of their experience which may be different from their male counterparts runs the risk of being perceived as invalid, as 'not real'. The educational slogan, 'Begin with the experience of the learner' takes on new dimensions in this context, for uniquely female experience frequently does not count in male terms, and therefore is not used as the starting-point for female learners. Female experience can be consigned to the realm of non-data. James Britton (1973) has deplored the practice of not taking the experience of the learner into account and criticizes the attitude prevalent in some schools which he calls 'the fresh start' policy. Those who follow this policy assume that their own view of the world is the norm and students who do not share this view are often classified as deficient, even as 'culturally disadvantaged', and are subjected to a 'fresh start'. Not only is it insensitive and inhumane, declares Britton, to rule that the experience of some students is null and void, and to demand that they repudiate it, it is also educationally counter-productive. 'In so far as they succeed in outlawing the kinds of learning that have developed,' says Britton of the 'fresh start' advocates, 'they will, at worst, induce total apathy – a loss of the old learning and nothing to take its place', and he goes on to add that 'To many a child it must seem as though a comprehensible, explorable and eventually knowable world gives way to one that is known to the teacher but to no one else' (Britton, 1973, p. 4).

Few would dispute Britton's thesis. To be unable to use one's own experience as a basis for operating in the world is to be lost, to be without reference points, to be handicapped in any learning situation. Yet it seems that this is often what women are required to do in a society, and an educational institution, where only male experience is counted as real. To paraphrase Britton, it must seem to many women that what may begin as a comprehensible, explorable and eventually knowable world gives way to one that is known only to men. And of course this can disadvantage women.

Women are constantly subjected to a 'fresh start' in education where the male version of experience is perceived as the norm, with the result that female differences can be classified as deviation and deficiency, and discounted. Both directly and indirectly women can be deprived of the opportunity to use their own experience as a reference point. Male control of talk, in coeducational settings, can result in the repudiation of female experience; and where males are not present, the male-centred curriculum, which is frequently passed off as pertaining to the human condition, can exclude a female version of the world.

In commenting on the literary curriculum (where women's experience could be taken into account if desired), Elaine Showalter (1974) has said, 'Women students will . . . perceive that literature, as it is selected to be taught confirms what everything else in the society tells them; that the masculine viewpoint is considered normative and the feminine viewpoint divergent' (p. 319). But it is not necessarily literature where the greatest sins of omission are committed; women's experience is left out of almost every part of the curriculum. History and the social sciences have also made a selection on the basis that the male is the norm, while even mathematics and the sciences, as embodied in textbooks and presented by teachers, have often presented a male view of the world (Scott, 1980). They have ignored the contributions which women have made to their construction so that women have few means of bringing their own experience into the curriculum and are led to believe in the myth of their own inadequacy.

Mr X said that women have never been any good at science but we didn't believe him; why shouldn't women do science? But we couldn't find any; there were no women scientists in the library. We thought it would be good to go and tell him he was wrong, but we couldn't. Well, not that way. I suppose we could prove he was wrong if we were good at science, couldn't we? Aaahhh . . . but he wouldn't be impressed, he wouldn't change his mind by that. And anyway, I don't know if we could be good at it. He should know. (16-year-old Inner London comprehensive female student, 1978)

This young woman's experience did not count. Although she did not *feel* it as a condition of her existence that females could not do science, she had many sources telling her 'how it is' and telling her she was mistaken. As Elizabeth Fennema points out in relation to mathematics (in Chapter 11), it was boys who thought that girls could not do mathematics and while the girls may not have shared this view, the boys' view predominated. This student's experience gets little support. The teacher tells her 'how it is' and says women cannot do science. The 'subject' tells her 'how it is' through its presentation and says that women cannot do science (there were no references to women scientists in the library, not even to Marie Curie). Who is she to disagree with these authorities? Is it any wonder that she begins to doubt her own experience, to be puzzled about how it really is, even for herself? How long will it be before she declares that women cannot do science and thereby repudiates her own experience of the world?

Elaine Showalter has made a similar point, again speaking primarily of literature:

> What are the effects of this long apprenticeship in negative capability on the self image and self confidence of women students? The masculine culture, reinforced by the presence of a male author . . . is all so encompassing that few women students can sustain the sense of a positive feminine identity in the face of it. Women are estranged from their own experience and unable to perceive its shape and authenticity, in part because they do not see it mirrored and given resonance by literature. Instead they are expected to identify as readers with a masculine experience and perspective which is presented as the human one. (Showalter, 1974, pp. 319–20)

When a selection of prescribed A level texts in English in 1978 revealed that there were fifty-three male authors to two female authors (Walters, 1978) it is not difficult to appreciate the significance of Showalter's claims. Unlike the male student who can find himself and his own experience confirmed in the literary curriculum, who can find a 'match' between his own experience and the way literature tells him 'how it is', the woman student finds she is studying a different culture, to which 'she must bring the adaptability of the anthropologist' (Showalter, 1974, p. 319). The way she explains the world is not usually the way it is explained in the curriculum, and even literature can represent a 'fresh start'. She must begin anew to make sense of the world without benefit of her own experience, for it carries little weight and affords her few reference points or signposts to direct her in her task.

If this absence of women's experience were acknowledged, then perhaps it would be different. If the student who encountered the science teacher who claimed that women could not do science had been aware that women have been left out of the records of scientific achievement, then no doubt her response would have been different. She might not have been as ready to accept the teacher's version of 'how it is'. If the students who confronted an entire English course comprised of male authors concerned with male experience knew that this was not a reflection of women's contribution, but a reflection of the priorities of those who are responsible for curriculum selection, then perhaps they would be less likely to devalue themselves and their experience, to accept the myth of their own 'inferiority' and 'stupidity'. But such an acknowledgement is not made; indeed, it is even often actively resisted. And this is where we are back to the question of power. This is where there is no parity between male and female sex roles. This is where it is males who tell it 'how it is', and where females must take on the male version, even though it may conflict with, or repudiate, their own understanding of themselves and their world.

James Britton, a staunch supporter of the premise that educators should begin with the experience of the student, and a passionate believer in the capacity of literature to draw upon and expand that experience, might have condemned this 'fresh start' policy imposed upon females, had he been aware of, or acknowledged, its operation. The way in which females are treated within the curriculum and classroom practice is the very antithesis of the methods proposed by the adherents of language across the curriculum. While some gains have been made in the area of multicultural education, partly because of the language across the curriculum movement, and while intentional encouragement is given to students to utilize their own specific cultural experience, to express it in their own way, to tell it 'how it is' from their own standpoint,* the culture divisions between female and male are still largely overlooked and *both* sexes are usually required to tell it 'how it is' from the male point of view. This is even the case with multicultural education itself, where one could be forgiven for concluding that all students of different ethnic groups are male.

Not all educationists have remained oblivious to the repercussions of male control of language (written and spoken) in the classroom. Some feminists have documented the consequences of this control (see Clarricoates, 1978).

John Elliot has also indicated in his study on 'Sex role constraints on freedom of discussion' (1974) that in the class he was teaching there was a 'problem of non-participation among the girls' (p. 148). He took steps to remedy it and exerted pressure on the girls to talk and, as he says, 'This was met with nearly ten minutes silence' (p. 148). Some of Elliot's observations are interesting; he seems to be genuinely puzzled about the dynamics of interaction in his mixed sex classroom. He notes that when one girl finally did begin to talk, 'a boy called Dick came in to confront her with a critical question from which she retreated and backed down' (p. 149). The girls, however, did not seem to retreat and back down when talking to each other. In a single sex context, 'there were individual differences of interpretation' among the girls but when they emerged they were *not* followed by withdrawal and silence. While Elliot does not raise the possibility, I think it likely, however, that these differences served as a basis for negotiation and learning, because their experience was accepted by each other as valid and there was no overriding hierarchical structure which permitted any one girl to take control and to decree, without challenge, 'how it really was'. But this was not the case when the girls and boys were required to talk together. There the boys were able to decree 'how it really was', and the girls

*This is not to claim that such attempts have been successful, or even that they have gone far enough, only to suggest that multicultural education has been accepted as a legitimate area of educational concern.

were silenced. Elliot found this cause for concern and stated that 'Frequently at the root of the phenomenon of non-participation is a lack of confidence in one's capacity to think independently of others' (p. 154). No doubt few would disagree with him. What he does not state, however, is that educational structures foster this dependency in girls. He does not say that girls who do not have confidence in their capacity to think independently of others (males), and who manifest this in their silence, are behaving in a realistic manner. Given the 'evidence' they are presented with in society and in the school, they would be acting irrationally to draw any other conclusions. The 'deficiency' lies not in the girls, but in the expectations, and the roles, which society and education provide for them. *Anyone* who cannot make use of their own experience, who cannot tell it 'how it is' from their perspective and have this perceived as valid, will look to others for clues. Elliot's female students were no exception. The topic he was asking them to talk about was war!

This topic, very much defined as male territory I should think, reveals both the direct and indirect reinforcement of the repudiation of girls' experience and their language. Like so many other topics set for discussion in education, it enhances the male control of talk, encourages males to talk more, and with greater authority. It even helps them to appear to be better and more capable students. And this is one way in which language and gender operates in the classroom.

For the sake of argument, let us speculate on what might have happened if John Elliot had asked the class to discuss a topic defined as female territory. Let us ask ourselves what might have happened if he had asked, for example, that they talk about birth, about suburban isolation, about making a choice between family and career commitments. I think it likely that the boys would choose to be non-participants. I think it likely that they would have been obliged to look to the girls for the clues. But this would be an unusual, even an uncomfortable predicament for the boys, and their non-participation might have taken a very different form.

My own experience as a teacher suggests that the boys would not have been silent, they would have protested and deemed the discussion of such topics as 'unfair'.* Whenever I have attempted to provide a 'corrective' to the male biased curriculum I have found myself confronted with a disruptive class – of boys. I think John Elliot would probably have encountered similar problems. For the boys are used to having their experience legitimated as the substance of education, they are used to being in control of the talk, they are used to having the advantage when it comes to learning and they do not like it when they feel that their significance is being minimized or made marginal. This

*I have indicated what boys are likely to do when excluded from the content of the lesson in a chapter, 'Disappearing tricks', in Dale Spender and Elizabeth Sarah (eds), *Learning to Lose: Sexism and Education* (The Women's Press, 1980).

is not what they have been led to expect as their role. They will frequently try to turn it back to their own advantage:

Male 1.    I'm not going to talk about girls' stuff; that's stupid. It's just
           stupid having to talk about what it's like being at home all day
           with the kids. Anyway, they don't have to do it. They can get
           out, can't they? Make every day a holiday? Can't they?

Male 2.    Yeah, go to the football, or the pub. (Laughter)

Male 3.    Or play records.

Male 1.    Or meet their mates.

Female 1.  What about the housework, and the kids, and the shopping?

Male 3.    Well, they don't take long. Blokes could do that in half an
           hour. And then enjoy themselves. (Laughter, directed at
           females. Topic of suburban isolation abandoned; topic of the
           way males spend holidays introduced.)

(fourth-year English class, Inner London comprehensive school)

In this context, the girls were not allowed to begin to tell it 'how it is'. The few comments that they did make, initially, were treated with derision by the males, who protested and quickly changed the topic to one in which they dictated the terms, and in which their experience was drawn upon and that of the girls excluded. My own research indicates that this is not an atypical reaction when a teacher tries to introduce material which draws on the specific experience of females.

I think most teachers are familiar with this situation and take it into account when deciding what material to use in their classrooms. While teachers are expected to control classrooms, they are making realistic choices when they cater almost exclusively for the interests of the boys. When Katherine Clarricoates (1978) talked to teachers about this, they made the following statements:

I'd tend to try and make the topic as interesting as possible so that boys won't lose their concentration and start fidgeting. (p. 357)

It's a bit harder to keep the boys' attention during the lesson . . . at least that's what I've found so I gear the subject to them more than I do the girls . . . (p. 357)

It's easier to pull the girls in than it is to pull the boys in, so I try a topic that's usually got quite a lot for the lads. (p. 359)

So do most teachers of mixed sex classes. In a sexist society where boys by virtue of their sex are accorded more significance than girls, teachers make nothing less than a sensible decision when they take male supremacy into account. It is easier to deal with the resistance of those without power – particularly if that resistance is channelled into an expression of silence and passivity – than it is to deal with the resistance of those with power.

But while teachers persist with this practice, sexism is maintained and reinforced; the power differences of the sexes are perpetuated. Males continue to be accorded authority and to have their experience validated, and to be confirmed, without justification, as the superior sex, while females have their experience invalidated and their inferiority constructed and confirmed. In the classroom males continue to monopolize talk and to define its parameters. And females continue to be confronted with the evidence that they do not count. While this state of existence has been persistently and emphatically acknowledged as a crucial area of educational concern for those who are neither white nor middle class, it does not seem to have penetrated that the same problem arises for those who are not male.

To have one's experience discounted, one's view of the world relegated to the realm of non-data, is to be deprived of the means of making sense of the world and to be reduced to guesswork when it comes to making decisions. To be deprived of the opportunity to use language to learn, to be unable to 'talk things into place', is to have one's image-making, symbolizing and thinking skills impaired. We know this. We have designed policies aimed at eliminating these practices – for boys.

'Rejection of speech implies rejection of the speaker,' says James Britton (1973, p. 5) and those who have their language, their experience and themselves rejected – as most girls do daily in mixed sex classrooms – seek protection in silence. Those who have their experience, their language and themselves validated – as most boys do by both students and teachers – are encouraged to assert themselves even more. This is one way sexism is fostered and developed, one way in which *the sexes are made unequal*, and it is a way which is utilized daily in educational institutions.

My experience as a woman informs me that the world is not comprised exclusively of males and that males do not even constitute the norm, the yardstick, or the desirable human being. And any education system which continues to base its theory and practice on the belief that males are the paradigmatic human beings is to be condemned.

I do not seek to persuade some of my male colleagues of the error of their ways for I have no reason to believe that it will be productive. In the last five years they have had ample opportunity to familiarize themselves with research in this area and their continued refusal to accept such research as legitimate (and to change their ways) reflects poorly upon them. Their failure to include women in educational theory and practice cannot be attributed to ignorance.

Were sex roles symmetrical, a matter of difference rather than dominance, such a state of affairs would not have persisted. Both men and women would be able to tell it 'how it is' from their own perspective. But it is men who have the powerful sex role, and it is men who reinforce that power by telling it 'how it is', and it seems that they are unlikely to surrender that power simply because they have been asked politely to do so.

Some males will perhaps repudiate this account of the invisibility of women – their language and their experience – as the substance of education, precisely because it is not *their* experience of the world. They will be tempted to deny its authenticity and to put me right by telling *me* 'how it *really* is'. Such rejection, however, will simply confirm my hypothesis. Feminists have also learnt how to play the 'research game' and with feminist research, the double bind is no longer something which is confined to women. This is one attempt to deconstruct the inequality of the sexes and is I hope far more challenging than the documentation of sex roles.

# References

Barnes, Douglas (1972). 'Language and learning in the classroom', in Language and Learning Course Team, Open University. *Language in Education: a Source book*. Routledge & Kegan Paul, pp. 112-18.

—— (1976). *From Communication to Curriculum*. Harmondsworth: Penguin Books.

Britton, James (1973). 'What does the school do with language?', in Australian UNESCO Seminar. *The Teaching of English*. Canberra: Australian Goverment Publishing Service, pp. 4-9.

Byrne, Eileen (1978). *Women and Education*. Tavistock.

Clarricoates, Katherine (1978). 'Dinosaurs in the classroom - a reexamination of some aspects of the "hidden" curriculum in primary schools'. *Women's Studies International Quarterly*, vol. I no. 4, pp. 353-64.

Daly, Mary (1979). *Gyn/Ecology: the metaethics of radical feminism*. Boston: Beacon Press.

de Beauvoir, Simone (1972). *The Second Sex*. Harmondsworth: Penguin Books.

Department of Education and Science (1975). *A Language for Life*. (The Bullock Report). HMSO.

Dubois, Betty Lou and Crouch, Isabel, (1975). 'The question of tag questions in women's speech; they don't really use more of them, do they?'. *Language and Society*, vol. 4, pp. 289-94.

Elliot, John (1974). 'Sex role constraints on freedom of discussion: a neglected reality of the classroom'. *The New Era*, vol. 55, no. 6. pp. 147-55.

Flanders, N.A. (1962). 'Using interactional analysis in the inservice training of teachers'. *Journal of Experimental Education*, vol. 30, no. 4, pp. 313-16.

Jacklin, Carol Nagy (1980). Comment made at conference, 'Sex Differentiation and Schooling', Cambridge, UK, January, 1980.

Kramer, Cheris (1975). 'Women's speech: separate but unequal', in Barrie Thorne and Nancy Henley (eds). *Language and Sex: Difference and Dominance*. Rowley, Mass.: Newbury House, pp. 43-56.

Kramarae, Cheris (ed.) (1980). 'The words and voices of women and men'. *Women's Studies International Quarterly*, vol. III Nos 2 and 3, special issue.

Lakoff, Robin (1975). *Language and Women's Place*. New York: Harper & Row.

Rosen, Harold (1971). 'Towards a language policy across the curriculum: a discussion document prepared and introduced by Harold Rosen on behalf of the London Association for the Teaching of English', in Douglas Barnes, James Britton, Harold Rosen and the LATE. *Language, the Learner and the School*. Harmondsworth: Penguin Books, pp. 119-59.

Scott, Marian (1980). 'Teach her a lesson' in Dale Spender and Elizabeth Sarah (eds). *Learning to Lose: Sexism and Education*. The Women's Press.

Showalter, Elaine (1974). 'Women and the literary curriculum', in Judith Stacey, Susan Bereaud and Joan Daniels (eds). *And Jill Came Tumbling After: Sexism in American Education*. New York: Dell.

Spender, Dale (1980a). 'Talking in class' and 'Disappearing tricks', in Dale Spender and Elizabeth Sarah (eds). *Learning to Lose: Sexism and Education*. The Women's Press.

—— (1980b). *Man Made Language*. Routledge & Kegan Paul.

—— (ed.) (1981). *Men's Studies Modified: the Impact of Feminism on the Academic Disciplines*. Oxford: Pergamon Press.

—— and Sarah, Elizabeth (eds) (1980). *Learning to Lose: Sexism and Education.* The Women's Press.

Walters, Anna (1978). 'Women authors and prescribed texts'.W.A.S.T.E Papers, presented at National Association for the Teaching of English Conference, York, March/April, 1978.

# 8 Guidance and Pastoral Care

## Michael Marland

## The importance of pastoral care

Much of the discussion of sex stereotyping and schools has been in terms of teaching materials and the curriculum. There is another hugely important facet of the work of schools. A school does not just teach; it endeavours to help pupils to learn. This learning support is vital, for pupils have to *use* schools, and most are not able to do so by mere virtue of the skills they bring to school with them. 'Personal, educational and vocational guidance' is a central part of the function of a school (Marland, 1974, Chapter 1; Best et al., 1980). In the USA the main burden of this task is typically given a professionally additionally trained and administratively separated staff, while in the UK, typically again, the function is merged in with the general teacher's role. The first solution offers narrower but more powerful counselling, especially for educational guidance; the second is potentially more integrated with the full range of learning and growing experience, but is often very weak. From the point of view of this book the results of the US system are easier to recognize and assess – and to change. Many observers would agree with the criticism that: 'Counselling services provided for students generally support and reinforce stereotyped attitudes and behaviours about appropriate roles for males and females in society' (Saario, 1976, p. 9). We have fewer specific studies of the guidance element of pastoral care in the UK, but I have no doubt that it is a very strong part of a school's sex stereotyping. Whether guidance is given specifically through guidance departments and counsellors, or disseminated through a school's pastoral care and teaching structure, it is a potent force for sex differentiation.

# Coping with feedback

A central guidance task is to help pupils use feedback from teachers, whether informal comments or specific grades and analyses of completed assignments. We have a fair idea that boys and girls tend to react differently to peer-group and adult feedback as Barbara Licht and Carol Dweck discuss in Chapter 6. It certainly seems that one component of being successful at school is being able to interpret and use positively adult feedback.

The repeated 'must try harder' of teachers' exhortations does little. It is an essential pastoral task to help pupils 're-attribute', as Licht and Dweck put it. Class teachers or tutors should therefore study with their pupils the marks, grades and comments of other teachers, help pupils to understand the point of them, and, above all, be able to re-frame those comments as self-formulated advice, and to incorporate that into their learning.

The tutor (or in the USA the home-base teacher) in the secondary school is the key person, and this task has to be done on a group and not only an individual basis (see, for instance, Blackburn, 1975, and Hamblyn, 1978). Such work is part of the larger responsibility for teaching study skills.

There is, it appears, a special responsibility here to girls. The work of Carol Dweck and her colleagues described in Chapter 6 has shown that feedback is given differently to girls and boys, and that girls can develop what is aptly termed 'learned helplessness'. The pastoral task is to re-teach, or, to use their phrase, to give 'attribution retraining'.

# Expectation of success

Anxiety can be valuable and indeed it should be, for it is the quality we use to sharpen ourselves to cope better. However, too much anxiety can be debilitating, and can be applied differently to different of our tasks, to be 'domain-related'. It is fairly clearly sex-related, and typically girls develop 'mathematics anxiety', as Margaret Sutherland makes clear in Chapter 5. It can be shown that such anxiety can be avoided by adequate teaching, flexible approaches, special help and attitudinal support. This last is very much a guidance task, an essential part of full pastoral care.

# Subject choice

Whatever the arguments for extending the core, or for producing homogeneous option choices that oblige all pupils to retain at least one language, science, craft and humanities, say, there will always be some choice. The complementary worrying points are that pupils develop their ideas very early – before we start guidance! The research on primary pupils, all from the USA so far, is quite frightening in this respect: children as young as two-and-a-half 'display stereotypic concepts of sex-appropriate traits, beliefs, and adult roles'; from 'pre-school through elementary school, children set highly sex-typed, occupational goals'; 'beginning in second grade and persisting through the twelfth grade, children perceive social-verbal and artistic skills as feminine, whereas spatial, mechanical, and athletic skills are viewed as masculine'; 'beginning at age twelve, boys predict that science and mathematics will be relevant to their work styles. In contrast, girls predict that science and maths will have little relevance to their lives' (Wittig and Petersen, 1979, p. 265). This means that the high school year-by-year considerations of electives, or the secondary-school third-to-fourth year option choices in the UK, grow out of already stereotyped views of roles, suitable occupations, and likely subject preparation for them. The guidance given is pitted against years of background attitude hardening.

It would be bad enough if the problem were merely that girls and boys have established attitudes by the time they make subject choices. But a variety of studies have shown that the guidance system of secondary schools builds on and exaggerates these earlier ideas. In the USA mathematics and science are electives throughout the high school year, and it can be shown that guidance counsellors believe that courses in mathematics and sciences should be encouraged for males rather than females (Casserly, 1975, p. 30).

The studies of guidance in the UK have not especially focused on the difference between the sexes. Their general findings have been the weakness in guidance (Reid et al., 1974; Hurman, 1978; Wood, 1976; Ryrie et al., 1979). In such circumstances the peer-group and societal sex stereotypes are likely to flourish. This is amply confirmed in a study of 30,000 Scottish pupils, which certainly found that the more open the choice the more sex differentiation there is likely to be (Gray et al., 1979).

There is further evidence that not only do boys and girls choose differently as a result of pressures, but even that the choices they do make in subject options are unequally responded to: girls do not want physics as often as is desirable, but they are allowed to study it even less than they choose it. For instance, girls rating physics high in their preference scale are less likely than boys with the same level of prefer-ence for physics to actually study it, whereas girls rating biology low in a preference scale are more likely to study it than boys with the same level of preference (Keys and Ormerod, 1976, p. 350). This must reflect teachers' stereotypical influence, and anecdotal evidence and personal observation suggest that it is unwittingly differentiating. I have myself known, for instance, a girl recommended not to consider being a vet 'as it is so messy', and another one advised to take home studies instead of chemistry at 15 'because you have so many difficult subjects'. Neither remark, I believe, would have been made to a boy.

Similar steering of girls away from subjects linked with jobs that are perceived as being 'masculine' is reported by Bennett (1981).

My suggestions for facing this problem do not include removing choice, for not only do I think that choice within education is an essential part of it and anyway necessary to allow growing adults to shape their own lives, but also because to do that is only to avoid the problem or hide it temporarily.

Steps can be taken, although the early ones on this list depend on a continuity between primary and secondary phases possible in North American school systems, but not in almost all parts of the UK:

1. Occupation portrayal must start in the youngest years, and specific learning about occupations be seen as a part of the general curriculum (as indeed it should long have been) from age 6. This specific teaching would, of course, not suffer from parodies that creep through the hidden curriculum from readers, picture books, and the periphery of general humanities teaching.

2. The subjects that will be presented as separately timetabled labels in older years should have 'tasters' for younger children, to endeavour to make them attractive to all before specific prejudices are established.

3. Cross-age tutoring of one sort or another should be used to bring successful older students or young workers in non-stereotypical subjects or occupations before pupils throughout their schooling. Regular arrangements need to be set up for that.

4. Additionally schools should have methodical series of atypical adult visitors to speak, discuss, join in. Such a scheme, called 'Visiting Women Scientists Programme' is organized in the Greater Manchester area by the 'Girls in Science and Technology Affirmative Action Programme' in Manchester.

5. 'Choosing' should be part of the curriculum; that is a specified educational aim should be 'teaching pupils the processes of choice'. This would be a curriculum aim embodied in a number of teaching syllabuses from various subjects (for example, crafts, design and technology is a very good vehicle) and in the 'pastoral curriculum' (for a description see Marland, 1980). This would include occasions for focusing the theory and process of choosing: the need to know all the available items; self-assessment; and a knowledge of the outcome of various choices.

6. A very thorough organization of the process of actually choosing subjects, so that this both benefits from the tuition given earlier under (5), and acts as a paradigm for subsequent choice.

7. Individual counselling for pupils of both sexes to help them consider non-stereotypical choices.

8. The labelling, describing and image-building of subjects to de-emphasize their previous sex-stereotypical associations. There is ample evidence from studies of testing that results can be affected by the presentation of a test as 'male' or 'female'. Re-labelling is

obviously not easy over short periods when the attitudes have been developed over years of socialization but, as one study commented: 'It is encouraging that the negative effects can be reduced even for a short time by such simple manipulations' (Unger and Denmark, 1975, p. 417). Thus both the syllabus and the label of sex-stereotypical subjects can be shifted towards their being androgynous.

9. Single-sex classes could be used as a transition; the arguments are discussed in Chapter 12.

At the moment in both the UK and USA subject or course choice is rightly seen as a manifestation of the sex differentiation of schooling. I am suggesting not only that if schools organized themselves to reduce the sex differentiation subject choice will be an indicator of success, but, more than that, the process of preparing for and following up subject choice should be an important part of the actual school process of reducing overall sex differentiation: subject choice can be the core of this.

## Working with parents

A part of a school's pastoral work is to relate to parents. This has never been as successful as those of us responsible for schools would have liked, or even have declared it to be! The duty towards parents involves listening to them, informing and interesting them and, at least in community schools, facilitating or organizing activities for them. There must also, however, be an educating task, though this has to be sensitively done and with appropriate humility. It can be difficult to reconcile with the listening and responding role. For instance, how does a school committed to reducing sex differentiation respond to that section of the Muslim population that wishes to retain a different role for their girls?

I can see no alternative to the school's adopting a persuasive stance. Indeed the evidence is that parents are far less likely to have sex-stereotypical wishes for their children than teachers readily suppose. A school therefore needs to have a programme of talks, discussion groups, events and publications that help parents know of the career opportunities for girls and help them re-focus their attitudes to sex differentiating aspects of schooling.

## References

Bennett, Y. (1981). Report of research for the EDC presented at the British Association for the Advancement of Science, September 1981.

Best, Ron, Jarvis, Colin and Ribbins, Peter (1980). *Perspectives On Pastoral Care*. Heineman Educational Books.

Blackburn, Keith. (1975). *The Tutor*. Heinemann Educational Books.

Casserly, P.L. (1975). *An Assessment of Factors affecting Female Participation in Advance*

*Placement Programs in Mathematics, Chemistry, and Physics*. Report to the National Science Foundation, NSF Grant No. GY-11325 p. 42.

Ernest, J. (1976). *Mathematics and Sex*. Berkeley: University of California, p. 30.

Gray, John, McPherson, Andrew and Raffe, David (1979). 'Collaborative research in Scotland: a new departure'. *Educational Research*, vol. 21, no. 3, pp. 178–85.

Hamblyn, Douglas (1978). *The Teacher and Pastoral Care*. Oxford: Basil Blackwell.

Hurman, A. (1978). *Charter for Choice*. Monographs in Curriculum Studies 3. Windsor: NFER Publishing.

Keys, Wendy, and Ormerod, M.B. (1976). 'A comparison of the patterns of science subject choices for boys and girls in the light of pupils' own expressed preferences'. *School Science Review*, vol. 58, no. 203, pp. 348–50.

Marland, Michael (1974). *Pastoral Care*. Heinemann Educational Books.

—— (1980). 'The pastoral curriculum', in Best et al. *Perspectives On Pastoral Care*. Heinemann Educational Books.

Reid, M.I., Barnett, B.R. and Rosenberg, H.A. (1974). *A Matter of Choice: Study of Guidance and Subject Options*. Windsor: NFER Publishing.

Ryrie, A.C., Furst, A. and Lauder, M (1979). *Choices and Chances*. Dunton Green: Hodder & Stoughton.

Saario, Terry Tinson (1976). 'Title IX: now what?', in Allan C. Ornstein and Steven Miller. (eds) *Policy Issues in Education*, Lexington: Lexington Books, D.C. Heath. Reprinted for the Ford Foundation.

Unger, R.K. and Denmark, F.L. (eds) (1975). *Woman: Dependent or Independent Variable*. New York: Psychological Dimensions, p. 417. Cited in Wittig and Petersen (1979).

Wittig, Michele Andrisia and Petersen, Anne C. (1979). *Sex-Related Differences in Cognitive Functioning*. Academic Press.

Wood, Robert (1976), 'Sex differences in mathematics attainment at GCE ordinary level'. *Educational Studies*, vol. II, no. 2, pp. 141-60.

# 9 Sex Differentiation and Careers

*Jackie Bould and Barrie Hopson*

## Myths about women at work

A number of myths are commonly held to be true:
1. Since the Equal Pay Act came into force in 1975, women earn as much as men.
   In 1979, average gross weekly earnings were: for women – £61·80; for men – £98·80 (Department of Employment, 1979).
2. Most women work for pin money.
   The 1974 Family Expenditure Survey (Department of Health and Social Security) showed that without the contribution made by a woman's earnings, the number of families living below Supplementary Benefit level would have trebled.
3. A woman's place is in the home.
   Women make up 40 per cent of the labour force. An EEC survey (Commission of European Communities, 1975) found that 'a majority of women, be they single or married' would positively prefer to be in paid employment.
4. Since the Sex Discrimination Act, women have equal opportunity in work.
   A report by Audrey Hunt in 1975 showed that a 'majority of those responsible for the engagement of employees start off with the belief that a woman is likely to be inferior to a man in respect of all the qualities considered important'.
5. Married women and mothers are not reliable workers.
   A study by the Industrial Training Research Unit in five clothing firms showed that turnover and absenteeism among part-time working mothers was lower than among the younger full-time workers (Haggar, 1973).

6. Women only work until they marry.
   Married women make up the majority of working women and are increasing as a proportion of the work force (Department of Employment statistics, 1974).

These are examples of some of the attitudes commonly expressed about women at work; they are extensions of the stereotypes which our society reinforces about women.

Sex-role stereotyping provides a picture of women and men at work which is not necessarily based on fact, and its influence is like that of stereotyping in other areas of life; it provides artificial boundaries which suggest that behaviour which does not conform to the sex stereotype is in some way deviant. Sex-role stereotyping begins to influence our lives from birth and can be observed as a powerful influence within schools. Some of the consequences of stereotyping in schools are reflected in restrictions upon the freedom of occupational choice and career development for girls and boys.

Before considering the role of the school as a determinant of career choice, and its contribution to the reinforcement of sex-role stereotypes in the world of work, it is necessary first to consider what we know about vocational development and the way in which this knowledge influences careers work in schools and careers services.

## Some theories of vocational development

In 1951, Ginzberg published the first real attempt to organize the available literature concerning vocational development. Prior to this, he had been able to identify three general approaches. The first approach emphasized the external influence of chance as a major factor; the second approach was more concerned with 'internal' factors of unconscious motivation. Both these approaches are incomplete and cannot be used satisfactorily to produce general working theories. The third approach Ginzberg called talent-matching theories. These focus attention on the assets of an individual and match these assets against the requirements of occupations. Talent-matching theories appear to have provided the cornerstone for vocational guidance work in this country.

However, two major weaknesses are apparent in this approach. First, it ignores the provision for people to develop their own self-concepts, and secondly, it does not allow for the development of ideas over a period of time. As the talent-matching approach does not take cognisance of the developmental nature of occupational choice, vocational guidance has in the past tended to be postponed until the latest possible moment in schools.

A number of researchers (for example, Super, Tiedeman and O'Hara, Borow, Tennyson and Klaurens and Holland) have developed these ideas to produce more comprehensive theories of vocational development which Lorraine Hansen (1979) summarizes with the following list of implications for schools:

1. Career development is a continuous, developmental process, a sequence of choices which form a pattern throughout one's lifetime and which represent one's self-concept.
2. Personal meanings or psychological determinants of work (what it means in the life of an individual in relation to their values and life-style) may be far more important than external job characteristics.
3. Career development involves a compromise, a reality-testing which involves role identification, role taking and role exploration, assessment of self and of opportunities, and of the economic conditions of society.
4. Career patterns of individuals may be influenced by intelligence, sex, location, socio-economic level, economic conditions, and the changing nature of the world of work in an advanced technological society.
5. Career development is part of human self development involving different developmental tasks at various life stages, and individuals varying in their readiness for such tasks or their vocational maturity.

Some recognition of these implications is now being made in schools with planned careers programmes being introduced lower down the school, but generally careers work is still confined to a small school team with little time and resources available to implement and monitor the more extended careers work suggested by recent research (*Education in Schools - a Consultative Document*, Equal Opportunities Commission, 1977).

However, most of the research on vocational development has been related to the traditional approaches of men and boys to work. As Tennyson (1968) points out in his review of career development literature, much of the present knowledge cannot be generalized to large segments of the population, including women. Super (1957) has more recently made attempts to identify some of the career patterns for women. He distinguishes between:

1. Conventional - that is full-time work until marriage leading to full-time housewife; perhaps this should now be amended to suggest full-time work until the first child followed by full-time housewife.
2. Interrupted - this pattern includes the return to work as children grow older.
3. Double track - this pattern describes full-time work after the birth of children by utilizing child-care facilities.

Such studies are still in their infancy and as little follow-up work has been done in this country, this work has not been translated into careers work in schools.

It would be very useful for those involved in careers work to have more information in such areas as: the ways in which women and men view work differently, both for themselves and for the opposite sex; the ways in which women and men view work in relation to their roles outside work; and possible alternative patterns of work for women and men as technology develops and unemployment becomes an increasingly common feature of our lives.

These are suggestions for further research which could give careers teams help in providing more effective careers programmes in schools, but there is already some knowledge and information available about differences for girls and boys in occupational choice, and for women and men at work, which have implications for careers work. This chapter examines this information in terms of ability, attitudes and aspirations of girls and boys, and how differences in these areas and in occupational opportunity lead to the wide differences which we see when we examine the roles of the sexes in employment. The last section of the chapter considers practical ways in which schools can help reduce the effects of sex-role stereotyping, so as to maximize each student's chances of using her or his potential and provide them with opportunities to discuss new potentials within themselves.

There are frequent references to observations made as part of a research project at the Counselling and Career Development Unit at Leeds University. This two-year project which was funded by the Equal Opportunities Commission began in 1977 and was concerned with examining the differences in school for girls and boys in Yorkshire and Humberside. Fourteen schools were visited from primary to secondary level in different economic and geographic areas, and through discussion with school staff and pupils alongside participant observation the following areas of school life were examined: school structure, school policies, teachers' attitudes and behaviour, pupils' attitudes and aspirations, the curriculum, out-of-school activities, resource materials. The outcome of this research has been to focus on teachers' attitudes and behaviour, and an in-service short course for teachers has been designed.

## Abilities and attainments

In discussions with school teachers at all levels and in all types of school, it was found that differences in abilities for girls and boys were often accepted as a natural phenomenon arising from innate ability and the influence of home. Associated with this attitude was a general reluctance among school staff to accept the responsibility of school in influencing and reinforcing differing abilities for girls and boys.

In primary schools teachers tended to expect girls to develop more quickly and apply themselves more diligently than boys. 'After all, it's only natural that boys prefer to be active and play football outside,' said one teacher. 'In fact, I find that the quiet boys who want to just sit and read can give us more trouble than the boisterous ones higher up the school.' The situation in junior and middle schools showed the first signs of some of the differences for girls and boys which are seen in later examination results. Curricular differences, particularly in craft areas and physical education, were not uncommon in these schools and the expectation of the staff was that the boys would be 'catching the girls up' in terms of academic ability. However, none of the schools visited was able to back up these thoughts about the differing abilities of girls and boys with comparative test data. These expectations were all based on experience and seemed likely in the terminology of Rosenthal and Jacobsen (1968) to produce a 'Pygmalion effect' – that is, the self-fulfilling prophecy.

In secondary schools there is considerably more information available on the differences in attainment between boys and girls, a sample of which is considered below. How much these differences can be attributed to inherited abilities and biological sex differences, the authors do not propose to argue in this chapter. However, even if such differences were to have their roots in biological phenomena, there are significant influences in all areas of our society which reinforce and cement the differences between the sexes, and it is not until we are able to reduce these influences to a minimum that we are able to say conclusively that sex differences are 'natural and not to be tampered with' in the words of one headteacher.

Table 9:1 shows the CSE entries for 1978 and the entry and pass rates for O level 1976. The picture which emerges from these statistics follows the stereotypic image of girls and boys. From discussions about sex differentiation in schools with secondary-school staff, it was found that it was often these differences in examination performance which gave staff most cause for concern.

A detailed discussion of the differences in examination figures in particular subject areas is covered more fully in other chapters. However, in relating these figures to their implications for occupational choice, two major factors are of importance:

1. Craft areas still tend to be recognized as traditionally male or female, for example, entries for CSE needlework and related subjects were predominantly from girls, representing 99·74 per cent of the total entries. In metalwork and related subjects, boys' entries represented 99 per cent of the total. Domestic science subjects are often given respectability for a boy when linked to a career interest in catering; rarely is a similar link displayed between needlework and tailoring, for example. For girls, participation in traditional male crafts is increasing but a continued interest into an occupation related to these crafts is still an unusual choice.

2. Boys predominate in entry numbers and success rate in mathematics, physics and chemistry. Girls show greater success and entry numbers in languages.

Table 9:2 shows a comparison of A-level results from the Department of Education and Science Education Survey 21 (DES, 1975). From these figures it can be seen that the trends seen at 16 continue through advanced-level courses.

If these figures are compared with the entry requirements for certain careers (Table 9:3); it can be seen that many school-leavers are further restricted in their occupational choice by offering to employers a limited range of subjects and examination successes.

These examples of career qualification requirements have been chosen to highlight a number of restrictions upon occupational choice

**Table 9:1    CSE entries (1978) and O-level entries and pass rates (1976) for boys and girls**

WEST YORKSHIRE AND LINDSEY REGIONAL EXAMINATION BOARD
ENTRIES FOR CSE 1978

| Subject | Girls | | Boys | |
|---|---|---|---|---|
| Domestic science and related subjects | 4122 | (82%) | 889 | (18%) |
| Needlework and related subjects | 3570 | (99·74%) | 9 | ( 0·26%) |
| Metalwork and related subjects | 16 | ( 1%) | 1 649 | (99%) |
| Technical drawing and related subjects | 76 | ( 2·5%) | 2 936 | (97·5%) |
| Woodwork | 182 | ( 3·3%) | 5 301 | (96·7%) |
| Total | 7966 | | 10 784 | |

Source: Letter from the West Yorkshire and Lindsey Regional Examining Board in reply to a request from J. Bould.

COMPARISON OF MALE AND FEMALE ENTRIES AND PASS RATES IN VARIOUS
GCE O-LEVEL EXAMS IN JUNE 1976 (ALL BOARDS)

| Subject | Sex | Entry | Percentage pass (A B C Grades) | |
|---|---|---|---|---|
| English literature | Females | 141 000 | 64 | Higher female entry and |
| | Males | 106 000 | 54 | pass rate |
| English language | Females | 203 000 | 65 | Higher female entry and |
| | Males | 183 000 | 56 | pass rate |
| French | Females | 84 000 | 64 | Higher female entry and |
| | Males | 66 000 | 58 | pass rate |
| Religious studies | Females | 40 000 | 63 | Higher female entry and |
| | Males | 25 000 | 51 | pass rate |
| Chemistry | Females | 30 000 | 60 | Higher male entry and pass |
| | Males | 60 000 | 61 | rate |
| Physics | Females | 25 000 | 58 | Higher male entry and pass |
| | Males | 86 000 | 59 | rate |
| Mathematics | Females | 87 000 | 56 | Higher male entry and pass |
| | Males | 116 000 | 60 | rate |
| Biology | Females | 86 000 | 56 | Higher female entry |
| | Males | 61 000 | 61 | Higher male pass rate |

Source: Murphy, R.J.L. (1978) Sex Differences in Objective Test Performance. Unpublished Associated Examining Board Research Report.

with particular implications for girls and boys. The traditional male crafts of engineering, construction and motor trades at craft level require abilities in the subjects in which boys have traditionally shown interest and success; whereas secretarial work and nursery nursing emphasize the academic strengths of girls. As technology is becoming an increasing part of our everyday life, certain careers are reflecting this trend by asking for technical qualifications. Such careers as hair-

Table 9:2    Corrected percentages for comparison of pupils taking
particular A-level courses

| Subject | All boys | All girls | Boys single-sex | mixed | Girls single-sex | mixed |
|---|---|---|---|---|---|---|
| Mathematics | 41 | 15 | 37 | 41 | 19 | 12 |
| Further pure mathematics | 9 | 3 | 9 | 9 | 5 | 2 |
| Physics | 41 | 9 | 36 | 43 | 12 | 7 |
| Chemistry | 30 | 13 | 27 | 31 | 15 | 11 |
| Biology | 16 | 21 | 16 | 18 | 21 | 21 |
| English literature | 23 | 53 | 28 | 21 | 48 | 55 |
| French | 8 | 24 | 11 | 5 | 23 | 25 |
| German | 3 | 9 | 3 | 2 | 8 | 10 |
| Geography | 27 | 22 | 23 | 29 | 24 | 20 |
| History | 23 | 28 | 26 | 20 | 28 | 28 |
| Economics | 22 | 8 | 26 | 22 | 6 | 9 |
| Art | 9 | 15 | 7 | 9 | 15 | 15 |
| Music | 2 | 4 | 2 | 2 | 3 | 1 |

Source:  Department of Education and Science (1975), Table 8.

dressing, catering and nursing, which have been predominantly female careers, are now looking for evidence of scientific study; careers such as radiography and dietetics require A-level science qualifications. Girls are increasingly finding that areas of work which have previously been open to them will now be closed unless they have physical science subjects and/or mathematics to offer. Included in the list of examples are careers such as accountancy and architecture. These careers do not necessarily require study of sciences or mathematics to advanced level and could be seen as areas of work needing skills in which girls are traditionally very competent, such as language and design ability. However, these areas are still dominated by men. For example, women formed only 4·3 per cent of the membership of the Royal Institute of British Architects in 1974, and nearly 4 per cent of the membership of the Institute of Chartered Accountants up to January 1980.

As the economy has moved from a position of full employment to one of high unemployment, employers are finding that they have greater numbers of applicants for each vacancy and can, therefore, be more selective. One of the consequences of this situation is the use of the pre-entry test which is particularly apparent in the typical male craft areas, where a knowledge of mathematics and physics can be vital to comprehend the test questions. Another consequence is the raising of entry qualification levels. For example, chartered accountancy demanded five O levels twenty years ago, rising to two A levels currently, with an intention of reaching all graduate entry in the near future. Teaching itself has risen through a similar series of increasing entry requirements over an even shorter period of time.

How do the abilities of school-leavers and the entry requirements for

Table 9:3   Examples of career qualification requirements

| JOB TITLE | MINIMUM ENTRY REQUIREMENTS | |
| | Level | Subjects |
| --- | --- | --- |
| *Craft level opportunities* | | |
| Engineer | CSE grades 2–5 | Mathematics, physics and craft |
| Motor trades | | subject preferred |
| Construction | | |
| Hairdressing | No minimum required | Study of science subjects |
| Catering | | preferred |
| Clerical work | No minimum required | Study of mathematics and English required |
| Secretarial work | CSE 1–4 or O levels preferred | English, possibly typing |
| Sales work | No minimum required | Study of mathematics and English |
| Agriculture | CSE grades 2–5 | English, mathematics required with science subjects preferred |
| Nursery nursing | CSE 1–3 or O levels preferred | English |
| | | |
| *Technician level opportunities* | | |
| Nursing (SRN) | O level (usually 3) | English (Welsh) language and science subjects preferred |
| Physiological measurement technician | O level (usually 4) | English, mathematics and science preferred |
| Animal nursing auxiliary | O level (usually 3) | English and mathematics or science |
| Police (cadet entry) | O level (usually 4) | English and mathematics |
| Computer operator | O level (usually 5) | English and mathematics |
| | | |
| *Professional level opportunities* | | |
| Chartered accountant | A level (usually 2/3) | English and mathematics (at least to O level) |
| Architect | A level (usually 2/3) | English, mathematics and/or science (at least to O level) |
| Medicine and surgery | A level (usually 3) | Usually biology, chemistry and physics |
| Radiographer | A level (usually 2) | Physics |
| Dietician | A level (usually 2) | Chemistry and another science |
| Social worker | A levels (usually 2/3) | |

Source: Various career publications – list compiled by J. Bould.

careers actually affect the career choice of girls and boys? The answer is not readily available. No national statistics on the entry of young people into employment have been produced since 1973. This is in part due to a change in the National Insurance system in 1975, but also as a result of a failure to agree about the ways entry to employment should be classified. Department of Employment surveys have been conducted, sampling 10 per cent of the school-leaver population, but the results have not yet been published. This lack of information severely restricts our knowledge of national trends in types of employment entered and training undertaken.

Table 9:4 shows the entry by industry of girls and boys into employment in 1973 and the type of training undertaken by school-leavers in 1974.

The figures show clearly the concentration of girls and boys into specific industries. For example, construction trades – 90·7 per cent boys, 9·3 per cent girls; distributive trades – 44 per cent boys, 56 per cent girls. If a more detailed breakdown was undertaken, showing the actual job descriptions and job titles, these differences would be even wider. For example, many of the girls entering the construction

**Table 9:4   Industry analysis of girls and boys entering employment (1973) and training undertaken by school-leavers (1974)**

| Industry Order<br>(standard industry classification 1968) | Boys | Girls |
|---|---|---|
| 1.  Agriculture, forestry, fishing | 4 834 | 827 |
| 2.  Mining and quarrying | 1 157 | 153 |
| 3.  Food, drink and tobacco | 2 492 | 2 287 |
| 4.  Coal and petroleum products | 204 | 90 |
| 5.  Chemicals and allied industries | 1 750 | 1 898 |
| 6.  Metal manufacture | 3 266 | 1 058 |
| 7.  Mechanical engineering | 8 943 | 2 387 |
| 8.  Instrument engineering | 880 | 494 |
| 9.  Electrical engineering | 4 951 | 2 268 |
| 10.  Ship building and marine engineering | 2 408 | 177 |
| 11.  Vehicles | 3 744 | 830 |
| 12.  Metal goods not elsewhere specified | 5 707 | 1 802 |
| 13.  Textiles | 1 969 | 2 096 |
| 14.  Leather, leather goods and fur | 287 | 174 |
| 15.  Clothing and footwear | 1 172 | 2 897 |
| 16.  Bricks, pottery, glass, cement, etc. | 1 229 | 735 |
| 17.  Timber, furniture, etc. | 3 234 | 673 |
| 18.  Paper, printing and publishing | 4 475 | 2 395 |
| 19.  Other manufacturing aids | 1 346 | 996 |
| 20.  Construction | 21 887 | 2 239 |
| 21.  Gas, electricity and water | 1 962 | 914 |
| 22.  Transport and communication | 6 884 | 3 634 |
| 23.  Distributive trades | 18 523 | 23 317 |
| 24.  Insurance, banking, finance and business services | 6 491 | 18 917 |
| 25.  Professional and scientific services | 5 090 | 15 524 |
| 26.  Miscellaneous | 15 344 | 11 054 |
| 27.  Public administration and defence | 10 303 | 7 211 |
| Total | 140 532 | 107 047 |

**Table 9:4** *cont'd*

| *Training* *(designations of school-leavers 1974)* | *Boys* (000s) | *Girls* (000s) |
|---|---|---|
| Apprenticeship | 118·2 | 15·5 |
| Professional | 3·5 | 2·2 |
| Clerical | 19·2 | 96·3 |
| Employment with planned training: | | |
| over 12 months | 26·4 | 13·5 |
| 8 weeks to 12 months | 20·5 | 27·5 |
| Other employment | 86·9 | 80·9 |
| Total | 274·7 | 235·9 |

Source: Department of Employment (1974), and Careers Service statistics.

industry will do so as clerical assistants and secretaries, many of the boys in the distributive industry will be employed in delivery or portering jobs.

Women are, in fact, concentrated into relatively few working areas. In 1977, nine million women were working outside the home and of these, over half worked in three service areas: 17 per cent in distributive trades; 23 per cent in professional and scientific areas (typists, nurses, technicians, secretaries, teachers); and 12 per cent in miscellaneous services (laundries, catering, dry cleaning, hairdressing).

Table 9:4 also indicates the different levels of training undertaken by girls and boys, which shows that the majority of jobs which girls enter offer little or no training. The clerical grouping which comprises 40·8 per cent of girls and 7 per cent of boys entering employment masks a wide variety of training patterns from a filing clerk with a very limited period of training to a highly skilled secretarial post with training lasting a number of years. In fact, only 10 per cent of girls under 18 in employment attended day-release courses as opposed to 40 per cent of the boys.

The consequences of limited subject choice and ability within these subjects combined with career entry requirements serve to provide a vital component in restricting the freedom of occupational choice. Both girls and boys are limited to some extent but it is girls in particular who find themselves in a position of offering inappropriate school subjects for many careers, and hence facing limited opportunities in terms of variety of occupations and training given. It is a situation which will demand far more than simply offering all craft subjects to girls and boys, and making sure that careers literature states that 'opportunities are open to girls and boys', which are the remedies which some schools think should suffice to bring about change. Possibilities for further development in schools are discussed later.

# Attitudes

A growing body of research literature reflects not only the impact of external or cultural barriers, such as discrimination on career development (Guttentag and Bray, 1976), but also the internal psychological barriers which inhibit development and choice. The literature suggests that significant attitudinal and behavioural changes on the part of educators, students and parents may be necessary for individuals to expand the range of options they know and are willing to consider. Among such internal variables which have been studied are self-concept and self-esteem, sex-role identification, locus of control, achievement motivation and attributions of causes for success and failure in self and others (Follett et al., 1977).

A number of studies have very direct implications for school work. Garai and Scheinfeld in 1968 found that 'boys have a clearer concept of their future occupational roles, are more realistic in their vocational planning and less frequently engaged in unrealistic fantasies and pipe-dreams about future happiness than girls'. Their studies also concluded that men desire jobs which give: 'power, profit, independence and prestige'. Women look for: 'interest, work with people or work helping others'. Another American study shows that despite the higher school grades which American girls earn, they are significantly less likely than their male peers to believe that they definitely have the ability to do college work. Since several studies indicate that individuals who have higher expectations actually perform better on achievement tasks and set higher aspiration levels for themselves, this variable is an important one. Maccoby and Jacklin (1974) go on to report that although females and males do not differ when young in their beliefs about the extent to which they have some control over their own destinies, by the time they reach college, women begin reporting less control over their own fates.

In careers work generally in this country there is little agreement about the way in which attitudes such as these influence career choice and therefore little cognisance of differing attitudes towards work is taken in the training of careers teachers and careers officers. Although discussion among those involved with careers work is full of references to experiences of pupils' attitudes towards work, or often lack of it, there is still much we need to know and much which is controversial about career development. This is an area which needs extensive research and development if we are to make careers work in schools more effective.

A variable which has been more widely reported, and the effects of which are more apparent, is the role of aspirations and expectations upon career choice.

# Aspirations and expectations

One of the central aims of a careers programme in school is to encourage students to utilize their potential to the full in making 'aware' decisions. A careers officer or teacher often tries to encourage discussion with a pupil about his/her aspirations prior to a discussion about vocational choices. However, there is a growing movement among those concerned with vocational guidance, supported by Donald Super's work (Super, 1975), towards the belief that it is very difficult for pupils to develop aspirations about their choice of work in a vacuum; a framework of possibilities and limitations is needed as a support for an individual's aspirations to develop. In schools, aspirations among pupils are often inextricably linked with their expectations; a compromise process between fantasy and reality.

Such a theory would be supported by conversations during the research project with children in their earliest years at school about what they wanted to do when they left school. Most girls replied that they wanted to be nurses, teachers, look after animals or become mothers and grandmothers. Most boys wanted to become soldiers, sailors, airmen, policemen, or follow their father's occupation, and two replies mentioned Action Man and James Bond. The question did not ask specifically about career choice. However, the boys only listed occupational choices, whereas, the girls included the roles of mother and grandmother, but did not mention their mother's occupation as a possibility for themselves. This arose in part from many of these young children having mothers who had interrupted their working life or who worked part-time. In response to questions put to the 'prospective nurses' about whether they would also consider becoming doctors, 'No', came the replies, 'women aren't doctors – that's for men'. This reply was even offered by a young girl whose mother was a doctor.

Such influences stemming from within and outside the home, for example, the images presented to children in the media about the desirable roles for men and women, can be very powerful as Kirchener and Vondracek showed (1973). A study of girls between the ages of 3 and 6 showed that they had already begun to realize that certain adult positions were not open to them. By the time careers work is undertaken on a formal basis in schools, that is some time between the ages of 13 and 15, aspirations may often be totally aligned with expectations, and decisions have already been made with crucial implications for future employment and life-style.

Many pupils have potential for further academic work or extended vocational training but girls in particular have often decided to deny that potential by preferring a job which demands no further academic challenge and little training. The thought of a three- or four-year apprenticeship training to a school-leaver at 16 or a five- or six-year medical training to a school-leaver at 18 can be daunting to both girls and boys, but for many boys, an extended training is considered a necessary evil to acquire a vital skill. For girls, training appears to be much more of an option, and possibly even wasteful if aspirations tend towards early marriage, home-making and giving up paid employment. Certainly, some girls view training as a risk in terms of cutting across social development and acceptance by peer groups. The figures for training contained in Table 9:4 clearly show the consequences of such expectations.

But why do girls and boys have such different aspirations?

A review of what is known about women beyond school and at work provides a clearer picture of what girls can expect.

## Further and higher education

One in 10 female workers under 18 attends day-release courses as opposed to 1 in 4 males under 18.

Engineering and technology students at non-advanced level comprise 2 per cent girls, 98 per cent boys.

Engineering and technology students at degree level comprise 4 per cent girls, 96 per cent boys.

In 1975 women comprised 35·3 per cent of the total undergraduate population.

In 1925 this figure was 31 per cent, although the figure did go as low as 25 per cent in the mid 1950s.

## Pay

The New Earnings Survey 1979 (Department of Employment, 1979) showed that the average gross weekly earnings for men are £98·80 and for women £61·80.

## As part of the labour force

Nearly 40 per cent of the labour force in Britain is female and of these almost 70 per cent are married.

There is a significant increase in the number of mothers of young children taking up paid employment. In 1975, 55 per cent of married female workers had children – an increase of just 10 per cent in ten years.

## Unemployment and special measures

In the six years 1973–78 female unemployment rose as a percentage of total unemployment from 16·2 per cent to 29·4 per cent. The numbers of women unemployed have risen much faster since 1975 than those of unemployed men, and indications are that this trend may continue. Younger women are especially affected; since 1973 the proportion of female unemployed school-leavers has risen from 35·3 per cent to just under 50 per cent.

The Manpower Services Commission 1979 gives the following details for participants in the 1978/79 programmes.

In the Job Creation Programme women averaged 24 per cent of the work force.

In the Work Experience Programme girls were 56 per cent of the participants.

In the Youth Opportunities Programme girls were 50 per cent of participants.

In the Special Temporary Employment Programme women were 25 per cent of participants in 1978/79.

Most girls can, therefore, anticipate at least twenty or thirty years of paid employment, even if they become unemployed for a time or choose to have a break. Why then, do so many girls cling to the ideal that their future fulfilment will be achieved as soon as they can give up work to tend a family, when for most girls this is clearly an unrealistic position?

Lorraine Hansen (1979) suggests a number of barriers to career aspirations and development which are perpetuated in the media and reinforced in schools and which tend to develop the sex-role stereotype further.

*Barriers for women*
(a) Lack of career orientation. Paid work is not supposed to be as important for women as work inside the home.
(b) Focus on marriage. Women expect to marry and be taken care of and are not ready for the economic, social and emotional independence they may face through separation, divorce or widowhood.
(c) Role conflicts. Women are dichotemized into opposites – traditionals or pioneers; housewives or career women. There is an expectation that men will be able to fill the multiple roles of worker, husband and father with no role conflict but no similar expectations exist for women.
(d) Institutional bias. A lack of women in non-traditional subjects in school and occupations, few women in top management and administration provides an absence of alternative role models for women.

*Barriers for men*
(a) Primary school and family bias. The largely female environment of elementary school years provides a limited role model for young boys.
(b) Messages which restrict male emotionality. Men are not supposed to cry, show too much emotion, spend too much time with children, or get too close to other men.
(c) 'Vocational success is everything' messages. Men are supposed to put career success first and their domestic arrangements should be made to support this success. Men are still expected to train for one career after full-time school education and continue in that chosen field until

retiring age. Changes in technology and employment patterns suggest that relatively few men will be able to follow this traditional pattern.

Schools have a vital part to play in providing an accurate picture of men and women at work to challenge some of these barriers and to reduce the power of media messages which can limit an individual's potential and hence career development.

## What can schools and careers services do?

A number of implications for schools as a result of sex differentiation in vocational development have already been suggested. School can act to redress the balance of negative influences from other areas of society about sex- and work-role stereotypes, but can also have a very positive role to play in extending the options open to girls and boys.

The following table lists examples of ways in which schools can help to reduce sex-role stereotyping in all areas of school life. These examples are all ways which were observed as part of the EOC research project and are not confined to the influence of a careers team.

**Table 9:5 Helping and hindering influences to reduce sex-role stereotyping**

| HELPING | HINDERING |
| --- | --- |
| *School structure* | |
| Positive discrimination in favour of male staff and use of fathers (especially in primary schools) | Predominantly female staff in schools |
| Use of outside female speakers | Men in all senior posts (especially in secondary schools) |
| | Predominance of men in mathematics/science departments |
| Discussion of issues with pupils, for example, whether metalwork is a boy's subject, and needlework for girls only; and visits outside school to show that subjects are appropriate to both sexes | Predominance of one sex in craft areas, for example, only female domestic science teachers and male metalwork teachers |
| Positive encouragement to mix groups | Segregation of boys and girls in class, during breaks, queueing, playgrounds |
| | Responsibility given to pupils in 'stereotyped areas', for |

**Table 9:5** *cont'd*

| HELPING | HINDERING |
|---|---|
|  | example, girls responsible for social activities, boys for 'heavy' work |
|  | Limited craft areas, science laboratories, etc. |
| *School policies* | |
| Common disciplinary system | Boys receiving physical punishment, girls verbal only |
| Shared pastoral-care responsibility | Pastoral care split, for example, female teacher deals with all girls' problems and vice versa |
| Equal recognition for achievement, for example, prestigious netball cup, or girls playing football! | Recognition of different achievements for girls and boys, for example, football cup |
| School rules apply to all pupils | Girls receiving stricter school rules about uniform, code of conduct |
| Involvement with parents and managing bodies in school policies, and activities to promote exchange of ideas and climate for change | Lack of involvement with families and community so that school becomes detached and unaware of outside influences |
| A questioning school policy, for example, an awareness of girls' and boys' achievements and the formation of a working party to examine school practices | An acceptance of the *status quo* based on lack of information |

*Teachers' attitudes, behaviour change and use of language*

| | |
|---|---|
| Expectations for all pupils as people, not based on sex, for example, some girls and boys do not like metalwork but they will not know unless they have been given every encouragement to try it | Self-fulfilling different expectations for girls and boys, for example, 'girls don't like metalwork'; 'boys find needlework too fine' |
| Little reference to groups of girls and boys as a general reference group | Use of girls' groups versus boys' groups as a means of discipline or to produce a competitive element |
| Careful use of humour | Use of sexist humour |
| All pupils known by first names | Boys known by surnames; girls |

**Table 9:5** *cont'd*

| HELPING | HINDERING |
|---|---|
| as a mark of respect for all pupils | by first names |
| | Teachers not wanting to teach one sex or the other |
| Girls and boys encouraged to play with the whole range of toys | Play limited to sex-linked activities, for example, girls – Wendy house/craft; boys – mechanical/special toys |

*Pupils' attitudes and aspirations*

| Encouragement and support for widening horizons | Accepting limited aspirations, for example, in careers terms, in school work |
|---|---|
| Providing a forum for challenging sexist comments and humour | Ignoring peer-group comments which suggest that one sex is inferior to another |
| Provision within timetable for looking at the roles of men and women and encouragement to form own ideas in relation to these roles | Avoidance of 'social education' within timetable |

*The curriculum*

| Early health education programmes for both sexes | No health education or split health education for boys and girls |
|---|---|
| As much mixed physical education as possible; positive encouragement to try all sports and achieve in all areas | All sports and physical education split, and rigid differences between girls' activities and boys' activities. |
| A system of rotating crafts so that boys and girls can sample every area or have a free choice of subject | Subjects specifically designated for girls or boys, for example, metalwork – boys; child care – girls |

This area is an extensive one and can be more comprehensively covered by teachers with a specific subject interest or teachers with an overall interest in the curriculum.

*Out-of-school activities*

| Work-experience is an ideal opportunity for pupils to try a range of jobs and work environments | Work-experience limited by letting pupils only try jobs traditionally done by their own sex |
|---|---|
| Timetabling outside activities to avoid clashes of interest | Football practice run after school at the same time as the dance club/keep-fit |

**Table 9:5** *cont'd*

| HELPING | HINDERING |
| --- | --- |
| *Resource materials* | |
| Careful choice of visual aids to provide a balanced portrayal of the sexes | Visual material displayed showing stereotypical roles for example, 27 occupations – all men |
| Using books, television, films as a stimulus for encouraging discussion about sex roles | Using very outdated material with no discussion about its relevance today |
| Displaying a wide range of books and suggesting alternative titles to girls and boys | Having a library divided into books for girls, books for boys |

Careers departments and careers teams would help to reduce the influence of stereotyping in career choice and development if:

1. All staff in schools, particularly careers staff were to receive training, not only in the basics of careers work but also on the effects of sex-role stereotyping.
2. The aims and objectives of a careers programme included mention of the issue of sex-role stereotyping and indicated materials and methods which staff could implement to reduce possible effects.
3. Attempts were made to introduce elements of careers work into the curriculum, not only in the early years of secondary education but also in middle and primary schools.
4. The range of careers information and job knowledge were extended to show men and women in non-traditional work areas by
   (a) Visits to employers
   (b) Speakers from industry
   (c) Work-experience
   (d) Careers material. If the careers material which is available shows men and women in predominantly sex-typed areas, then reference can be made to this in open discussion and this stimulus used as a basis for further work on differences for men and women at work.
5. All pupils had an opportunity to explore the consequences of decisions which they are asked to make, particularly at the time of choosing subjects.
6. Attention was given to the concept of teaching skills which enable pupils to choose the life-style they really want. Such a programme should include discussions about the alternative life-styles available to women and men and how work relates to life-style.
7. Schools liaised more closely with local industry to discuss opportunities. For example, there are now local and national opportunities which discriminate positively to encourage pupils to consider

careers outside the traditional areas. The Engineering Industry Training Board runs such a programme – the Technician Scheme for Girls. Such innovatory schemes could be given special recognition and discussed with pupils, staff and parents.

8. Support was given to pupils who are considering making decisions in a non sex-stereotyped way. It is important to remember that the consequences of making such a decision, for example, peer-group pressure, family commitments, may not be felt immediately and that, as a result, support is needed on a continuing basis.

The effectiveness of measures to reduce the consequences of sex-role stereotyping, and intervention programmes, are being studied in a number of countries. Two studies have produced interesting findings for careers work:

1. Lisa K. Barclay (1974) undertook a study of the emergence of vocational expectations in pre-school children. She exposed these young children to only three, fifteen-minute lessons covering women's careers, and she discovered that, at least in the short-term, their perceptions of women's career roles were affected and that they recognized a wider field of career possibilities for women than they did before the lessons. The long-term effects have not yet been reported.

2. A Careers and Girls Project was mounted by the Education Department of South Australia (1978) as part of the Career Education Project to widen the perception of girls about possible future careers. Through a study which modified existing curriculum materials and teaching methods it was shown that:

    (a) Teachers can act to help students make more rational choices and that such action at any level of schooling can be successful

    (b) Sex stereotyping of behaviour, activities and career choices is not inevitable and unchangeable

    (c) Teachers in school can modify the effects of such stereotyping in students through their work in the classroom.

These studies show that attempts to reduce sex-role stereotyping in occupational choice can be effective even at the most basic level. A neglect of these issues can produce an equally powerful effect. By doing nothing, the influence of school will continue to contribute towards unsatisfactory career choices which lead to personal dissatisfaction at work and at home and to wastage within the economy.

# References

Barclay, Lisa K. (1974). 'The emergence of vocational expectations in pre-school children'. *Journal of Vocational Behaviour*. vol. IV, no. 1.

Commission of European Communities (1975). European Men and Women: a Comparison of their Attitudes to Some of the Problems Facing Society. Brussels.

Department of Education and Science (1975). *Curricular Differences for Boys and Girls*. Education Survey 21. HMSO.

Department of Employment (1974). *Gazette*. HMSO. May.

—— (1979). 'New Earnings Survey'. *Gazette*. HMSO. October.

Department of Health and Social Security (1974, 1975). *Health and Social Service Statistics for England*. HMSO.

Education Department of South Australia (1978). *Careers and Girls Project*. Woolman, South Australia.

Equal Opportunities Commission (1977). *Education in Schools – a Consultative Document: the response of the EOC* Manchester: EOC.

Follett C., Watt M.A. and Hansen L.S. (1977). *Project Born Free*. Technical Report No. 3. Newton, MA: Education Development Center, USA.

Garai, J.E. and Scheinfeld, A. (1968). 'Sex differences in mental and behavioural traits'. *Genetic Psychology Monographs*. 77, pp. 169–229. USA.

Ginzberg, E. (1951). *Occupational Choice, an Approach to a General Theory*. New York: Columbia University Press.

Guttentag, M. and Bray, H. (1976). *Undoing Sex Stereotypes*. New York: McGraw-Hill.

Haggar, A. (1973) *Recruiting School Mums. Industrial and Commercial Training*.

Hansen, Lorraine Sundal (1979). 'School curriculum, developmental career guidance and changing roles of women and men'. Paper prepared for the International Conference on Guidance through the Curriculum, Cambridge 1979.

Hunt, Audrey. (1975). *Management Attitudes and Practices Toward Women at Work*. Office of Population Censuses and Surveys. HMSO.

Kirchener, R. and Vondracek, S. (1973). 'What do you want to be when you grow up? Vocational choice in children aged three to six'. Paper presented at the Society for Research in Child Development.

Maccoby, E. and Jacklin, C. (1974). *The Psychology of Sex Differences*. Stanford: Stanford University Press.

Manpower Services Commission (1979). *Opportunities for Girls and Women in the MSC Special Programmes for the Unemployed*. New Opportunity Press.

Rosenthal, R. and Jacobson L. (1968). *Pygmalion in the Classroom*. New York: Holt, Rinehart & Winston.

Super, Donald E. (1975). *The Psychology of Careers*. New York: Harper & Row.

Tennyson, W.W. (1968). 'Career development'. *Review of Educational Research*.

# 10    Curriculum Matters

*Michael Marland*

## Curriculum planning

For too many 'curriculum' means a list of subjects. The result is that curriculum planning is then taken to mean: 'Which subject do you add to which?' The content of each is either taken for granted or delegated to the subject team to work out unilaterally. The relationship between them seems to be 'integration' or nothing. Curriculum debate then becomes arguing about lists of subjects.

If we are willing to go behind those lists we need a workable definition of curriculum. Here is that of Lawrence Stenhouse:

> A curriculum is an attempt to communicate the essential principles and features of an educational proposal in such a form that it is open to critical scrutiny and capable of effective translation into practice. (Stenhouse, 1978, p. 14)

The point about 'open to critical scrutiny' is vital to the concern of this book. If every school had an overall curriculum plan that met this definition, its deficiencies in terms of sexual balance would be clearer and therefore more remediable. At the moment we are struggling in schools with such an inadequate notion of curriculum planning that the concerns of sex equality have no leverage on the workings of the school and no way into the planning activities of the school. Indeed, I should say that the difficulties encountered by girls in British and American schools are a manifestation of the general failure to plan whole curricula. *In an unplanned situation, underlying prejudices can easily rise to the surface.* Most of those in schools and outside who have tried to tackle the problems of sex differentiation in schooling have been obliged to work on the detailed surface of the curriculum: classroom lessons. Much of this is done with good effect, but working at the surface requires a huge investment of effort for very little return. For one thing, it is an effort required continually with every new lesson: fundamentals are not changed.

Dale Spender's crucial objection (Chapter 7) is that the male version of the curriculum is posing as the human condition (see also Spender, 1981). This will continue to be so, and there will be no way of changing it, until a proper whole-curriculum plan is instigated. I would go as far as suggesting that there is virtually no curriculum planning in the United Kingdom. Even in the small primary school a pupil can go from year to year, with what is learnt varying as she moves from teacher to teacher. The autonomy of the UK classroom teacher in the primary school is one of the biggest blocks to sex equality in education. In secondary schools, curriculum planning is weak in vertical continuity, and almost non existent in whole-school terms. In the US there is a much more thorough attempt. State laws usually determine some general principles, and School Boards add others. Vertical continuity is usually good, with single curriculum guides, 'K through 12', giving details from the youngest classes to the oldest. However, it is rare for these vertical shafts to be planned with cognisance of each other: indeed they are frequently incompatible. Thus 'Science K–12', 'Language arts K–12', and 'Library and media skills K–12' each have ambitions beyond themselves, but none has proper relationships. Indeed, US curriculum planning, while infinitely better than in the UK within subjects, is the supreme example of the notion that education is the aggregating of separate courses.

Proper curriculum planning involves listing what a school considers should be learnt and then distributing those aspects into teacher teams. Through-planning up the years has to be complemented by whole-school planning across the subjects. Such planning requires the detailed listing of the concepts, skills, facts and attitudes that the school (or school system) hopes pupils will have achieved by a certain stage, say the end of compulsory schooling. These lists are the foundations of curriculum planning, and are logically prior to and hierarchically superior to syllabuses devised by subject teams. These overarching curriculum statements allow the educator concerned with removing sexual differentiation to build in the basic requirements of a curriculum for all.

Thus a 'subject' becomes a collection of elements from the range of overall whole-school curriculum policies that cluster helpfully: a subject cannot be planned on its own, for if it is there will be both gaps and exaggerations. It has to be planned within whole-school policies. If this is done, the argument, for instance, about whether or not girls should do technical drawing (or drafting in the USA) is a logically subsequent one to deciding whether school pupils should be visually literate, and if so what this involves. If a school had such a whole-school approach, the question of technical drawing or not would be less acute, as the entire burden of visual literacy, or graphicacy, would not rest on one timetable slot.

In the UK the strongest arguments for whole-school planning have been concerned with language, and are summed up in the phrase 'language across the curriculum' (Department of Education and Science, 1975; Marland, 1978). The US has a similar (though rather narrower) movement calling for whole-school approaches to reading: 'reading in the content areas' (Herber, 1970). Both movements have the same message: you cannot leave language and reading to chance; language and reading cannot be taught only by the English teacher or the teacher of language arts.

Consider the case of mathematics. For a variety of reasons many girls find difficulties. Earlier chapters have discounted genetic disposition, and the concept of a difference in visual-spatialization has been challenged. Usually, however, the mathematics difficulties of girls are grouped into an undifferentiated mass. Supposing we concentrate on reading in mathematics. My observation is that somewhat more girls find mathematics reading difficult than boys. Why? And what can be done? We know from full textual analysis (Bruner, 1976) that the reading material in mathematics is substantially different from that in the normal reading of other subject books – and even more different from that in fiction: the text has a considerably lower redundancy level, for instance. Such modes of reading are simply not taught in schools (compare Lunzer and Gardner, 1978; Marland, 1978, Ch. 5), which give considerable tuition only in narrative. My hypothesis is that lacking any tuition or practise in the reading required for mathematics, those who find such reading difficult are handicapped in that subject – and among that group are more girls than boys.

There are no doubt other sub-aspects of mathematics which are difficult to more girls than boys. We therefore need to break down the undifferentiated mass called 'mathematics' to isolate these (see Hart, 1981). I suspect that they include measuring, ratio, decimal notation and, more generally, problem-solving. If, as I suspect, it is aspects such as these that cause a great part of the difficulty, there needs to be pre-learning experiences for these, and reinforcement across the curriculum. Without such whole-school curriculum planning, those lacking external reinforcement or adequate pre-learning experiences will be those who will fall by the wayside. Lack of overall curriculum planning leaves the subjects at the mercy of extraneous influences, and sex stereotyping is one of these.

My argument, therefore, is that a school must face these issues initially in the core of its curriculum, and from that work to the syllabuses, and thus to the learning materials and the classroom. Much of the current reactions to sex stereotyping endeavours to do the reverse, and work back from the classroom to the curriculum. I should suggest that whole-school policies are of particular importance to sex differentiation, for in the curriculum vacuum left by their absence the prejudices flow in. The failures from the point of view of sex equity of classroom teaching in topic, content, attitude and materials are a major manifestation of the failure of curriculum planning. That failure leaves gaps and creates highlights; certain matters are not taught at all, and others are overstressed or warped. *We will never have an equal curriculum until we have a planned curriculum to make equal!*

## Balance, freedom, and choice

'Balance' is a healthy-sounding word in curriculum discussion, but it can mask the truth. If past teaching and external experience have been differentiated, and therefore the individual's range of skills is already *un*balanced, a 'balanced' curriculum at the most leaves the differences untouched, and in many cases probably exacerbates them. Most public debate stops at the superficial level of providing a balanced diet – without any consideration of whether existing deficiencies require special attention. Particularly noticeable in the UK is the fairly extensive provision of remedial reading but the staggering dearth of remedial mathematics, thus providing work to help mainly the boys, but leaving the great weakness of many girls untouched! If it can be shown that a group of pupils have suffered a lack in the past, it should follow that that group is given a compensatory boost now.

For instance, it is fairly clear that girls are offered far less or no craft experience with resistant materials and with three-dimensional work in most primary schools. The importance of three-dimensional craft experience is clearly put for the primary years by HM Inspectorate (1975):

> Provision for constructional activities, indoors and out, is less commonly found. This lack of three-dimensional experience at the early stages may leave unharnessed the interest and energies of some children; they could thereby be at a disadvantage at a later stage in forming spatial concepts in mathematics and some basic notions in physical science. The girls are less likely than the boys to gain this experience out of school since they are more likely to be encouraged to join in just those kinds of activities about the house that the school also provides; the boys stand a better chance of being encouraged to share their fathers' interests in such activities as carpentry, thus extending their experience.
>
> Mechanical and spatial experience is necessary for young girls just because their verbal powers grow more quickly than those of boys. Experience suggests, on the other hand, that boys are probably at a disadvantage because their more robust interests rarely form a basis for early reading material. (HMI, 1975, pp. 2–3)

By their 1978 survey HMI were stating:

> There is no justification for differentiation between the curriculum for boys and for girls because of traditional differences in social roles; such differentiation as does still occur, for example in craft work which limits girls to using soft materials, is unusual and should cease. (HMI, 1978, p. 114)

This being so, it is up to schools to compensate. As the National

Foundation for Educational Research commented in 1976:

> If girls do lack spatial or mathematical concepts, whether because of home or school environment or innate qualities, it is up to the school to make up for these rather than reinforce them . . . Early restriction in mechanical and spatial experience may be the cause of later rejection of scientific subjects.

*For unbalanced early stages lead to balance only if there is a compensating imbalance.*

Compulsion in the curriculum is a key question, too rarely discussed carefully. We believe in the freedom of the individual to determine her or his own future, but we are nervous about tracing the roots of that source back. How can you choose that which you do not know? How can you know that which you do not learn? How can you learn that which is not put before you and you are compelled to learn? Thus the paradox of educating young people is that true later choice depends on earlier compulsion.

This argues for a compulsory range of learning, in which what is important is the content (which includes skills and attitudes) rather than the subject labels, and in which the possibilities of later choice are seeded. Such a compulsory range need not continue to the age of 16 in its full scope but undoubtedly some elements of it need to.

In this discussion the word 'core' can be confusing: to the extent that the metaphor is a useful one it should label not a group of timetabled subjects, but a list of concepts, skills, attitudes and facts which are required. They might be learnt through the vehicle of, for example, commerce or history. This is particularly important for sex differentiation as the range of skills must be insisted upon for all pupils.

Consider science as an example. What do we mean when we say 'a science must be compulsory'? We seem to have two separate reasons, and not to have translated what they mean into curriculum content. One is that if pupils give up school science at 14-plus they will never have access to science in a university or to a scientific career. We also sometimes mean that pupils who do not study this subject will have an inadequate understanding of the workings of the world. Before we can properly investigate content, we need to have explored the connection, if any, between these two aims. To accept one, however unconsciously, as the basis for science syllabuses, but to accept the other as the basis for a compulsory choice is both misleading and dangerous. Indeed, this confusion is one of the reasons why in the UK a large proportion of girls do biology or human biology as a fourth- and fifth-year option: the compulsory rule of 'one science' has been crudely imposed and pointlessly followed.

I would suggest that we need in the early years a far more rigorous approach to balance and compulsion, one that does not easily allow deficiencies to go unnoticed or unworked on. This would mean a differently unbalanced curriculum emphasis for each individual, and would, among other things, go some way to ensure that the stereotypes do not control the individual's balance of learning.

In later years choice must be allowed, for through choice the individual is creating herself or himself. However, the underlying curriculum planning must be such that the choice is of activities and modes of learning, but that these do not deny access to key aspects of the curriculum, for example, science and mathematics.

## Subject planning

As a result of the failures of overall curriculum planning, the within-school subject planning can be dangerously warped. For instance, the early approaches to science in the primary school can be so structured as to alienate girls from the start, and to differentiate sharply in presumed interests. For instance, there are schools in which by the age of 8 simple approaches to science are introduced, but for boys via astronomy and space travel and for girls via nature study (Ormerod, 1975).

In the UK, the science subject teacher's obsession with practical work, while a healthy corrective to entirely lecture- and note-based approaches, has altered the nature of the subject. I have on record, for instance, a remark by an able head of science that the school could not teach human biology because the method by which he and his team believed science should be taught was not suitable for the teaching of human biology: thus the subject should go rather than the method be altered! Religious education is another subject which, left to itself, casts around for a subject matter and rationale, and often ends up with peculiar mixtures. Stevi Jackson has shown the unacceptable in 'How to Make Babies: Sexism in Sex Education' (Jackson, 1978). Design technology, to take a further example, is often poorly prepared to take the curriculum burden expected of it by the school, and for which there is no proper school-department planning.

All this means that no subject team can properly plan their syllabuses in isolation from whole-school policies. If they do, the true balance of the curriculum is irrevocably lost. Leaders of subject and pastoral teams have to devise their syllabuses in a way which is consistent with whole-school policies, and gives individual teachers a clear brief. This will involve ensuring that the perspective adopted by the syllabus is not stereotypical. The basic questions need to include: Is the place of women in this activity recognized in the topics taught? Is the range of learning material balanced? Is the style of teaching dissected equally to the present requirements of boys *and* girls?

## Attitudes and the curriculum

If the curriculum is to be 'open to critical scrutiny and capable of effective translation into practice', there is hope that curriculum planning can pay proper regard to conscious teaching of attitudes. Obviously, the teaching of attitudes is already carried out in all classes in all schools, albeit often unwittingly. It is this unconscious teaching of ill-defined attitudes, undisciplined by articulation in advance and critical scrutiny by other colleagues, that is responsible for much of the harm. For the denial, deliberately or by default, that a curriculum includes attitudes is opening the door still wider to prejudice and the effects of stereotypical attitudes.

We know that attitudes are developed early. Lisa Barclay's work on careers shows that around the age of 5 and 6 attitudes towards sex role and occupation are being developed (Barclay, 1974), and Ormerod has shown similarly that attitudes towards science are largely established by 14 (Ormerod, 1975). The development of favourable attitudes to the social implications of science, for instance, affect the pupil's attitude towards physics and chemistry as school subjects (not, interestingly, biology). The school curriculum planner has to take this into account, and consider what attitudes are being conveyed, implicitly or explicitly. Similarly attitudes are created as part of the curriculum towards reading, writing, mathematics, practical work and a range of careers. The curriculum is, among other things, an image builder.

The reality of the 'hidden curriculum' is now widely accepted. I would argue that as much as possible should come out of the hidden into the ostensible curriculum, so that it can be critically and professionally scrutinized and related to wider aims. This applies especially to the creating of images and the teaching of attitudes: *the informal and the hidden curriculum is the agent of sex stereotyping, especially in its teaching of attitudes.*

## Understanding of work

The vicious circle of sexist schooling is that occupational stereotypes affect attitudes to skills and subjects being taught; those attitudes affect success in those subjects; and that in its turn irrevocably affects the possibility of future higher education and training, and ultimately careers. Thus the apparently trivial stereotypical details of the primary school affect the final career possibilities, often via what Lucy Sells (Sells, 1976) so rightly calls 'the critical filter of Maths'.

To break this vicious circle, many approaches are required, but a key one is the providing of a proper education for the world of work. What most of us do at the moment is to give careers advice which is too late, too little and too narrow. The school curriculum simply does not adequately cover how people earn their living. In junior schools there is no methodical attempt at all; in secondary schools, nothing until the third or fourth year. Whole aspects of the curriculum shun the topic as far as they can. For instance, the literature offered in English lessons explores families, love and growing up, but rarely the relationship between earning a living and making a life.

Paradoxically it can be shown that the very realism and good sense of the girls is part of their undoing: while young boys are revelling in fantasy versions of how they might spend their adult lives, girls are establishing likely aspirations. The first keeps possibilities open, whereas the second inhibits.

The approach of schools to industry and commerce is an example where new approaches are needed. We so arrange things that only those likely to go into business offices are taught about the commercial aspects of the modern world – and thus prejudice and stereotype are unchecked. Instead we need a fully worked out curriculum plan from 5 to 16 that explores all occupations and gives a balanced picture. Studies of, for instance, how young people (and their teachers!) think of industry (Schools Council, 1981) are revealing. The large majority of pupils brought up in schools in, for example, suburban London have an erroneous view of what industry is, concentrating only on heavy manufacturing. What people actually do in their working lives is neither known nor taught. Again, this offers open space for external stereotypes. A school should have a methodical plan of education about occupations (perhaps a better phrase than 'careers education') from at least the youngest secondary years, and preferably from the primary school. This would endeavour to teach about what people actually do in a variety of occupations, and would thus reduce the crude links of commerce – office work – girls; management – being ruthless – boys; and so on. The sex-stereotypical opting of pupils especially at 14-plus is substantially the result of weak or non-existent teaching of what certain walks of life are really like. For example, many industrial/commercial managers have as much responsibility for the care of their staff as workers in the so-called 'caring professions'.

## Topics chosen

From one point of view, the whole of teaching is a series of decisions about what topics, large or small, teachers will put before pupils, whether as possibilities for choice or as compulsory assignments. For the learner, schooling is a series of assignments, small and short or large and longer. For most pupils there is little or no coherence over the range of assignments, for they relate fairly loosely to what is anyway a fairly loose curriculum plan in most schools.

In the first place a so-called 'free choice' of topics or assignments, as practised in both junior school topic work and secondary-school CSE folders, to take two examples, tends to encourage pupils to choose more sex stereotypically than they would otherwise have done. This process is analogous to the play activities described by Lisa Serbin (pp. 33–5): boys choose 'girlish' toys equally with others when they are on their own, but revert to expected type when observed. Free choice of topics has established itself for understandable reasons as an essential element in 'progressive' teaching approaches, for, the argument goes, thus a pupil's interests can be harnessed to create genuine motivation. This is undoubtedly so, but there are two factors that can be overlooked but which should be considered to slightly modify the argument:

1. The almost parodying effect that peer-group pressure, and the expectations the individual considers peers of the same sex to hold, has on the so-called free choice. The latter is an especially powerful effect of what Alex Dickinson, founder of Community Service Volunteers, calls 'the prison of the peer group'.

2. The progression of choice up the years: as a pupil moves from teacher to teacher in the junior school and across the subjects and up the years in a secondary school, the books read, the stories written, and the topics chosen are not monitored. My impression is that if they were to be we should be horrified by the sheer limitations imposed by the apparently 'free' choice. It is as if pupils get locked into a sequence of preferences, always moving towards the sex stereotypical, and each choice predetermining the next.

The effects of this process can easily be seen in English lessons in primary or secondary schools. The class reader, for instance, of first-year secondary used to dominate much of the sequence of lessons. This had many faults, and most teachers of English in the UK have moved towards a more flexible reading pattern. Even if there is a single title chosen for a part of the work, various arrangements of class libraries, book boxes, or library visits are used to facilitate *personal* selection by each pupil. Yet, how personal is the choosing? Apart from the peer-group pressure described above, the initial selection of books available usually shows a polarity, and this is heightened by book jacket, title, and blurb, which are often angled by publishers firmly to one sex or another.

Anyone who has observed the choices then made will have regretted the scrabbled haste as books are plucked from the shelf, leafed through rapidly, and discarded as quickly. Rarely is even the blurb made use of; rather some vague impression is gathered from any illustrative material and the opening lines. Although there is a sense in which the book thus obtained has been chosen 'freely', there is a deeper sense in which it has not been truly chosen at all, and in these circumstances the sex link is often the aspect hooked on to. Similar effects can be seen in:

1. *Drama lessons*, where self-chosen groups are usually single sex, and then feel obliged to choose ostentatiously sex-linked scenes to improvise.

2. *Humanities*, where a choice of aspects of, for instance, a period in social history is often given to groups in the class. The topics are, consciously or unconsciously, devised by the teacher as having sex-linked attractions. Again, groups of pupils are obliged by the polarity of the offering and the pull of their presumption of their peers' inclinations to plump for the obviously sex-stereotypical, often as crudely as the girls settling for 'fashion' and the boys 'transport' in the given era!

3. *Needlecraft* (or the fabric component of home economics), in those schools where mixed classes take the subject, when the teacher often devises quite different choices of assignments, perhaps leatherwork belts and gingham aprons. Offered to the pupils as free choice, such selections are self-perpetuating, leading to the expected choices and amplifying any differences there may have been in attitudes.

I would argue then that ill considered 'free choice' between stereotyped alternatives with inadequate pupil preparation can create a travesty of its aims and a greater sexual differentiation. Instead I should like to see a greater use of fixed assignments, very carefully devised so as not to be ostentatiously labelled as 'boyish' or 'girlish'. In craft, design and technology lessons, in the early years of secondary school, for instance, the series of design exercises can range from ball games to devising propellant devices for self-designed boats and testing their speed along a water trough. In dance, as a compulsory subject started young, the whole-class and group activities can be deliberately suited to all. In English and humanities, despite the often outspoken intentions of the teachers, sexual differentiation most frequently flourishes, and here assignments need very great care.

## Teaching and learning materials

We now have available a range of studies of many aspects of existing material available for pupils (see, for example, Children's Rights Workshop, 1976; Dixon, 1977 and 1982; Zimet, 1976; Froschl, 1973). Careful analysis of early pre-school books, reading schemes, picture books, children's fiction, and most textbooks in the humanities, foreign languages, mother tongue, and sciences has shown very heavy sex-role stereotyping. It is more contentious to argue that formal studies of literature from middle secondary upwards reveal similar biases, for those responsible for selecting and teaching literature in university genuinely consider that they are selecting according to 'the common pursuit of true judgement', using only objective literary criteria. However, there have been studies in the USA (Beaven, 1972, pp. 48–68) of the literature of literature classes, and they reveal a definite bias. There have been no detailed studies that I know of in this country, though informal surveys (for example, Rose, 1979) show the same bias. It is surprising that apparently well read and thoughtful university teachers, examiners, and school teachers defend the present choice as the proper selection from the best that has been written. It is less surprising that the selection is so strikingly unbalanced when you consider how it comes about.

Literature is, to use I.A. Richards' phrase, 'a storehouse of recorded values'. Although many writers have been ahead and above their age, most writers even of the first rank, have been people of their times. Thus the values they have recorded by writing as they have done, and about the characters they have chosen, are values growing out of their age, and their writings thus embody the views of their age. As most ages have been times when definite and limited roles of lesser status have been standard for women, these books inevitably speak of this lesser status through character, plot, incident and language – sometimes ostentatiously, but (and perhaps more powerfully as a result) often almost unnoticeably through the smaller details and phrases.

There is, though, also a secondary process which further reinforces this partiality: literature is always to some extent mediated between the creator and the reader by the editorial machinery of an age – publishers, editors, reviewers, teachers, examiners, publicists, librarians, and more recently by broadcasters. These middle people are more likely than the writers to have the prejudices of their age, for their prime task is to understand and feed the needs of the age. These people therefore amplify the writers' limitation of perspective by a host of mediating influences, many of them powerful. They select which authors and which of their writings will be published; they increase or decrease the reputation of writers; they ensure the reprinting, anthologizing, and continuation of certain works and not others. It has taken recent research and the work of the great feminist publishers of very recent years to reveal to even the most committed feminist the immense range and richness of women writers, women characters, and women's concerns in literature. It is hardly an exaggeration to say that what has been revealed is a hitherto 'lost' literature. Women writers have often been obliged to become invisible.

The combination of these points has meant that the literature normally available for reading, and even more that presented for close study, reflects both a more unequal view of male/female roles than we would hold now, but also than a true cross-section of literature would represent. Thus we carry a double burden. The literature presented to pupils is largely by men and about men (for example, 3 per cent of A-level authors are women). Indeed it has been said that in US high schools women characters are central to the literature studied only if they are to die or marry (or both). Studies of our CSE, O- and A-level set texts produce similar results. The cumulative picture of the sexes gained by pupils as they grow from early readers to set texts is that women do not often create literature; they do not hold important public positions or carry responsibilities outside the home; they are there to tend their men and, most important, to find fulfilment not through themselves but through others. They are not allowed independent sexuality, independent means, independent occupations, independent satisfaction or independent lives. Despite the fact that the majority of teachers of reading and literature in schools are women (not so, of course, in the more prestigious universities), the strength of these processes is so great that the majority of books studied are heavily masculine-orientated. One researcher has put it thus:

Women students will . . . perceive that literature, as it is selected to be taught, confirms what everything else in society tells them: that the masculine viewpoint is considered normative and the feminine viewpoint divergent. (Showalter, 1974, p. 319)

It is therefore as if our aims of reducing the stereotypes of sexual differentiation are not only hampered by the chain of influences shown here, but that the teaching of literature can actually do harm by amplifying society's stereotyped prejudices – and thus the cycle restarts. I describe it thus: the stereotypes of the author's society are picked up by the author, who writes about them and from that point of view; which is filtered into even more stereotyped presentations by middle people, who publish that which suits society's views; from which an even more limited selection is made by teachers anxious to select according to their pupils' experience; which is further sharpened by classroom approaches, which further enhance the stereotypes by relying heavily on pupils' existing views and experiences; so that each year's school-leavers continue the stereotypes, as public opinion is then reaffirmed by a further in-put of recent school-leavers.

As an editor of school editions for some fifteen years I have had experience of how this comes about. A series I am responsible for is designed to bring to classrooms the best of modern literature, largely contemporary, that is likely to appeal to 15- and 16-year-olds. In its early years there was definitely a masculine bias in authors, central characters and stereotyped appeal. This is partly because of the received view of literature, and it was reinforced by the development of British writing, as the rise of 'regional' fiction in England in the late 1950s and 1960s provided good adult novels which were often accessible to pupils of modest ability. Because of the dominant part of the cultural tradition from which they had come, these books were (with the exception of Shelagh Delaney, whose work was less impressive and there was less of it) by men. Thus Sillitoe, Barstow, Naughton and Chaplin filled the volumes as they filled the CSE lists of the time. Of course there were outstanding women writers, and by the 1970s one could actually almost say that in the UK women writers dominated the literary scene. Curiously, though, their stylistic tradition was a more complex one, and language, narrative method and style appeared to be less easy for pupils, perhaps less direct. Lessing, Lavin, Tindall, Drabble, Taylor, for instance, are excellent writers, but harder to get pupils into.

But for whatever reason, the bulk of anthologies, school editions, and set texts deny the position of the female author, the female chief character (*Shane* is available for schools, but not Charles Portis' *True Grit*, a Western with a girl as the chief character!) and surface appeal for girls. Similarly, studies of language used, as Dale Spender points out in Chapter 7, show that the bias is carried into the educational texts and the school-produced worksheets in all subjects and activities.

There seem to be two main difficulties in coping with the challenge: (a) perceptual; (b) logistical. In the first instance, many teachers do not perceive the problem, denying its existence even when analyses demonstrate it. Only a school with good in-service seminars can hope gradually to change this. Secondly, much of the reading and learning material is poorly chosen in the UK, where teachers carry most of the burden. The only objective research on how teachers select books put it boldly: 'Few teachers were aware of the difficulties of skilful book selection or adopted a methodical approach to the problem, so that their choice of sources was often a haphazard or arbitary one.' (Vincent, 1980, p. 155.) Also school-produced material is often done hurriedly, with insufficient vetting by colleagues, and frequently by teachers inexperienced as writers or materials producers. It is often weaker than the books it is designed to replace.

It cannot be said of most British schools that there is a stocking policy, or even that the diet of reading material is monitored. Few schools have carried out the exercise of gathering together all the reading material of one pupil for, say, one month and considering it, asking the question: 'Does this seem a reasonable diet?' When schools have done this, they have, I fear, been shocked from many points of view by what they have found (including how little, how unvaried, what reading levels, and how dull!). Among the points revealed is the picture of sex stereotyping that emerges.

A school intending action requires a programme such as this:
1. A written materials policy growing out of the whole-school policies
2. Careful selection procedures in library and departments, with in-service work in LEA and school to support it (compare Committee of Enquiry under Chairmanship of Lady David, 1981, pp. 23–4)
3. Proper library leadership, whether by professionally qualified librarian or teacher librarian, with the time to carry out the task
4. Guidance in the in-school preparation of learning material, with a language guideline, possibly abbreviated from one used by a major publishing house (such as McGraw Hill in Children's Rights Workshop, 1976, pp. 45–56; Women in Publishing; Scott Foresman in White, 1974; and National Council of Teachers of English)
5. A scrutiny and weeding out of blatantly poor and biased material in library and classroom.

Finally, there is no way of avoiding the use of all biased material, and that which is allowed to remain should clearly be used by teachers in ways in which pupils can analyse its limitations.

## Women's studies

The thought of a course on 'Women's Studies' in a secondary school makes some people laugh and others indignant – 'Proselytizing the young!' they declare. Yet I have already argued that affirmative action is required to adjust the imbalance left by the past. There are many arguments to support this reluctance to introduce a special study; indeed it risks precisely the kind of separation of focus that I have argued against. However, after considerable hesitation I have come to believe that there are good reasons for introducing women's studies (1) as one examination option, (2) as a module in fourth- and fifth-year English work for all, and (3) as a module in some part of the humanities core.

The main argument is simply that righting the balance in the presentation of themes and the selection of learning material is not fully possible (as we have to work to a considerable extent with existing syllabuses and material), and even to the extent that it is possible it does not achieve very much for the imbalance is so great. The evidence of feminist research and feminist publishing is that previously history, sociology and literary criticism have all overlooked important aspects of the contribution of women (see especially Spender, 1981). This is a point that many people find difficult to accept, and indignantly sneer at as propaganda. However, it does not take much reading of more recent history, literary criticism or sociology to realize that there has been a staggering selection of material by virtue of who records, what they think fit to record, which of those records are published and preserved and, especially from our point of view, which have been thought fit to bring before school pupils. Take one small instance from my own experience. For twenty-five years I had been teaching poetry of the First World War to secondary pupils, considering that I brought before my classes a selection of the best and most appropriate poems. However, only with the publication in 1981 of an anthology specifically devoted to poetry by women on that theme (Reilly, 1981), did I realize that I had simply been ignorant of some suitable material. It wasn't that I (or the anthologizers from whom I taught) had read and rejected: we had not known. The same is true of the selections of poetry more generally: many women poets are simply unknown (compare Cosman, Keefe and Weaver, 1978; and Stetson, 1981).

The point is well put in a different context by Vera Brittain. The *selectivity* of history extends deep into such subtle and intimate aspects of life as attitudes. She writes of close friendship:

> The type of friendship which reaches its apotheosis in the story of David and Jonathan is not a monopoly of the masculine sex. Hitherto, *perhaps owing to a lack of women recorders*, this fact has been found difficult to accept by men, and even by other women. (Brittain, 1980, pp. 117–18, my italics.)

The 'lack of women recorders' has produced a situation that will take generations to re-balance. I therefore argue that specific attention to the imbalance is required and this can be much assisted by women's studies.

What are women's studies? The subject has been defined in the standard British introduction (itself designed for further and higher education):

> An awareness of female achievement is part of what Margherita Rendel has described as the main emphasis of women's studies, that of 'completing the record'. Such an emphasis may result in the discovery of long forgotten

women artists or writers. Women's studies is also about correcting the bias, implicit or explicit, in traditional subject areas. This bias may manifest itself in anthropology and archaeology, for example, by a neglect of female skills because the things that women made in pre-historic societies were often perishable (such as textiles) and have thus not survived for subsequent generations to discover. Sociology, too, has shown its bias by analysing society predominantly in terms of industrial organisation. This has meant looking at work outside the household and ignoring or rather neglecting the work done in the home, and the role of the family, thus excluding the contribution of the majority of women. The awareness of bias is bound up with creating a 'feminist understanding of the relationship between the sexes', which is how Diana Leonard Barker defines the area of women's studies. Women's studies, however defined, depends upon a concept of female inequality. It can be said to be both the exploring and the understanding of that inequality, although when we come to the question of what to do about removing that inequality the answers are much harder to find. (Bristol Women's Studies Group, 1979, pp. 4-5)

In the USA such an approach has been translated into high school courses. Florence Howe, introducing an anthology *High School Feminist Studies*, puts the claim as centrally as this:

The energy, imagination and information in this book respond to a deep-felt need to improve the heart of the high school curriculum – literature and language, history and social studies. We read literature, as one student put it, to 'find out what to do with our lives'. We read history to learn about the past so that we may understand the present and plan for the future. But what if women are omitted from the history recorded in textbooks? What if, as a study by Mary Beaven has indicated, the portraits of women provided in the high school literature classroom are harmful to students? The high school years are critical for the future of females and males alike, not only for what they enable students to understand about human relationships between women and men and among members of families, but also for what they enable students to envision of the world of work. For many students, these are the last years of required schooling, the years preceding important choices: marriage, vocation or college. Half don't or can't choose college, and a larger proportion of the talented who don't go on are women. Who controls those choices? What influence could or should the high school curriculum have on those students? Directly or indirectly, the courses described in this volume answer those questions. (Howe, 1976, p. vii)

Both that book and a single volume devoted to the women's studies curriculum of the Group School in Cambridge, Massachusetts (Gate, 1979) are published evidence of the many USA high school courses. Such courses are 'electives', and pursued, it might be said, by the committed few (although often, as in the Group School, which is an 'alternative' high school for students from working-class low income backgrounds, for the less academically oriented).

In the UK there are now very many courses in adult education, undergraduate, diploma and some post-graduate courses, together with a variety of more specialized courses like 'New Opportunities for

Women' (for a complete list, see Bradshaw, 1981). There are very few school courses though there is an interesting starting-point in a London University Board G C E alternative O level which has an optional section, 'Women in Society in Britain since 1850'. Although this is only one subject, and an optional one at that, of one examination syllabus, a study of this shows some possible approaches. There is also a Mode III C S E course, 'Women in Society', taught in a few London schools, including Kidbrooke and Langdon Park. There are a few sixth-form general studies or liberal studies courses which include women's studies.

As long ago as 1967 I devised and taught a mini version of such a course as a six week general studies unit (Marland, 1969, pp. 124-7). Starting with Schopenhauer and the entry on 'women' in an early nineteenth-century edition of the Encyclopaedia Britannica, the course covered 'the commercial view', 'women on the screen', 'fashion' (with a visit to the costume court of the Victoria and Albert Museum), and a reading of Ibsen's *The Doll's House*. It included a group study of different aspects. The overall themes were stated to the students:

> *Women and Society: students' course outline*
> An enquiry into some aspects of the place of women in modern society, posing the following questions:
> What view of feminity does our society hold?
> How do women themselves feel about this role?
> To what extent is the attitude to women that is held in our country at this time universal? How does it compare with other countries at other times?
> How has the present attitude developed?

This was but a beginning, but I have no doubt that intellectually sound courses could be devised to fit into the U K option and examination systems.

The existence of one such option has a powerful effect on a school and the rest of its curriculum: the pupils from this group gain special expertise, insight and confidence, and *they take this with them as they scatter into other options*. The presence of one such well-informed pupil in a commerce, social studies, literature or history class can help the teacher of that class and those students to adjust their perspective from time to time.

However, options and special courses are what they are labelled, and inevitably they stand to one side of the mainstream. I should wish to see units in both the lower-school core humanities, probably in the third year, and in the fourth- and fifth-year English core. The former would highlight the concept of 'record' and 'value', and contrast 'standard' and 'feminist' accounts, and would look, however briefly, at the relationship between women and society in different eras. The latter would concentrate on women writers, possibly using a specifically feminist anthology suitable for the age-range (see Healy, 1983). It is important to note the effect of context in anthologizing and presenting literature. The juxtaposition of stories and poems gives them a different effect. Compare, for instance, Doris Lessing's story, *The De Wets Come to Kloof Grange* in its original volume (*African Stories*) with its placing in the adult feminist collection, *In the Looking Glass* (Dean, 1977). Compare also Gillian Tindall's powerful story, *The Visitor*, in its original volume (Tindall, 1973) with its effect in Maura Healy's collection for schools. In each case the story gains in my view a new sharpness and power from its context.

No doubt in a quarter of a century's time both the compulsory module and the optional course will have phased themselves out. In the shorter term, however, both would contribute to the overall effect of decreasing sexual differentiation in the secondary school. Then, perhaps, we shall have women properly within studies rather than requiring women's studies.

## Classroom methods

Most of the contributors to this book have been concerned with the actual details of the way adults react to young people. The details of classroom manner and methods matter, and the closer and more methodical the observation of teachers' activities in the classroom, the clearer this becomes. For instance, in as much as there are mean differences between girl and boy achievements it can also be said that there are mean differences in optimum classroom teaching styles. Girls, it is fairly certain, do better in the classroom if lessons and learning activities (a) have frequent and immediate feedback; (b) have clearly articulated structure; and (c) if the pupils are given clear information about what is expected of them. No doubt that would be true of all pupils, for such conditions are likely to lead to more effective learning more generally. The point is, though, that in our society, and under the socialization and early education processes that we experience, a weakness in these aspects particularly affects girls.

I take this fact to be a specific example of what is clearly a general fact: the ineffective classroom is one in which (among other things) those with a deficit in the learning activity get even further behind, and prejudice pushes up as the rocks around which the lessons must navigate. Weak classrooms are prejudiced classrooms. Take a small point like seating in a mixed classroom. If free choices are allowed, boys and girls will group separately. Is that what we want? I fear that mixed-ability classes allow all forms of external, societal pressures to work more strongly. The evidence is that learning gains are greatest when there is more specific teaching. In their different ways the classroom observation of both Bennett (1976) and Rutter (1979) support this. Other studies have revealed how hard-working teachers can be misled into giving very little continuous help. Vera Southgate Booth, for instance, has shown that the sheer business of some teachers prevents uninterrupted teaching. For instance, she finds the modal

length of time spent hearing a pupil read is only thirty seconds
(Southgate Booth, 1981). I want to suggest that in mathematics and
science in particular, non-specific, ineffective teaching is particularly
powerful in its effects, for it allows those with general background
support to forge ahead. This effect, my hypothesis goes, is similar in
the way it works to the effects of class. Therefore, classrooms which do
not provide more specific teaching are classrooms where family background plays a greater part in determining results. Elizabeth Fennema
shows in Chapter 11 that much of the deficit that can be found in girls'
mathematics performance can be explained simply by the fact that
where mathematics courses are optional, girls do fewer. My suggestion
is that in primary classrooms, where supposedly there is little or no
choice, ineffective teaching is producing a similar comparative effect.
(The fact that the results in modern languages go the other way
deserves much closer attention than it has been given.)

I therefore argue that more teaching, more specific teaching, and
better teaching (which is in effect simply managing the classroom so
that there is more actual teaching) smoothes away much of the prejudice. Even teacher expectation looms higher the looser things are.
The weaker the teaching strength, the more societal, family and
teacher prejudices are strengthened.

Finally, the texture of teacher/pupil interaction needs a self-
conscious scrutiny. The expectations of boy/girl differences which we
all bring to our work lead us to a host of unconscious variations in style
of speaking, type of assignment, way of encouraging or reprimanding,
mode of relating. The differences in teachers' reactions recorded by
Barbara Licht and Carol Dweck in Chapter 6 indicate really major
differences coming from the minute-by-minute responses of teachers
unaware of what they are doing. Close observation of an A Level
English class by Michelle Stanworth (1983) showed a similar set of
differences in the messages that the teachers gave about male/female
worth. As she puts it in summary: there are 'subtle ways in which classroom encounters bring to life and sustain sexual divisions. Part of that
learning involves the regeneration of a gender hierarchy' (Stanworth,
1983, p. 49). Teachers working together in schools can monitor each
other and in school-focused in-service work help each other change this
unintended but powerful classroom effect.

# References

Barclay, Lisa (1974). 'The emergence of vocational expectations in pre-school
   children'. *Journal of Vocational Behaviour*, vol. iv, no. 1, January.
Beaven, Mary (1972). 'Responses of adolescents to feminine characters in literature'.
   *Research in the Teaching of English*, Spring, vol. 6, no. 1.
Bennett, Neville (1976). *Teaching Styles and Pupil Progress*. Open Books.
Bradshaw, Jan, Davies, Wendy and de Wolfe, Patricia (1981). *Women's Studies in the
   UK*. Women's Research and Resources Centre, 190 Upper Street, London.
Bristol Women's Studies Group (1979). *Half the Sky*. Virago.

Brittain, Vera (1980). *Testament of Friendship*. Virago/Fontana.

Bruner, Regine Baron. (1976). 'Reading mathematical exposition'. *Educational Research*, vol. 18, no. 3, p. 208.

Children's Rights Workshop (1976). *Sexism in Children's Books*. Writers and Readers.

Committee of Enquiry under the Chairmanship of Lady David (1981). *The Supply of Books to Schools and Colleges*. Booksellers Association and Publishers Association.

Cosman, Carol, Keefe, Joan and Weaver, Kathleen (1978). *The Penguin Book of Women Poets*. Allen Lane. (Viking Press and Penguin Books, 1979.)

Dean, Nancy and Stark, Myra (1977). *In the Looking Glass*. New York: G.P. Putnam's Sons.

Department of Education and Science (1975). *A Language for Life* (The Bullock Report). HMSO.

Dixon, Bob (1977). *Catching Them Young*. Pluto Press.

——(1982). *Now Read On*. Pluto Press.

Froschl, Merle and Williamson, Jane (1973). *Feminist Resources for Schools and Colleges*. New York: The Feminist Press.

Gate, Barbara, Klaw, Susan and Steinberg, Adria (1979). *Changing Learning, Changing Lives*. New York: The Feminist Press.

Hart, K.M. (ed) (1981). *Children's Understanding of Mathematics: 11–16*, John Murray.

Healy, Maura (1983). *Women*. Longman Imprint Books.

Herber, Harold, L. (1970). *Teaching Reading in the Content Areas*. Englewood Cliffs, NJ: Prentice-Hall.

HM Inspectorate (1975). *Curriculum Differences for Boys and Girls*. HMSO.

—— (1978). *Primary Education in England*. A survey by HM Inspectors of Schools. HMSO.

Howe, Florence (1976). *High School Feminist Studies*. New York: The Feminist Press.

Jackson, Stevi (1978). 'How to Make Babies: Sexism in Sex Education'. *Women's Studies International Quarterly*, vol. 1, no. 4, pp. 342–52, Pergamon Press.

Lessing, Doris (1964). *African Stories*. Michael Joseph.

Lunzer, E. and Gardner, K. (1978). *The Effective Use of Reading*. Heinemann Educational Books.

Marland, Michael (1978). *Language Across the Curriculum*. Heinemann Educational Books.

—— (1969). *Towards the New Fifth*. Longman.

NCTE. *Guidelines on Non-sexist Language*. National Council of Teachers of English, 1111 Keynon Road, Urbana, Illinois, 61801.

Ormerod, M.B. (1975). 'The writing on the wall: is chemistry's popularity declining?' *Chemistry in Britain*, vol. 14, no. 3, pp. 127–32.

Reilly, Catherine (1981). *Scars Upon My Heart*. Virago.

Rose, Joy (1979). 'Set books, set roles'. *Women and Education*, no. 16, Summer.

Rutter, Michael et al., (1979). *Fifteen Thousand Hours*. Open Books.

Schools Council Industry Project (1981). *Pupil Attitudes to Industry and the Trade Unions* and *Teacher Attitudes to Industry and the Trade Unions*. Available from Schools Council Industry Project.

Scott Foresman and Company (1974). 'Guidelines for improving the image of women in textbooks', in Bob White. *Non-Sexist Teaching Materials and Approaches*. New Childhood Press.

Sells, L.W. (1976). *The Mathematics Filter and the Education of Women and Minorities*. Paper presented at the annual meeting of the American Association for the Advancement of Science, Boston, Massachusetts, February 1976.

Showalter, Elaine (1974). 'Women and the literary curriculum', in J. Stacey et al. *And Jill Came Tumbling After: Sexism in American Education*. New York: Dell.

Southgate-Booth, Vera (1981). *Extending Beginning Reading*. Heinemann Educational Books.

Spender, Dale (1981), *Men's Studies Modified*. Pergamon.

Stanworth, Michelle (1983). *Gender and Schooling*. Hutchinson, in association with the Explorations in Feminism Collective.

Stenhouse, Lawrence (1978). *An Introduction to Curriculum Research and Development*. Heinemann Educational Books.

Stetson, Erlene (1981). *Black Sister, Poetry by Black American Women, 1746–1980*. Bloomington: Indiana University Press.

Tindall, Gillian (1973). *Dances of Death*. Dunton Green: Hodder & Stoughton.

Vincent, Kate (1980). *A Survey of the Methods by which Teachers Select Books*. CRUS, Occasional Papers 3. British Library Board.

White, Bob (1974). *Non-Sexist Teaching Materials and Approaches*. New Childhood Press, c/o Photography Workshop, 152 Upper Street, London N1.

Women in Publishing Industry Group. *Non-Sexist Code of Practice for Book Publishing*. Women in Publishing Industry Group, 19 Novello Street, London SW6.

Zimet, Sara Goodman (1976). *Print and Prejudice*. Dunton Green: Hodder & Stoughton.

# 11 Success in Mathematics

*Elizabeth Fennema*

Is it true that females are successful in mathematics or is it true that females are failures in mathematics? If one reads much of the current literature or listens to much of the current rhetoric, one would have to conclude that females are remarkedly unsuccessful in mathematics or at least much less successful than males. Maccoby and Jacklin (1974, p. 352) conclude that one of the few sex differences that are fairly well-established is 'that boys excel in mathematical ability'. In a 1979 publication, Nash (1979) states that males excel in quantitative performance (p. 263). Throughout the United States, there is an upsurge in interest in solving the 'problem of women and mathematics'. Major funding institutions are giving money for research dealing with the issue, and/or intervention programmes that will solve the 'problem'. Anxiety clinics for mathematics anxious women are increasing day by day. Obviously, one could intuitively conclude that females do not succeed in mathematics and action must be taken to ensure that they start experiencing success. However, as with many generalizations, such a simplistic statement while having a portion of truth behind it, is far from representing the whole truth. First, let us examine the bases of the belief that females are not succeeding in mathematics.

There is an impressive body of research literature that apparently supports the belief of male superiority in mathematics. The variable of sex has often been included in mathematics education research and any review that has been done of research in mathematics education includes a discussion of sex differences. Just examine a few statements published before 1974 from well-respected writers. 'Sex differences in mathematical abilities are, of course, present at the kindergarten level and undoubtedly earlier' (Aiken, 1971, p. 201). 'The evidence would suggest to the teacher that boys will achieve higher than girls on tests dealing with mathematical reasoning' (Glennon and Callahan, 1968, p. 50). 'From junior high school and beyond . . . boys now surpass girls in studies involving science and mathematics' (Suydam and Riedesel, 1969, p. 129). Basically, all reviews concluded that while there might not be a sex-related difference in young children, male superiority was evident by the time learners reached upper elementary or junior high school. In addition, males were definitely superior in higher level cognitive tasks which assume increasing importance as one progresses to advanced mathematical study.

While the reviews quoted dealt with learning in the United States, results from the International Study of Achievement in Mathematics (IEA) indicated that the phenomenon of sex differences in mathematics learning was not restricted to the US. In this study conducted in 1964 in twelve countries, results showed that overall males surpassed females in mathematics achievement. Males scored higher on the mathematics tests in all populations both on computation and on verbal problems (Husén, 1967).

However, when mathematics educators look at the literature, different conclusions result. In 1974 I reviewed thirty-six studies and concluded that while there was little evidence that sex-related differences in mathematics existed before or during secondary school, there was a trend that males excelled in higher level cognitive tasks and females in lower level cognitive tasks. In 1977, in a further analysis of the literature, I stated that:

> There are no sex-related differences evident in elementary school years at all cognitive levels from computation to problem-solving. After elementary school years, differences do not always appear. However, starting at about the 7th grade, if differences appear, they tend to be in the males' favor, particularly on tasks involving higher level cognitive skills.

There also (Fennema, 1977) was some evidence that sex-related differences in mathematics learning in high school were not as large in 1976 as they had been in previous years. Schonberger (1978) reviewed problem-solving literature and concluded that better male performance was rarely found and was usually limited to students of higher ability and to certain types of problems.

It appears that the belief about male superiority in mathematics is no longer accepted as valid in all situations. What are some explanations of this change in belief? One explanation might be that females are now learning mathematics to levels more comparable with males, and there is reason to believe that there is some truth in this. All cognitive differences between the sexes are growing smaller (Maccoby and Jacklin, 1974) due, perhaps, to the changing role of women. However, the major explanation for lessening sex-related differences in mathematics learning lies in the way in which the problem is being studied. Before 1974, most studies which reported male superiority in mathematics learning (Wilson, 1972; Flanagan, 1976; Husén, 1967) used random samples of females and males enrolled in secondary schools. Since traditionally, females have not chosen to study mathematics as often as have males in advanced secondary-school classes (Husén, 1967), a population of males who had spent more time studying mathematics has been compared to a population of females who had studied less mathematics. Since the single most important influence on learning mathematics is studying mathematics, it would indeed be strange if males did not score higher on mathematics achievement tests than did females. In studies since 1974, when the amount of mathematics studied was carefully controlled (Fennema and Sherman, 1977; Fennema and Carpenter, 1981) and when re-analyses of extant data controlled for the number of mathematics courses in secondary school (Wise, 1978), few significant differences in mathematics achievement between females and males have been found.

There have been strong sex-related differences in the percentage of females and males who are enrolled in mathematics classes in secondary schools. In 1964, Husén reported that in the twelve countries studied in the International Study of Achievement, the ratio of males to females enrolled in mathematics at the end of secondary education ranged from 1·73 to 7·13 with an average ratio of 3·70 (Husén, 1967, p. 234). Basically, these data are similar to those reported by Fennema and Sherman (1978) for the 1974–75 school year. What the current situation is concerning the number of women who elect mathematics courses remains largely unknown at least in the US, and the data are elusive or unavailable. Isolated informal reports indicate that more women are electing advanced secondary-school mathematics courses while other reports indicate just the opposite. Enrolment by women in mathematics-related post-secondary-school curricula such as engineering appears to be growing.

Although only symptomatic of the effects of many variables, electing not to study mathematics beyond minimal requirements is currently a direct cause of many females' non-participation in mathematics-related occupations. The one variable which can be positively identified as causing sex-related differences in mathematics usage in adults is the differential number of years females and males spend formally studying and using mathematics. Such a simple explanation of such an important problem seems too good to be true. However, I believe strongly that if the amount and quality of time spent learning mathe-matics is somehow equated for females and males, educationally significant sex-related differences in mathematics performance will at least partially disappear.

Although the solution to the problem is easy to state, achieving the solution is not simple. The first step is to gain an understanding of the causes of females' decision not to study mathematics. Involved in these causes is the cognitive acquisition of mathematics by females, as well as the attitudes or affective beliefs held by females, male peers, parents and educators toward females as learners of mathematics. The cognitive and affective components are so intertwined that it is difficult if not impossible to separate them. Not only are they intertwined, but they are developed over a period of years in a complex social matrix which involves home, community and school. Therefore, in seeking to understand why inequity exists in the representation of the sexes in occupations related to mathematics, one must study the cognitive and affective components affecting the acquisition of mathematical skills and knowledge in the social environment where they are developed.

Although intellectually interesting to discuss, at the present time, it is impossible to study the totality of causative behaviour. However, it has been possible, and indeed profitable, to select variables which exert major influence and to study the development, interrelationships and effects of these variables upon the learning of mathematics.

## The cognitive variables

'Mathematics is essentially cognitive in nature; and the principal, distinguishing goals or objectives of mathematics instruction are (and should be) cognitive ones' (Weaver, 1971, p. 263). Since mathematics is a cognitive endeavour, the logical place to begin to look for explanatory variables of sex-related differences in mathematics study is in the cognitive area. It is well-accepted that the cognitive variables of general intelligence and verbal abilities are highly important in the learning of mathematics. However, these two variables are not helpful as possible explanations of sex-related differences in mathematics. No differences exist between males and females in general intelligence. While there appears to be some female superiority in certain verbal skills in children, (Maccoby and Jacklin, 1974) by the time learners reach the secondary school, males and females possess approximately equivalent skills in verbal areas which are related to the learning of mathematics (Fennema and Sherman, 1977). Therefore, general intelligence and verbal skills are not helpful variables in understanding differences in mathematics between females and males.

One cognitive variable that may help to explain sex-related differences in mathematics performance is spatial visualization, a particular subset of spatial skills. Even though the existence of many sex-related differences is currently being challenged, the evidence is still persuasive that in many cultures, male superiority on tasks that require spatial visualization is evident, beginning during adolescence (Fennema, 1975; Maccoby and Jacklin, 1974). Spatial visualization involves visual imagery of objects, movement of the objects or changes in their properties. In other words, objects or their properties must be manipulated in the 'mind's eye', or mentally. The relationship between mathematics and spatial visualization is logically evident. In mathematical items, spatial visualization requires rotation, reflection or translation of rigid figures. These are important ideas in geometry. Many mathematicians believe that all of mathematical thought involves geometrical ideas (Bronowski, 1947). Therefore, if spatial visualization terms are geometrical in character and if mathematical thought involves geometrical ideas, spatial visualization and mathematics are inseparably intertwined.

Not only are spatial visualization skills related to ideas within the structure of mathematics, but spatial representations are being increasingly included in the teaching of mathematics. For example, the Piagetian conservation tasks which are becoming part of many school programmes, involve focusing on correct spatial attributes before quantity, length and volume are conserved. Most concrete and pictorial representations of arithmetical, geometrical and algebraic ideas appear to be heavily reliant on spatial attributes. The number line, which is used extensively to represent whole numbers and operations on them, is a spatial representation. Illustrating the commutativity of multiplication by turning an array 90 degrees involves a direct spatial visualization skill.

Although the relation between the content of mathematics, instruction in mathematics, and spatial visualization skills appears logical, results from empirical studies which have explored the relationship are not consistent. Many factor analytic studies have explored this relationship and several authors have reviewed the literature. Some investigators have definitely concluded that spatial skills and learning of mathematics are not related while other authors feel that data indicate a positive relationship (Fennema, 1975). Even less is known about the effect that differential spatial visualization skills have on the mathematical learning of females and males. One indication that spatial visualization is an important consideration is the concurrent development of sex-related differences in favour of males in mathematics achievement and spatial visualization skills. However, the Fennema–Sherman studies (1978) specifically investigated the relationship between mathematics achievement and spatial visualization skills and these data do not support the idea that spatial visualization is helpful in explaining sex-related differences in mathematics achievement. In these studies of females and males enrolled in mathematics courses, grades 6 to 12, few sex-related differences in either mathematics achievement or spatial visualization skills were found. The two were related similarly ($r \simeq 0.5$) for both sexes, and spatial visualization appeared to influence both females and males equally to continue studying mathematics (Fennema and Sherman, 1978).

I am currently engaged in gathering data about how mathematics learning is dependent upon spatial visualization. It appears evident to me that tasks which measure spatial visualization skills have components which can be mathematically analysed or described. From such an examination, one could hypothesize a direct relationship between mathematics and spatial visualization. An item from the Space Relations portion of the Differential Aptitude Test (Bennett, Seashore and Wesman, 1973) requires that a two-dimensional figure be folded mentally into a three-dimensional figure (see Figure 11:1). The spatial visualization test called the Form Boards test requires that rigid figures be rotated and translated to a specified location. The Cubes test requires rotation of a three-dimensional shape, a cube. The activities required by those items can be described as mathematical operations. Yet this set of operations is only a minute subset of mathematical ideas which must be learned, and indeed one could go a long way in the study of mathematics without these specific ideas.

The hypothesis that I and my colleagues are currently investigating is that the critical relationship between mathematics and spatial visualization is not direct, but quite indirect. It involves the translation of words and/or mathematical symbols into a form where spatial visualization skills can be utilized. Let me illustrate what I mean. Consider the following problem:

A pole, 5 meters long, has been erected near the bank of a lake. Two and a half meters of the pole have been hammered down into the bottom of the lake; one half meter is above the surface of the water. How deep is the lake? (Werdelin, 1961)

For children of 11 to 12 years of age, this is a moderately difficult problem. You must add the lengths of two pieces of the post and then subtract that length from the total length: $2\frac{1}{2} + \frac{1}{2} = 3$ and $5 - 3 = 2$. Keeping track of the steps and sequencing them accurately is not easy. Consider the problem from a spatial visualization perspective. If one can visualize in one's mind what is involved, a picture like that shown in Figure 11:2 might be seen. The solution of the problem then becomes simpler. One has an image that enables one to move the

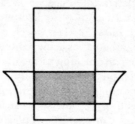

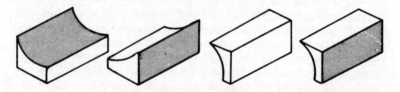

**Figure 11.1**

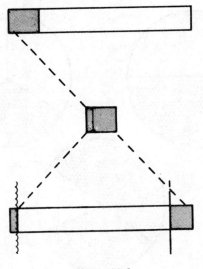

**Figure 11.2**

pieces above and below the water together, then that length can be sub-tracted from the total length in order to get the correct answer. Once the problem can be visualized, spatial visualization skills can be utilized as a major aid in attaining a solution.

Consider a symbolic problem met by children of the same age: ½ + ⅓. While it can be solved totally with symbols, children of this age, because of their developmental level, often have trouble really under-standing the symbolic process involved. Now look at the problem represented pictorially much as it could be visualized in the mind (Figure 11:3). Once it is visualized in the mind, spatial visualization skills can be utilized and the answer more easily found.

We know that females tend to score lower on spatial visualization tests than do males. What we do not know is if females differ from males in their ability to visualize mathematics – in the translation of mathematical ideas and problems into pictures. Also not known is if good spatial visualizers are better at this translation than are poor spatial visualizers. However, I am increasingly convinced that there is no direct causal relationship between spatial visualization skills and the learning of mathematics in a broad general sense. While I am continuing to investigate the impact of spatial visualization skills, I am less convinced than I was that spatial visualization is important in helping understand sex-related differences in the studying and learning of mathematics. (For an update on current thought, see Fennema and Tartre, 1982.)

In American schools, classrooms do not appear to use mathematical representations which either encourage or require the use of spatial visualization skills. While some primary mathematics programmes

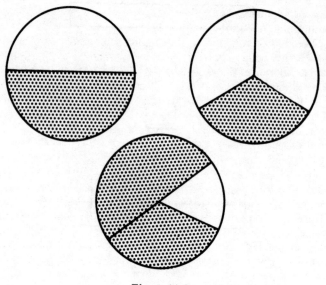

**Figure 11.3**

encourage the use of concrete and pictorial representations of mathematical ideas, by the time children are 10 to 11 years old, symbolic representations are used almost exclusively. Perhaps boys, more than girls, utilize the concrete representations during primary years and thus develop higher skills in using spatial visualization in learning mathematics. As far as I know, however, no one is investigating such a hypothesis.

Whatever influence that spatial visualization skills have on the learning of mathematics it is subtle, to say the least. It is providing an interesting area of investigation and discussion, but I do not foresee that an emphasis on the development of spatial visualization skills will do very much to eliminate sex-related differences in mathematics.

## Other variables

If sex-related differences in mathematics cannot be explained by cognitive variables, are there other variables which will help? At least two variables that I label as affective and at least one educational variable provide important insight into why females elect not to study mathematics beyond minimal requirements.

Affective variables have to do with feelings, beliefs and attitudes. The affective domain is a complicated one and has received less attention than the cognitive domain because of its characteristics. Variables within this domain are difficult to define, measure and understand. All too often, all affective variables have been lumped together into one large conglomerate and labelled as attitudes. However, this type of combining often masks many important things.

There has been an increasing amount of literature published which deals with various affective variables and their relationship to sex-related differences in mathematics study (Fox, 1977; Fennema, 1977; Reyes, 1980). Two well-defined variables (confidence and perceptions of usefulness) are closely related to studying mathematics and one other complex variable (causal attributions) has been hypothesized to be an important determinant in electing to study mathematics (Wolleat, et al., 1980).

Confidence in learning mathematics is related to self-esteem in general. High confidence in mathematics appears to be located at one end of a continuum and anxiety toward learning mathematics at the other end. Confidence in mathematics is a belief that one has the ability to learn new mathematics and to perform well on mathematical tasks. It often is measured by Likert-type scales which include items such as: 'I am sure that I can learn mathematics'; 'I can get good grades in math'; or 'I'm no good in math' (Fennema-Sherman Mathematics Scales; see page 177).

The literature strongly supports the fact that there are sex-related differences in the confidence–anxiety dimension. It appears reasonable to believe that lesser confidence or greater anxiety on the part of females is an important variable which helps explain sex-related differences in mathematics studying (Fennema and Koehler, 1982).

In the Fennema–Sherman study, at each grade level from 6 to 11 (Figure 11:4) boys were significantly more confident in their abilities to deal with mathematics than were girls. In most instances this happened when there were no significant sex-related differences in mathematics achievement. In addition, confidence in learning mathematics and achievement were more highly correlated than any other affective variable and achievement ($r \simeq 0.40$). Confidence was almost as highly related to achievement as were cognitive variables of verbal ability and spatial visualization.

While evidence exists in abundance that there are sex-related differences in this confidence–anxiety dimension related to mathematics, much is unknown about its true effect. The relationship between spatial-visual processes and the confidence–anxiety dimension has not been explored. What effect do feelings of confidence have on cognitive processes involved in learning mathematics and in solving mathematical problems and vice versa? Are feelings of confidence stable within individuals across time and across a variety of mathematics activities? Does lessening anxiety increase either learning or the willingness to elect to study mathematics? Do low levels of confidence affect females differently than they do males? Are there really sex differences in confidence toward mathematics, or (as many have hypothesized (Maccoby and Jacklin, 1974)) are females just more willing to admit their feelings than males?

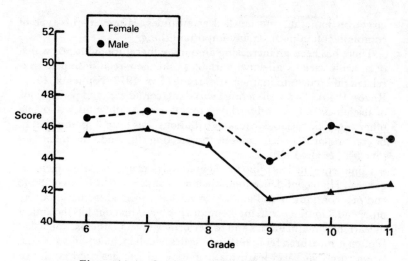

Figure 11.4    **Confidence in learning mathematics**

Currently there are many studies underway which will help in answering these questions. Until the results of these are available though, one must just accept the evidence that females, across a wide age-range, do report more anxiety and less confidence toward mathematics than do males.

Certainly no one knows why many females develop a lack of confidence in their ability to do mathematics. Even when females succeed in mathematics, they attribute their success to factors other than their own ability, such as luck, much more than do males (Wolleat, et al., 1980). It seems logical to believe, however, that when young girls feel mathematics is inappropriate for females, they will feel anxious about succeeding in it as they must, at least partially, deny their femininity in order to achieve in mathematics.

Another affective variable which helps explain females not electing to take mathematics is the perceived usefulness to them of mathematics (Figure 11:5) (Fox, 1977; Casserly, 1975). Mathematics is a difficult subject and not particularly enjoyable for many learners. Why should one study it if it is of no future use? Females in secondary schools as a group indicate that they do not feel they will use mathematics in the future. Males, as a group, are much more apt to report that mathematics is essential for whatever career they plan. This sex difference in perceived usefulness is also closely related to the stereotyping of mathematics as a male domain (Figure 11:6). Currently, the main users of mathematics in careers are male. If females do not see mathematics-related careers as possibilities, they will also not see mathematics as useful.

Females, more than males, respond negatively to such items as: 'I'll need mathematics for my future work' or 'Mathematics is a worth-

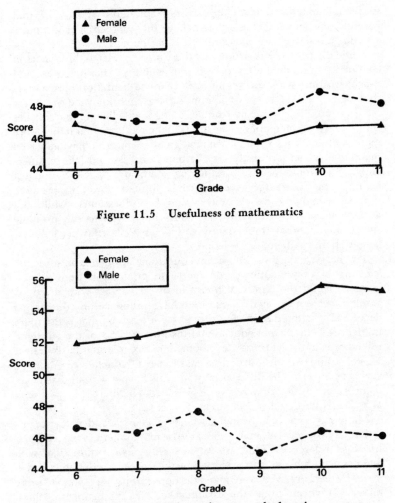

Figure 11.5   Usefulness of mathematics

Figure 11.6   Mathematics as a male domain

while and useful subject' (Fennema–Sherman Scales).

In addition to indicating more negative beliefs than do males on these specific affective variables, females also report that they perceive that parents, teachers and counsellors are not positive towards them as learners of mathematics. In addition, males more than females, starting at least as early as grade 6 (12 years of age) stereotype mathematics as a male domain at much higher levels than do females.

The cross-sex influence on all aspects of behaviour is strong during adolescent years. Since males stereotype mathematics as a male domain, they undoubtedly communicate this belief in many subtle and not so subtle ways to females, which influences females' willingness to study mathematics. Evidence also exists in abundance (Fox, 1977) that parents, teachers and counsellors believe that mathematics is a more appropriate activity for males than it is for females.

While the evidence is strong that there are sex-related differences in confidence in mathematics, perceived usefulness of mathematics, and causal attributions of success and failure in mathematics, I am always somewhat puzzled as to what implications such knowledge has for planning change. I have no trouble saying and believing that females should learn mathematics to the limits of their ability, that if they were more confident they would learn mathematics better, if they perceived mathematics as more useful or attributed success and failure differently they would persist in studying mathematics. Certainly just having that knowledge gives me only limited power to promote change. Changing beliefs and action by adolescents, while not impossible, is difficult. However, educational systems can promote such change, and an understanding of how schools influence females' beliefs about mathematics is helpful.

Teachers are the most important educational influence on students' learning of mathematics. From entry to graduation from school, learners spend thousands of hours in direct contact with teachers. While other educational agents may have influence on educational decisions, it is the day-by-day contact with teachers that is the main influence of the formal educational institution. Part of the teachers' influence is in the learners' development of sex-role standards. These sex-role standards include definitions of acceptable achievement in the various subjects. The differential standards for mathematics achievement is communicated to boys and girls through differential treatment as well as differential expectations of success.

Many studies have indicated teachers treat female and male students differently. In general, males appear to be more salient in the teachers' frame of reference. Teachers interact with males more than with females in both blame and praise contacts. More questions are asked of males by teachers. Males are given the opportunity to respond to more high cognitive questions than are females (Reyes and Fennema, 1982).

High achieving girls seem particularly vulnerable to teachers' influence. One major study (Good, Sikes and Brophy, 1973) indicated that high achieving girls received significantly less attention in mathematics classes than high achieving boys. On the other hand, many girls who have been accelerated in mathematics report positive teacher influence (Casserly, 1975) as a cause of their success. This influence was manifest by teachers being 'sex-blind' in the treatment of girls. Teachers treated males and females alike and had high expectations for females as well as males.

# Changing schools

Can schools be changed so that females elect to study more mathematics? All too often comments are addressed to me that imply that schools alone cannot do much. The argument goes like this. Because the studying of mathematics is stereotyped male, and because stereotyping of sex roles is so deeply embedded in society, schools are powerless to improve females' studying of mathematics until society changes. Let me say as loudly and emphatically as I can that that argument is fallacious. Schools can increase females' studying of mathematics. Let me cite some evidence that shows strongly that schools can be effective. There are two intervention programmes in the US that have been intensively evaluated. The first programme, called 'Multiplying Options and Subtracting Bias', is one that I have assisted in developing. The rationale behind this programme is that merely telling high school females about the importance of mathematics is insufficient. Forces which influence these girls to make their decisions are complex and deeply embedded in societal beliefs about the roles of males and females. Asking females to change their behaviour without changing the forces operating upon them would place a very heavy burden on their shoulders. What should be done is to change the educational environment of these females so that they are enabled to continue their study of mathematics beyond minimal requirements. This environment is composed of several significant groups of people: mathematics teachers, counsellors, parents, male students, and the female students themselves. 'Multiplying Options and Subtracting Bias' was designed to change these significant groups' beliefs about women and mathematics as well as to change each group's behaviour.

The programme is organized round four workshops: one each for students, teachers, counsellors and parents. Each of the four workshops is built around a unique version of a videotape designed explicitly for the target audience. Narrated by Marlo Thomas, the tapes use a variety of formats, candid interviews, dramatic vignettes and expert testimony to describe the problem of mathematics avoidance and some possible solutions. The videotapes and accompanying workshop activities make the target audience aware of the stereotyping of mathematics as a male domain which currently exists, females' feelings of confidence toward mathematics, the usefulness of mathematics for all people and differential treatment of females as learners of mathematics. Discussed specifically are plans for action by each group. The workshops, each of which is about two hours long, are designed to have an effect on a whole school.

Nine Midwestern high schools from urban, suburban and rural/suburban areas were selected for the field testing of the videotape series. The evaluation period covered the spring term of the 1977–78 academic year and the autumn term of the 1978–79 school year. Two or more ninth-grade classes of algebra students and two or more tenth-grade classes of geometry students from each of the sample schools participated in the collection of baseline data during the spring of 1978. No pre-algebra or general mathematics classes were involved in the study.

During the 1978 autumn term, five schools were randomly assigned to be experimental schools and the four target audiences were shown the videotape series as part of a standardized workshop. Most of the algebra and geometry students who had contributed to the baseline data pool the preceding spring had moved to the next level of mathematics or had dropped out of mathematics. Both the enrolled and the non-enrolled students were shown the videotape, either in intact classes or in class-sized groups. The video workshop was also presented to all mathematics teachers and counsellors in these schools during the same time period. Small groups of parents participated in the video workshop in three of the experimental schools during the respective school's 'parents' night' programmes.

The workshop formats developed for the testing of the videotapes' effectiveness added little content in addition to that on the tapes. They consisted of a standardized introduction; the showing of the videotape; a 10-minute, structured discussion period; and a standardized conclusion. Each workshop fitted into the 45- to 55-minute class period found in the schools. Three trained staff members presented all the workshops.

The four schools not assigned to be experimental schools served as control schools. Approximately three weeks after the video workshops were presented in the experimental schools, both experimental and control school students were given a battery of instruments/questions similar to those completed during the spring term.

The data which had been collected during the 1978 spring semester formed the baseline from which the amount of change effected by the video intervention was measured. The control schools permitted a comparison of the amount of change in the experimental group to that arising from naturally occurring factors during the two semesters of the investigation. More than 700 students, 64 teachers, 39 counsellors and 28 parents participated in the validation study.

Data were collected on cognitive, affective and behaviour variables (see Table 11:1).

These data showed that changes of greater magnitude were obtained from the experimental group for several of the variables listed in Table 11:1. Female students in the experimental group increased their plans to study mathematics both in high school and after high school at levels significant beyond the ·01 level. Their amount of information as evidenced by increases on their Information Scale scores also increased to a level significant beyond ·01. Their perception of the usefulness of mathematics for their futures increased over the females in the control group by an amount significant at the ·05 level. A trend in the direction of lowered attributions of their failures to a lack of ability was also

Table 11:1   Categories of data collected from students

| 1. Cognitive | 2. Attitudes | 3. Behaviour with regard to mathematics |
|---|---|---|
| Information on sex-related differences in mathematics scale | Fennema–Sherman Mathematics Scales:[a] <br><br> 1. Usefulness of mathematics <br> 2. Mathematics as a male domain <br> 3. Effectance motivation in mathematics <br> 4. Mathematics <br> 5. Mother <br> 6. Father <br> 7. Teacher <br> 8. Counsellor[b] <br><br> Mathematics Attribution Scales[c] <br> 1. Success-ability <br> 2. Success-effort <br> 3. Success-task <br> 4. Success-environment <br> 5. Failure-ability <br> 6. Failure-effort <br> 7. Failure-task <br> 8. Failure-environment | Self-report of plans to study high school mathematics <br><br> Self-report of plans to study after high school mathematics <br><br> School-wide enrolments in mathematics classes |

[a]E. Fennema and J. Sherman 'Fennema–Sherman Attitude Scales: Instruments designed to measure attitudes toward the learning of mathematics by females and males'. *JSAS Catalog of Selected Documents in Psychology*, vol. 6, no. 2 (1976), p. 31.
[b]Scale was developed in the manner of the earlier Fennema–Sherman Scales for this study.
[c]E. Fennema, P. Wolleat and J. Pedro 'Mathematics Attribution Scale: an instrument designed to measure students' attributions of causes of their successes and failures in mathematics'. *JSAS Catalog of Selected Documents in Psychology*, vol. 9, no. 2 (1979), p. 26.

noted. The level of significance reached ·06 for this variable.

Male students who were members of the experimental groups also increased their plans to study mathematics during and after high school. The increases were not as great as those noted with female students – partly a function of their having reported plans to take more mathematics than females during the baseline period. Thus there was a ceiling effect on their potential for increasing their mathematics plans, particularly at the high school level. Male students also increased their level of information as indicated by the Information Scale scores. The extent to which males perceived mathematics as a male domain dropped. Because the attitudes of male students undoubtedly affect the election of mathematics by female students, this drop in stereotyping mathematics by males may indicate a positive development.

School-wide mathematics pre-enrolment statistics indicated that the proportion of all junior and senior year females enrolling in junior and senior year mathematics courses increased in the experimental schools while it decreased slightly in the control schools. The increase was greatest among junior year females. The higher the percentage of the school's population involved in the study, the greater the amount of change. The rural-suburban and suburban schools which had smaller student enrolments reflected more positive change in the pre-enrolment statistics.

The statistically significant results of this study were not obtained by offering the video workshop to students only. It should be recalled that the teacher influence tape was shown to all the mathematics teachers and the counsellor influence tape was shown to all the counsellors in each of the five experimental schools. We doubt whether having only the students view their videotape would have been as effective as reaching all the target audiences.

It can safely be concluded that exposure to the Multiplying Options and Subtracting Bias series can substantially influence students' attitudes about mathematics, the stereotyping of mathematics and their willingness to take more mathematics courses.

The other intervention programme is one developed, planned and implemented by the San Francisco Bay Area Network for Women in Science (now called the Math/Science Network). The Network is a unique cooperative effort undertaken by scientists, mathematicians, technicians and educators from thirty colleges and universities, fifteen school districts, and a number of corporations, government agencies and foundations. The goal of the Network is to increase young women's participation in mathematical studies and to motivate them to enter careers in science and technology.

Supported by the Women's Educational Equity Act of the federal government, seven conferences were held in the spring of 1977 and 1978 designed to increase the entry of women into mathematics/science-oriented careers. These one-day conferences consisted of a general session with a panel or main speaker, one or two hands-on science/mathematics workshops, and one or more career workshops which provided opportunities for interaction with women working in mathematics/science related fields. Invited to the conferences were junior high and senior high school girls. Subjects were 2215 females who volunteered to attend the conferences. Pre-and post-conference questionnaires were administered and responses analysed. The evaluators of the conferences concluded that

> the conferences (1) increased participants' exposure to women in a variety of technical and scientific fields, (2) increased participants' awareness of the importance of taking mathematics and science-related courses, and (3) increased participants' plans to take more than two years of high school mathematics. (Cronkite and Perl, 1978)

The two intervention programmes described indicate quite clearly that it is possible to change females' mathematics behaviour, and to do so in relatively short periods of time.

Some schools are remarkably more effective in persuading females to attempt high achievement in mathematics. Casserly (1975) identified thirteen high schools which had an unusually high percentage of females in advanced placement mathematics and science classes. She concluded that the schools had identified these girls as early as fourth grade and the school teachers and peers were supportive of high achievement by the females.

# References

Aiken, L.R. (1971). 'Intellective Variables and Mathematics Achievement: Directions for Research', *Journal of School Psychology* 9, p. 201.

Bennett, G.K., Seashore, H.G., and Wesman, A.C. (1973). *Differential aptitude tests forms S & T*, 4th ed., New York, Psychological Corp.

Bronowski, J. (1947). 'Mathematics', in D. Thompson and J. Reeves (eds). *The Quality of Education*, Muller, London.

Casserly, P.L. (1975). 'An Assessment of Factors Affecting Female Participation in Advanced Placement Programs in Mathematics, Chemistry and Physics' (Grant No. GY-11325). National Science Foundation, Washington, D.C.

Cronkite, R. and Perl, T. (1978). 'Evaluating the impact of an intervention program: Math-science career conferences for young women,' in *Proceedings of the Conference on the Problem of Math Anxiety*. Sponsored by the School of Natural Sciences, California State University, Fresno.

Fennema, E. (1975). 'Spatial Ability, Mathematics and the Sexes', in E. Fennema (ed.), *Mathematics Learning: What Research Says About Sex Differences*. ERIC Center for Science, Mathematics and Environmental Education, College of Education, The Ohio State University, Columbus, Ohio.

―――― (1977). 'Influences of selected cognitive, affective and educational variables on sex-related differences in mathematics learning and studying'. *Women and Mathematics: Research Perspectives for Change – NIE Papers in Education and Work*, no. 8, National Institute of Education, Washington DC, pp. 79–136.

―――― and Koehler, M.S. (1982). *The development of confidence in learning mathematics by girls and boys*. Paper presented at the Annual Meeting of the American Educational Research Association, New York.

―――― and Sherman, J.A. (1977). 'Sex-related Differences in Mathematics Achievement, Spatial Visualization and Affective Factors'. *American Educational Research Journal* 14(1), pp. 51–72.

―――― and Sherman, J.A. (1978). 'Sex-related Differences in Mathematics Achievement and Related Factors: A Further Study'. *Journal for Research in Mathematics Education* 9, p. 189.

―――― and Tartre, L. (1982). *The use of spatial skills in mathematics by girls and boys: A longitudinal study*.

Flanagan, J.C. (1976). 'Changes in School Levels of Achievement: Project TALENT Ten and Fifteen Year Retests'. *Educational Researcher* 5(8), p. 9.

Fox, L.H. (1977). 'The Effects of Sex Role Socialization on Mathematics Participation and Achievement'. *Women and Mathematics: Research Perspectives for Change – NIE Papers in Education and Work*, no. 8, p. 1.

Glennon, V.J. and Callahan, L.G. (1968). *A Guide to Current Research: Elementary School Mathematics*. Association for Supervision and Curriculum Development. Washington, D.C.

Good, T.L., Sikes, J.N., and Brophy, J.E. (1973). 'Effects of Teacher Sex and Student Sex on Classroom Interaction'. *Journal of Educational Psychology* 65, p. 74.

Husén, T. (ed.) (1967). *International Study of Achievement in Mathematics: A Comparison of Twelve Countries.* John Wiley/Almquist and Wiksell, New York/Stockholm, 2 vols.

Maccoby, E.E. and Jacklin, C.N. (1974). *The Psychology of Sex Differences.* Stanford University Press, Stanford, California.

Nash, S.C. (1979). 'Sex role as a mediator of intellectual functioning', in M.A. Wittig and A.C. Petersen (eds.). *Sex-related differences in cognitive functioning.* New York, Academic Press.

Reyes, L.H. (1980). 'Attitudes and mathematics', in M.M. Lindquist (ed.). *Selected issues in mathematics education.* Chicago, National Society for the Study of Education.

—— and Fennema, E. (1982). *Sex and confidence level differences in participation in mathematics classroom processes.* Paper presented at the Annual Meeting of the American Educational Research Association, New York.

Schonberger, A.K. (1978). 'Are mathematics problems a problem for women and girls?', in J.E. Jacobs, (ed.). *Perspectives on women and mathematics.* Columbus, OHIO, ERIC Clearinghouse for Science, Mathematics, and Environmental Education.

Suydam, M.N. and Riedesel, C.A. (1969). *Interpretive Study of Research and Development in Elementary School Mathematics.* Vol. 1, 'Introduction and Summary: What Research Says,' Final report, Project no. 8-0586. Department of Health, Education and Welfare.

Weaver, J.F. (1971). 'Seductive Shibboleths', *The Arithmetic Teacher* 18, p. 263.

Werdelin, I. (1961). *The geometrical ability and space factor in boys and girls.* Lund, Sweden, University of Lund.

Wilson, J.W. (1972). *Patterns of Mathematics Achievement in Grade 11:Z Population.* National Longitudinal Study of Mathematical Abilities, no. 17. Stanford University Press, Palo Alto, California.

Wise, L.L. (1978). 'The Role of Mathematics in Women's Career Development' Paper presented at the Annual Convention of the American Psychological Association, Toronto, Canada.

Wolleat, P.L., Pedro, J.D., Becker, A.D., and Fennema, E. (1980). 'Sex differences in high school students' causal attribution of performance in mathematics.' *Journal for Research in Mathematics Education*, 11(5), pp. 356–366.

# 12   Should the Sexes be Separated?

## Michael Marland

We know that in certain respects single-sex schools show less marked sex stereotyping. U K 16-plus and 18-plus national examination results show a proportionately higher take-up and success by girls in the stereotypical subjects of mathematics and physical sciences, and boys in English literature and foreign languages in single-sex schools than in mixed. Similarly subject choice is less stereotypical in single-sex girls' schools than in mixed (Ormerod, 1975, pp. 257–67; Department of Education and Science, 1975, p. 12; Martini, 1982, pp. 4–6).

These differences are consistent with two of the most likely ways in which socialization produces sex-stereotypical attitudes in pupils:

1. The adolescent develops attitudes which are a reflection of what she or he thinks peers feel, and tries to behave in ways calculated (rightly or wrongly) to win approval from peers. In this it is especially what the opposite sex is guessed to think that is the amplifying device. Thus in a boys-only school there is no reflection from girls about the relationship between success in languages and the masculine role; nor in girls-only schools do the physical sciences become part of the masculine image. This is argued persuasively by one commentator: 'The social structures of mixed schools may drive children to make even more sex-stereotyped subject choices, precisely because of the other sex and the *pressure to maintain boundaries, distinctiveness, and identity*' (Shaw, 1976, p. 137, my italics). And it feels like that to me after teaching for over twenty years in four mixed schools.

2. Although, and increasingly, teachers of both sexes work in single-sex schools, the chances of women teachers of mathematics and the physical sciences is higher in girls-only schools than in mixed schools, and similarly teachers of literature and languages are more likely to be male in boys-only schools than in mixed schools (though

this is probably a less marked variation). It is therefore likely that the leadership of strong and successful role models will encourage the pupils towards what would otherwise be non-typical sex efforts and choice.

These reasons are speculation that is at least consistent with experimental studies and the analysis of socialization by Maccoby and Jacklin (Maccoby and Jacklin, 1974, Chapters 8 and 9).

There is also the question of learning and teaching styles. If the language of the classroom, its topics, its disciplinary style, its methods of encouragement and criticism and its very learning material are boy-dominated, would it not be better to educate the girls separately? It would then be possible to adapt, say, the teaching of science and mathematics to their perceived needs.

In the U K the question has to be seen in the continuing glow of the great achievement of schools such as the Girls Public Day School Trust schools, which offered remarkably effective academic education to girls from the last quarter of the nineteenth century (Kamm, 1972). The popular British view that parents want single-sex education for their daughters, though more will accept a mixed education for their sons, probably has some truth in it (although I believe this relates to the historical fact that the most prestigious old foundations in the big cities and among the public schools are inevitably single-sex, thus falsely associating prestige and supposed quality with single-sex education).

The reputation of the all-girls school has been further enhanced by the fact that in many areas where there are mixed and single-sex schools the balance of the sexes is poor in the mixed schools. I have not seen wider figures for the sexual composition of so-called mixed schools, but the I L E A mean is 60 per cent boys : 40 per cent girls, with some schools being 70:30 or even more unbalanced. Eileen Byrne has spoken of many mixed schools being 'boys' schools with some girls', referring to the ethos and leadership. But how much truer is this when the actual numerical balance of boys and girls puts the girls in such a minority.

The argument for single-sex schooling for girls based on the reported academic success of girls-only schools needs cautious interpretation. The I L E A, with commendable and typical thoroughness, has analysed its examination results and shown that 'When different average ability of intake "is allowed for" there is no significant difference between examination achievement in the Authority's single-sex and mixed schools' (Martini, 1982, pp. 15–16). This investigation clearly showed that the apparently better examination results in I L E A of all-girls schools is actually an attribute of intellectual attainment and social background of the intake of pupils rather than of the organization into girls-only schools.

The argument has been extended to the mixed school, where it is reasonably pointed out that single-sex classes for certain subjects, such as mathematics or physics, could easily be organized within mixed schools. The first results in the U K of such a scheme for mathematics seem to follow the direction of single-sex schooling: girls in girls-only mathematics classes appeared to do better than in the parallel mixed classes. (The results must not be discounted, but are of a very small sample, and the effects of the special sets might themselves have been as strong as the sexual composition of the group.) The eight-form-entry Stamford School in Tameside, put the girls-only mathematics sets in its first year, and followed them through. The following table and commentary comes from the school's own report.

| | October 1978 (Initial selection test) | November 1979 | February 1980 |
|---|---|---|---|
| All-girls set | 58·9% | 55·1% | 54·7% |
| Girls in equivalent mixed set | 58·1% | 50·0% | 43·9% |
| Boys in equivalent mixed set | 59·0% | 59·0% | 56·4% |

The October 1978 scores indicate that at the time of the initial set selection there was little to choose between the girls in either set. By February 1980, the average score of the girls in the mixed set had fallen well behind that of the boys in the same set. In other words, these girls were conforming to the typical pattern for the school. The girls in the single sex set however achieved a far better average score than the girls in the mixed set, and were only slightly below the average score achieved by the boys. Whereas nine of the sixteen girls in the mixed set failed to achieve 40% in the February test, only four out of thirty-one girls in the single set failed to obtain this score. (Stamford School, private communication.)

A similar experiment for foreign languages teaching was set up in the second and third years of Henry Box School, Witney. The school reported:

> an immediate improvement in terminal test results by pupils in the segregated groups. At the end of year two the results of the single-sex groups were considerably better than those of the co-educational groups in comparison with their performance in their first year in mixed ability coed groups. This improvement was particularly marked among the boys. (Powell, 1979, pp. 23–4)

This is fascinating, and needs careful study, though it is to my mind by no means a straight argument for girls-only classes: the distribution of scores needs studying, and a study made of the low achievers in both groups. Elizabeth Fennema's demonstration of special mathematics workshops (Chapter 11) would suggest the same effect could be achieved by different means.

It is not surprising that these different trends have been put together to argue that single-sex education might be a positive benefit during mid-adolescence at least. It is not surprising that feminists, considering the evidence of male domination in so many aspects of education, should argue that the answer must be 'yes', and that the academic and career aspirations of girls would be favoured if they were educated separately. It is a persuasive argument, not unlike that advanced for black undergraduate universities (or even by some for high schools) on the grounds that a large enough number qualified for graduate school will come through only if, during the crucial stages, their education can be concentrated on specifically, away from the majority domination and with effective black role models present to give encouragement and inspiration. However, two things are clear:

1. The assumption that all aspects of progressive educational thinking inevitably lead to mixed-sex education cannot be sustained. A re-scrutiny of the evidence assembled by Dale (1969, 1971, 1974) in his interesting study leads me to the answer that from some points of view the mixed schools were less good: they had a lower emphasis on academic success and it could be argued that the 'social' benefits he found (by retrospective discussions with adults) are no more than stereotypical pressures in thin disguise.

2. With the current pattern of subject take-up and differential success, some measure of single-sex learning needs considering, even if particular schools reject it.

A move to single-sex schooling would be too major a task for an area to be seriously considered except at exceptional moments, and it is unlikely that the advantages would outweigh the disadvantages. However, the introduction of some single sex classes in an otherwise mixed school is clearly possible.

The first advantage is that a subject which at option choice normally puts off one sex can be dramatically re-named. Typically, the small take-up of stereotyped subjects by the other sex puts off and thus further reduces the few who were considering it. However, by putting in an option called 'Physics for girls' or 'Home economics for boys' the message that the first is for girls and the second for boys comes across clearly. It is then possible to put on a same-sex teacher, and give the material and style a deliberate slant towards the expectations of the appropriate sex. This reassures pupils and even allows group counselling if difficulties arise. The group identity and the very existence of problems and stereotypes can be used positively.

Secondly, even for compulsory subjects there could be sex grouping, perhaps for mathematics, science or languages. This would be justified if in a particular school it was clear that one sex as a group was turning off a subject. The new group could have its atmosphere adjusted to suit, and the assignments similarly given a special attraction to that sex. As well as the mathematics classes referred to earlier, I have seen this done with 'Fabric' with 13-year-olds. In the early days of mixing this craft in a mixed school that had previously taught needlework only to girls, the variation in skills and in interests between the sexes was found to be so great that it seemed wisest to split the group, choose teachers who wanted to work with the boys, and alter the assignments to suit their current attitudes. Although this was in a way giving in to stereotyped attitudes, it also reduced them by allowing the boys to find their own way without using their perception of the girls' reactions to colour their own.

I can certainly see occasions when there would be arguments for introducing some single-sex work into a mixed school. It may be very helpful for getting over a particular hurdle at a particular time. However, it has serious drawbacks:

1. It feeds stereotypes, and by slanting the curriculum, learning material and teaching style it is likely to increase the strength of the socializing of stereotyped attitudes.
2. It assumes that all the boys and all the girls have similar needs, when all the evidence is that typical tendencies are not shared by all members of one sex. Thus the advantages for some could be outweighed by the disadvantages for others.
3. Above all it masks the real need, which is to find out what it is about a certain experience which is offputting and to adjust the teaching. Rather than polarizing teaching styles, there should be a greater mix of styles and a greater flexibility to suit aspects of a subject and individuals. If, for instance, it is found that too quasi-practical a diet of Nuffield Science turns off many girls, the answer is not to put them in a non-practical class but to adjust the mixture: their reaction might well be a valuable indicator, not just a sex reaction.

Interestingly the report from Stamford School, Tameside, which I referred to earlier, noted that the improvement in the girls-only classes had led teachers to ask if they could obtain similar results in mixed classes:

> One of the major values of this exercise has been the interest it has sparked among many teachers now that an improvement in girl performance has been shown to be quite feasible. Classroom strategies for dealing with under-achievement are now more readily discussed. The curriculum has come under closer scrutiny for showing signs of male bias. It is more generally recognised that teacher expectation of boys peforming better could have an adverse effect on the girls.
>
> Clearly the motivation now exists to develop a school-based in-service training programme. This will be centred initially on the Maths and Science departments and will focus on improving the academic performance of girls. Hopefully, discussion will broaden to include general questions of under-achievement in all subject disciplines.

We have learnt from the experience of desegregating blacks in the USA that you do not stop separatism merely by putting different groups under one roof. The race point was a sharp and simple example of what is true of sexual discrimination. It appears to me, therefore, that single-sex classes have some value at some times but could be dangerous in the long run.

# References

Dale, R.R. (1969, 1971, 1974). *Mixed or Single-sex School*, 3 vols. Routledge & Kegan Paul.

Department of Education and Science (1975). *Curricular Differences for Boys and Girls*, Education Survey 21, HMSO.

Kamm, Josephine (1972). *Indicative Past*, Friends of the Girls' Public Day School Trust.

Maccoby, E.E. and Jacklin, C.N. (1974). *The Psychology of Sex Differences*, Stanford: Stanford University Press.

Martini, Richard (1982). *Sex Differences and Achievement*, ILEA Research and Statistics, RS 823/82.

Ormerod, M.B. (1975). 'Subject preference and choice in co-educational and single-sex schools', *British Journal of Educational Psychology*, vol. 45, no. 3, pp. 257–67.

Powell, Robert C. (1979). 'Sex differences and language learning: a review of the evidence,' *Audio-Visual Language Journal*, vol. 17, part 1, pp. 19–24.

Shaw, J. (1976). 'Finishing school – some implications of sex-segregated education', in D.L. Barker and S. Allen *Sexual Divisions and Society: Process and Change*, Tavistock.

# 13   Equality or Equity? – a European Overview

## Eileen M. Byrne

*My destiny must be out there someplace*
Malena, aged 20, Sweden, 1975

The thoughtful speaker was Malena, at the end of her training for technical work in the Saab factory as part of the Swedish experiment established in the late 1970s to open up the 'male' labour market to women and to abolish the sex cleavage we have so insidiously inherited (Advisory Council on Equality Between Men and Women, 1979). She had been asked to look ahead ten years to her new future, as part of the evaluation of the trainees, their families and their workmates. Malena had welcomed the skilled work and higher pay – but she and her husband Urho, for whom home was 'a safe and secure island', were now *both* having to reconcile home, work, and a career which led to more than work in a Saab motor factory, to enable them both to have an equal opportunity to develop as leader worker, as parent, as citizen, as creative and individual people. When the children begin to arrive, it will still, however, be Malena who will tend to perceive a long-term alternative of part-time or no work for herself, as the mother, even long after the children are semi-independent. Does not Urho, her husband – and the father – have an equal right to the full pleasure of being a homeparent, of part-time work, of fuller fatherhood for at least part of his children's formative years?

The conference for which this paper was prepared, was essentially indeed about the destiny that the education service shapes for Malena's successors and their need for an unfettered, less conditioned preparation for a changing work ethic, for swifter social changes and for increasing participation by women in government and politics and economic development, if we are to survive in peace and stability not only into the new decade, but into the new century which is just around the corner for today's children.

Jacqueline Nonon, head of the Women's Bureau of the Social Affairs Directorate of the Commission of the European Communities, puts it more bluntly. If we go into the twenty-first century without women's full potential, we shall fail: a rendezvous with history will be missed.

La transition d'un siècle à l'autre ne se
fera bien qu'avec les femmes; si elle se
fait sans les femmes, elle sera ratée: ce
sera un rendez-vous manqué avec l'histoire (Nonon, 1978).

This chapter aims to provide a backcloth against which the detailed studies in other chapters can be seen, rather than to attempt to deal in detail with current European trends. There are four broad themes against which I believe work both at national levels and in the school, college, or local environment can helpfully be set.

First, the *concept* of equality itself – how to achieve consensus on what in fact we are aiming for; how this matches the international agreements to which we among others are as a nation committed; and what the implications are for educational planners and educators. What is equality? What is equity?

Secondly, the direct and inescapable responsibility of national governments to create and *carry out with resources* a coherent national plan for the achievement of educational equality. In the United Kingdom, the biggest single hindrance in my view to the achievement of sex equality, regional and rural equality and racial equality, is the persistent refusal of government, central and local alike, to take any accountable responsibility whatever for ensuring the achievement of a national plan of education; for a common core to which every child has a right and for which every educator has a duty to provide; and for a national minimum standard of resources and good practice which is not dependent on the accident of the area of residence or on the particular philosophy of the head of the institution. There is a point at which defence of uncontrolled educational autonomy is in danger of becoming a hidden anarchy of non-provision. Unlimited delegation leads to planned inequality.

Thirdly, the need to understand better the full educational implications of the dual role for both sexes, and the concurrent urgency of curriculum reform for a compulsory common-core education for both sexes, for parenthood, or rather for a range of kinds of *family living* – since at any one time, by no means a majority of our citizens live in family situations with responsibility for young children; yet all will need the art of homemaking and of maintaining personal and satisfying relationships.

Fourthly, the need for positive discrimination (or for what is known in Scandinavia as 'temporary preferential treatment') in the curriculum as in training and in the labour market, if both sexes are to catch up with the areas of knowledge and skills in which we now know there to be major sex differences – whether these are innate or conditioned. The 1970s have seen some important innovative work in this field, and the decade has also seen a major international commitment to these principles, which a later section develops briefly.

## Equality or equity?

The weakness of the UK's attempts to achieve an educational equality programme is our consistent refusal to define precisely what we mean by equality. Even the Sex Discrimination Act is highly ambiguous in the wording of its education sections, and we have yet to see any proposals for amending the Act for which many of us have pressed now for many years. But most other countries have nailed some form of flag to the mast and their educators have, therefore, clearer guidelines which are reflected in their curricular planning, and which they can then monitor.

The Shorter Oxford Dictionary defines *equality* as 'the condition of being equal in quantity, amount, value, intensity, etc. . . . the condition of being equal in dignity, privileges, power', under which definition the planned provision for girls in most of our schools can hardly yet be said to be equal. *Equity* on the other had is defined as 'the quality of being equal or fair; impartiality', and is clearly set in the context of jurisprudence. This is a useful distinction, and a reflection of the major trend of the 1970s, which have seen a reassuring strengthening of legal, formal and constitutional equity both at national and international levels. Although formal equity does not necessarily result in factual equality in the 'Monday morning' situation of a classroom or staffroom, it is an essential prerequisite to a national acceptance of the need for rigorous monitoring and real application of what otherwise remain 'progressive' principles held by an enlightened minority. It follows that equality and equity are complementary rather than alternatives.

But how do we define equity (in the legal sense) or equality (in the Monday morning sense) for curriculum and planning? Uniformity or equivalence?

## Equal means the same

As long ago as 1967 the United Nations declared that equal means the same in its declaration to abolish sex discrimination:

> All appropriate measures shall be taken to ensure to girls and women, married or unmarried, equal rights with men in education at all levels, and in particular: (a) equal conditions of access to and study in educational institutions of all types, including universities and vocational, technical and professional schools; (b) the same choice of curricula, the same examinations, teaching staff with qualifications of the same standard and school premises and equipment of the same quality whether the institutions are coeducational or not; (c) equal opportunities to benefit from scholarships

and other study grants; (d) equal opportunities for access to programmes of continuing education, including adult literacy programmes and (e) access to educational information to help in ensuring the health and well-being of families. (United Nations, 1967)

In common with most of my European colleagues, I believe without reservation that *equal means the same* – that is to say, the same across sex, race, rural and urban children of similar abilities and aptitudes. It does not mean uniformity across the full ability range, or across genuinely different interests or personalities. But it does mean uniformity for boys and girls in all that relates to the common core of knowledge, skills, attitudes and experiences without which no one will survive in happy and fulfilled, efficient and adaptable adulthood. And that means that this country has to cease its comfortable evasion of the difficult but not impossible task of defining that common core – a task that even the Third World countries, leave aside our continental colleagues, have not been afraid to face. I am not, let me stress, talking of uniformity of detailed curricular content to the last historical date or set book, nor uniformity of teaching methodology; but that, for example, a core of homecraft and parenthood, technology and manual skills, mathematics and a balanced core of the sciences, at least one creative art, a modern language, and so on, should be the essential heart of the same compulsory education of all girls and all boys – taught together – up to the school-leaving age.

Or does equal mean equivalent? While the EEC commentary on the Community's Directive on Equality in Employment speaks of 'comparable' general education for both sexes and of 'comparable' educational and vocational guidance, the actual Directive later sharpens this to equal opportunity in access to all forms of vocational training. Article 3 of the Directive indeed makes it clear that equal access and standards must be according to ability and aspiration, not to sex.

> The implementation of the principle of equal treatment in regard to vocational training *requires access to all levels of general education, initial and advanced vocational training and retraining*, in accordance with their abilities and aspirations, whether such education and training is provided in institutions or on the job.
> In order to enable women to obtain the qualifications assuring them equal opportunities of employment, member states shall take steps to ensure that equal standards and level of general and technical education and vocational guidance, initial and advanced vocational training and retraining, shall be available *without discrimination based on sex*, or on marital or family status. (Commission of European Communities, 1975)

The view that equal means the same, was reinforced by the European Ministers of Education of the twenty-two Council of Europe countries who met in June 1979 at The Hague to debate equality of education for girls and women at their biennial Conference. This complemented the major initiative of the Commission of the European

Communities whose earlier commissioned study of equality of education for girls, completed in 1978 (Byrne 1979), was also presented to
the Standing Conference as one of four expert studies for debate. The
Ministers declared in their published statement after the conference
that: 'Because sex is becoming, and should become, less relevant in the
distribution of functions in adult life, the educational choices offered to
boys and girls should be the same.' (Standing Conference of European
Ministers of Education, 1979.) Ministerial speeches from the widest
variety of countries also endorsed the need for boys and men to take a
full and equal share in domestic responsibility, childrearing and family
life, and for the *common* curriculum, therefore, to educate both sexes in
this expectation.

## Planning for national equality

This heightens again the difference between the UK and its continental neighbours. Most other countries have defined some form of
national plans for coherent action over the next decade at least. These
without exception incorporate some definition of equality and of its
educational implications for action – which European Ministries
across the water are prepared actually to endorse with resources. As
long ago as 1972 the Nordic Ministers of Culture and Recreation, for
example, surveyed the whole effect of the education structure on sex
roles in educational materials and on the sex distribution in teacher
training and employment, and defined equality: 'Equality between
men and women is taken to mean equal worthiness of the sexes and a
balanced distribution of duties within the family, at work and in public
life.' (Nordic Council for SCEME, 1979). Within the Nordic group,
Norway and Iceland have in fact clearly legislated for sex equality in
education: 'Women and men shall be equally entitled to education.
Instruction in schools and other educational establishments shall be
organised to *ensure* equality of the sexes. Textbooks and other teaching
materials shall not discriminate against either sex.' (ibid.).

Note that they are not controlling or necessarily defining which
books to use on which course, but are prepared to monitor unsuitable
books in general. But where in the UK education service is there a
single point of accountability – central or local – that would ensure
equality, even after declaring it as a constitutional right? The Sex
Discrimination Act only guarantees a form of equality for those in coeducational schools and excludes children in single-sex schools and the
early test cases from 1978–80 under section 22 of that Act, aimed at
establishing that equal curricula between the sexes means identical
curricula equally offered and accessible, were lost in a welter of
ambiguity.

In Sweden the whole education and training system has now come to
be based on a concept of equality in which women and men are
expected to enjoy the same rights and freedoms within all life areas as

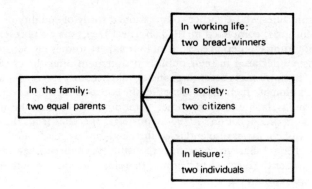

**Figure 13.1**

shown in Figure 13:1. The educational goal set before teachers is 'a whole and indivisible human being' evolving out of the dialectic between sensibility and objectivity, strength and weakness: rejecting sex-polarities on any 'normative' basis.

Denmark has also endorsed this in its recent major and seminal education discussion document for the 1990s called *U90*, in declaring that for the education service

> True equality resides precisely and expressly in the full respect of the originally given, unpredictable difference . . . accordingly an equality-oriented education becomes an individual-oriented education and not its contrast . . .
> All citizens must be entitled to the same amount of education . . . the same resource-equality . . . if not in the young years, then he or she must be *entitled* to retrieve the situation later on, for example, in the form of a preferential right of adult education. (Danish Ministry of Education, 1978)

The key word is *entitled*. Moreover, in all the Scandinavian countries, both boys and girls are given an identical education throughout the first cycle of secondary education, including both homecraft and textiles and the manual and technical basic skills.

The Danish authors of *U90* take for granted (as we do not) that equality means a *political* commitment – it is in their view essential that 'politicians establish that equality-orientation *is a central aim* that must be respected from first to last in the educational system', as a counter-weight to the traditional teaching matter and behavioural patterns in school which 'conceal remnants of previous periods' views on human beings and culture which were greatly characterised by acceptance of sex and class differences' (page 120). In Denmark, of course, the cross-timetabling of 'boys' subjects' and 'girls' subjects' was abolished in 1970 by amendment to the education legislation, and both sexes are now taught woodwork, textiles and homecrafts in coeducational classes. The 1975 Danish Schools Act made further proposals to counteract traditional sex roles.

The Dutch have also set out on their road, with a published discussion document sketching out the future of the education system as a whole over the next twenty-five years, *Contours of a future education system*. It defines equal opportunity not as uniformity, in the sense that again the individual differences between children must be recognized, but declares that equality requires equal options regardless of sex or social class in order to develop ability, interests and skills to the full, and that 'extreme care must be taken that a certain basic level and knowledge and skill . . . is attempted and indeed obtained' (Second Chamber of the States general, 1974–75) – and this common core is for both sexes.

The Dutch point of departure, however, is that educational establishments must themselves be made capable of giving form and content to changes in their own environment and work, and with Dutch logic and consistency, it is spelt out in a government memorandum that facilities must be 'related to each other and geared to each other in a *support structure*'. The Contours Memorandum identifies six means of doing so – all of which are accepted as a government responsibility for their enabling:

New approaches to initial teacher training
Refresher and retraining in new interchangeable sex roles
Innovation in guidance services (for teachers and students alike)
Improved research
Curriculum development
Improved dissemination of knowledge, information and expertise.

This proposed support-structure has a dual purpose – not only to support and service educational establishments, but also to enable the government to pursue a nationally coordinated policy to make innovation and reform a widespread reality in the Netherlands.

In outlining these examples of national planning for educational reform which includes sex equality and social class equality, I am not necessarily arguing that all is well in those countries, nor that *de facto* equality will automatically follow *de jure* declarations of intent – or equity. There are still worrying sex differences in the Netherlands (in particular), in Scandinavia and elsewhere as their Councils and Commissions for Equality regularly diagnose. Nevertheless, at least they are tackling the problem. Moreover, it is significant that it is those countries in which national standards *ensure* that both sexes follow a common-core curriculum up to 15 years, which includes homecraft and technical/manual crafts for both sexes, which also show a substantial and statistically significant proportion of girls entering non-traditional or 'male' areas of further education, training or work on leaving school. (That is to say, Germany, France, Denmark, Sweden.) I do not believe that this is coincidental.

The European Ministers at their 1979 Conference in fact also came to an unusually firm public conclusion that formal equality was indeed not enough. When they examined the mass of evidence presented to them on what girls could actually study and what they actually achieved, they went on record for the first time as recognizing now that 'formal equality in education has not been sufficient to achieve factual equality of opportunity for girls and women either in the educational system or in the life for which it is a preparation'. They recommended that there was a need for every country to commit itself to 'A *new overall policy* designed to *ensure* that in all areas of life equality between the sexes becomes a reality' and spoke of a 'coherent approach' in all forms of education – institutionalized and otherwise – which would complement social and employment policies for equality in each country. This is perhaps the more important where a country is starting with a major inherited problem, like the UK and the Netherlands. The Netherlands has a sex-segregated vocational training system and one of the lowest proportions of women in economic activity, in politics or in leadership of the industrialized countries. The UK has a secondary-school system in which girls may need to go to court to be allowed – let alone encouraged – to learn manual crafts or technical drawing.

The Ministers recognized in particular that 'Future European society cannot afford to leave a large part of its potential not fully realised' – that is the female potential – by the under-representation of women in scientific and technological work and in the leadership of education. This clearly means altering school and college practices – now and not at the millenium – to delete cross-timetabling on grounds of sex. It means developing compensatory programmes in mathematics and technical education, and *it means that government must devote resources for this*. We cannot continue to say that equality and the development of the brains in half the population of the UK in the fields most vital to our economic competitiveness with other industrialized countries, must wait 'until we can afford it'. Economically, we must find the resources or we will cease to be a viable nation. The corollary of the cumulative evidence available at international levels is that the UK must begin to accept some form of national, centrally defined and determined, policy standards of equality and of *resourced*, policy-based educational objectives, if we are to keep pace with our international neighbours.

## Education for the dual role

The relationship of the sharing of the dual role by both sexes to curriculum planning has been well debated and well rehearsed. It is encouraging that a third principle endorsed in the European Ministers' formal statement issued after their 1979 conference, declared that

> Education systems should . . . also prepare *all pupils* for the sharing of domestic and parental responsibilities and equip girls as well as boys to earn an independent living, to cope with the technical elements of practical life, and to participate in democratic decision-making and public life.

This has major implications for curriculum reform, for alternative methods of timetabling, and for the future of any single-sex school or college which perpetuates the existing mutual exclusivity of domesticity for girls and technical education for boys.

But culturally, as well as economically, we are facing regression, not progress, on the educative and social acceptance of the right of girls to full investment in training, in work, jobs, careers, whether or not they marry. All over Europe, female unemployment is rising at several times the rate of male unemployment. All over Europe, girls are relatively protected in academic, school and general education – but they are losing the battle for fewer and scarcer places on vocational training courses, except those traditionally reserved for women. Again, it is significant that those countries who have taken decisive steps to enshrine in their constitutions declarations of the rights of both sexes, happen also to be those with the most positive policies of training for women, of positive discrimination and of the highest proportion of women in leadership and non-traditional roles. Finland, for example, categorically defines the right of gainful employment as the main criterion of female independence, and Finland has the highest proportion of women M Ps in its government. It so happens that it has also produced some interesting analyses of the conflict of the dual role and of women's participation in decision-making. Riitta Auvinen's review of Finnish women in leadership endorses strongly that it is only when women begin *successfully* to compete with – and overtake – men, that pressure is exerted socially, publicly and personally by criticisms that women fulfilling a dual role – but not their male colleagues – are neglecting their (often by then well-grown) families (Auvinen, 1975). But when men have in turn competed with women in entering 'female' fields of training and employment, and then take over the leadership (as all over Europe the trend now shows they do) their 'threat' to women does not evoke parallel accusations of paternal deprivation and family neglect as their top posts lead them to be absent from the home more, and home even later in the evenings.

Evidence from Austria confirms the double standard of society's expectations of working women and working men. The Austrian microcensus of June 1973 into family relations examined the participation rates of wives, husbands and children in five main household tasks: shopping, washing dishes, cleaning the home, shining shoes and doing household repairs. The figures are differentiated by workdays and Saturdays, and by full-time working, part-time working and not working at all (that is, not in paid employment). Men, whatever their or their wives' working status, were only prepared to take from 13 per cent to 15 per cent of the shopping and shining shoes; and at no point more than 5 per cent of home-cleaning (even when men were part-timers). Men's acceptance of 85 per cent of work in household repairs (intermittent and essentially a sporadic weekend task) is in no way comparable with the daily and constant dishwashing, home-cleaning and shopping of which women did 85 per cent. Interestingly where women in paid employment *were* able to shed some household tasks, the statistics show that the work was transferred to the *children* and not to their husbands (Gaudart, 1975). This is confirmed by the evaluation of the Swedish experiment referred to below.

## Schools and parents

This double standard cannot alter until teaching staff in schools and colleges, educate boys as well as girls to the idea of mutual freedom, mutual merit, mutual right and mutual respect outside the home as well as within it. This means working with parents, of course. One important study from the Délégation à la Condition Féminine in France examined the role of mothers and fathers respectively in the guidance of their daughters and their sons in school subjects, career expectations and attitudes to their future roles in the family. The results will probably not surprise readers. Forty-four per cent of the parents thought that educational failure was serious for boys; none thought it mattered for girls since 'La fille a la remède de se marier' – girls could always fall back on marriage. The 31 per cent of parents who thought that choice of job and career was *more* important for boys and not important for girls, said candidly that it was because they believed that the boy *should* become the head of the family and the breadwinner, and that education for girls was mainly a matter of their personal development. One out of two of the mothers in the survey, perceived the essential characteristic of 'feminine' employment to be sporadic, unimportant, not requiring high qualifications and limited to the 'extended maternality' spheres regarded as 'suitable', that is teacher, nurse, child care (Délégation à la Condition Féminine, 1978). A second French research study confirms these findings. Parents from the Pas de Calais region with children in the fourth year of secondary schooling, expressed much more anxiety about sons' career choices than about daughters. The replies from the parental sample showed also a quite different pattern of parental expectation for girls and boys, a 'manifestation of an extremely strong interiorisation of the stereotypes of the masculine and feminine roles in society, that is of course, of the objective possibilities of the masculine labour market and its feminine homologue' (Beture, Département Socio-Economique, 1974). And 'même en rêve, les filles ne s'autorisent pas autant d'ambition que les garçons' ('Even in imagination, girls show less ambition than boys') (ibid).

## The concept of positive discrimination

The need of the education and training services, therefore, to counteract attitudes as well as inadequate skills and knowledge – in both sexes of course, but, for me, with decisive priority for girls until they catch up! – is, therefore, an important development which we have only begun in this decade, so far behind our transatlantic colleagues. Article 14 of the International Convention on human rights outlaws discrimination based on *unfounded* and alleged differences solely on grounds of sex. This applies (as does my 'equal means the same' principle) to all that relates to *basic* rights – the core, the foundation, the right to progression and to all educational services which are a key to unlocking further doors.

But we have accepted for centuries that to enable some who are handicapped either by innate disability, or by social disadvantage, or by accidental and temporary problems (illness, long-term absence from schooling) to achieve equal opportunity, they need extra remedial help – not a different base always, but additional compensatory education. Why is this so controversial when it is directed at girls and women? Remedial language help tends to benefit more boys because their language development is less advanced at a given stage. Why has the concept of remedial numerical and scientific education, which happens to benefit more girls, taken over a century to gain respectability? No European country has yet committed itself to a numeracy remedial programme equivalent to its language remedial programmes.

The Federal Republic of Germany launched a major national programme of compensatory programmes of education and training to train girls and women in mathematical, scientific, technical or craft skills for non-traditional 'male' employment, and evaluated the results by professional and sociopedagogic research teams – the result of which was debated together with analyses of similar programmes in Sweden, France, etc., at a World Congress mounted by UNESCO in 1980. The Germans had already declared their belief in full equality, but it should be said that the real motivation behind the new programme was their recognition that, with a declining birth rate, they will be desperately short of skilled technical labour by 1985. But so will Great Britain. Where is our parallel programme? The MSC and TSD programmes so far have been distinguished principally for the number of women on secretarial courses! The numbers on non-traditional training are infinitesimal, and again form no part of any definable national plan involving the Department of Education and Science in collaboration with the Department of Employment and the Department of Health and Social Security.

Similarly the Swedish 'temporary preferential treatment' programme writes a resources cheque which we do not. The Kristianstad project to train women in technical fields usually regarded as 'male', has now been evaluated in terms of effect on families as well as workplace (Advisory Council on Equality Between Men and Women, 1979). Sweden gives major subsidies to firms who train women in 'male' fields, for equal means the same in Sweden's social goals. Companies seeking regional aid must also now ensure that at least 40 per cent of the jobs *newly created* as a result of regional aid will be reserved for each sex, with back-up special training if need be. There is not space here to deal with the full findings of the Kristianstad survey, but let me dispel one myth of 'family deprivation' alleged to arise when mother works and takes on a dual role. The Swedish researchers themselves became conscious that the very way they framed their questions to the mothers on the effect on their children *presumed* the presence of problems by 'treacherously and biassedly' formed questions. But although the mothers were, therefore, 'on the alert, prepared at any moment to take the blame upon themselves (rather than on the absence of good solutions to child care and the negative effects of restrictive hours of work)' (ibid., p. 126), nevertheless, four positive and substantial results recurred in many families:

1. Children became more independent
2. Children had more (good) contact with fathers
3. Children took more responsibility for themselves and helped out more in the home
4. Children benefited materially from the improved family income.

Interestingly, the children's answers tended to confirm the recorded parental opinions.

Understandably, the Ministers at the Conference were more divided on affirmative action programmes, given the different social, cultural and demographic characteristics of the different countries. Nevertheless, the Ministers' formal statement does accept that actual 'measures should be taken in support of those women, or men, who wish to make non-traditional choices as regards subjects, courses or educational institutions'. A range of possibilities were mentioned in the Ministers' declaration. (Standing Conference of European Ministers of Education, 1979). These included:

> special *information* and *guidance* and special *incentives* to encourage the entry of women to traditionally male-dominated technical institutions and vocational courses;
> *compensatory curricular* programmes for girls and women, e.g., in technical subjects, mathematics, and in politics and civics for adult women;
> action to *encourage* employers to accept candidates of either sex regardless of tradition.

While accepting the inclusion of the qualifying words preferred by some countries of 'where national situations permit', the Ministers still took a generally supported view that 'positive discrimination, where national situations permit, might help in the short term to overcome the minority position of women in many areas of activity, including public administration, employment, policy within education, and those fields where women are conspicuously under-represented.' Within the overall concept of positive discrimination – or affirmative action – there was also Ministerial concern, reiterated in their statement, that special attention should be paid to the needs of groups at risk through 'compound disadvantage' – for example:

migrant women
women seeking their first employment
women wanting to return to employment after a prolonged break.

# The international organizations

I have stressed throughout the positive need for commitments by national governments to *ensure* educational equality and to courageous definitions of controversial issues. I do not suggest that all is well in any single country. There are strengths and weaknesses in each country surveyed by the Commission of the European Communities in its 1978 equality project (Byrne, 1979). This is why perhaps the major breakthrough in the 1970s is the growth of the role of the international organizations in bringing together expertise and knowledge of good practice, in publishing research reports and in providing both a forum for development of a clearer consensus, and a lever to persuade regressive governments to become more positively committed to action rather than theory.

At the UN World Congress in Mexico in International Women's Year, a decisive policy statement was approved by 89 votes to 3 by the delegates present, which laid a clear obligation on national governments to realize nine objectives by 1980, two of which are especially relevant here: (a) to *ensure* equality of access to all types and levels of education; and (b) *consciously* to orient school education and adult and continuing education to a revaluation of the role of women and men to *ensure* the 'full flowering of their personalities both within the family and in society'. This matches the directive issued by the Council of the Commission of the European Communities on equal treatment between men and women workers – binding on member states – already quoted. Article 3 of that Directive makes it clear that equal treatment at work has as its prerequisite, *exactly* the same access to all levels and standards of general and technical education, training, advanced training and vocational guidance. It is at least arguable that any differentiation of curricula on grounds of sex is in direct contravention of this directive. What mechanism has the UK education service for ensuring equal access and identical curriculum, especially in single-sex schools?

In 1977 the European Commission set up its first study on sex inequality at secondary level, completed in 1978, and this now forms the basis of a series of recommendations for a Community action programme to focus on a range of topics identified as of common interest across countries. These are mirrored by a series of current and earlier resolutions and reports from the Council of Europe, the ILO, the European Ministers (the 22). The recommendations centre on four

main areas which I suggest might form a blackcloth against which to set
more detailed discussions.

First, why do girls and boys act and achieve differently in single-sex
and coeducational environments? Both the European Commission
and the Standing Conference of Ministers recommended that priority
be given to research into relative performance in single-sex and mixed
schools and this is clearly a highly relevant area. Secondly, the
imbalance in the teaching force is worsening all over Europe, with
fewer women in leadership in direct proportion to the extension of
coeducation and of reorganizations into larger establishments. A
strategy is needed to deploy the teaching force more evenly at all levels.
Thirdly, the dissemination of the growing and rich pool of new
expertise is an increasing problem. How do we distil new ideas, good
practice and new evidence on sex differences – and the mythologies to
be replaced – to the field worker, the teacher in the classroom, the
careers officer in the High Street? Fourthly, there is universal agreement that little progress can be made without major changes to the
initial and in-service training of teachers and other workers with young
people, and this means a bridge between the expertise in the academic
sector, and the practitioners responsible for training and for teaching.

## Action

Which brings me back to the point of departure – how to move
forward on a national plane as well as in the schools and colleges. In
Sweden, for example, a report on equality has been sent to all universities and training schools by the Ministry with a request that students
and staff and other workers should discuss the new ideas and make
proposals. In the Netherlands, the Ministry has commissioned a five-
year plan from its Emancipation Commission and has already issued
some guidelines – and resources – for action. Germany has its
positive discrimination programmes. France has established a
common curriculum with homecraft for boys and technical education
for girls as well as vice versa. The UK is, so far as I can see, unique in
Europe in resolutely abrogating its responsibility to ensure a national
system of minimum education which incorporates sex equality, terri-
torial equality, and a common-core curriculum which does not depend
on where a child lives, which school it attends, what the philosophy of
the current head determines, or what resources the LEA has left after
the latest Rate Support Grant Settlement.

Successive governments since 1945 have indeed turned a Nelsonic
eye to Section 1 of the Education Act which *requires* the Minister 'to
*secure the effective* execution by local authorities under his (her) *control and
direction* of the *national policy* for providing a varied and comprehensive
educational service in every area.' [my italics] I am not arguing for
complete centralization of the detailed system – far from it. But the
corollary of total delegation by Ministers to local authorities is the

perpetuation of local variations in *basic* rights, not in innovative extras, and an abrogation of Section 1 of the 1944 Act. We need, therefore, still to pursue the question of what schools and colleges can do without waiting for government. But I still hold government ultimately responsible for making sure that it is done – everywhere, and not merely in progressive schools.

According to Goethe 'to act is easy, to think is hard'. I would reverse this maxim – although we should not so lose ourselves in day-to-day work as to lose our capacity for clear thought, neither is debate a substitute for deed. Arnold held that 'If we have the ideas firm and clear the mechanical details for their execution will come a great deal more simply and easily than we now suppose'. I hope that having read this book, readers will agree. And I hope that they will ensure that the Secretary of State also takes the message of his continental colleagues equally to heart. As the Bristol Women's Collective reminded us – 'Women hold up half the sky'. For our destiny, like Malena's, lies out there someplace too.

# References

Advisory Council on Equality Between Men and Women (1979). *Roles in Transition*. Stockholm: Advisory Council on Equality Between Men and Women.

Auvinen, Riitta (1975). 'Participation of Finnish women in decision-making', in *Research Symposium on Women and Decision-making*, No. 23. Geneva: ILO.

Beture, Département Socio-économique (1974). *Enquête sur la scolarisation au niveau 3ème CAP-BEP dans les arrondissements de Calais, Dunkerque et St Omer*. November 1974. Beture, France.

Byrne, E.M. (1979). *Equality of Education and Training for Girls' Studies*, Education Series No. 9. Commission of the European Communities.

Commission of the European Communities (1975). *Directive on Equality of Treatment Between Men and Women Workers*, 12 February 1975 (COM (75) 36 Final).

Danish Ministry of Education Central Council of Education (1978). U90, *Danish Educational Planning and Policy in a Social Context at the end of the 20th Century*. Danish Ministry of Education.

Délégation à la Condition Féminine (1978). *Attitudes et comportements des parents envers le problème de l'orientation scolaire*. Paris: Délégation à la Condition Féminine.

Gaudart, Dorothea (1975). 'The case of Austria', in *Research Symposium on Women and Decision-making*, No. 23. Geneva: ILO.

Netherlands, Second Chamber of the States General (1974–5, *Contours of a Future Education System* (13–459 (1–2)), pp. 89–97.

Nonon, Jacqueline (1978), to the Fifth International Congress of Women Engineers and Scientists, Rouen, 4 September 1978.

Nordic Council for Standing Conference of European Ministers of Education (1979). *Sex Roles and Education*. (CME/XI (79)6.)

Standing Conference of European Ministers of Education (SCEME) (1979), CME/HF (79) 8, June 1979.

United Nations (1967). From Resolution No. 2263 of the General Assembly of the UN, 'Declaration on the elimination of discrimination against women', 7 November 1967. The 1967 text has now been incorporated in the UN's 1979 *Convention on the Elimination of Discrimination Against Women* to which all European countries are signatories.

# 14 Towards a Programme of Action

*Michael Marland*

To a reader who responded, 'But most of these points argue merely for better schooling!' I should not disagree. In weak schooling, societal, family, and individual prejudices flourish; the atmosphere and working procedures of a poorly organized schooling system help the strongest flourish and leave the weakest to wither.

If schooling is to meet its obligation to girls and boys to allow them to be more fully and more skilfully themselves, to develop their talents, and to perceive the full possibilities of life, it must be carefully planned and effectively implemented. When we do not know what we are trying to do, have not articulated our aims, have not devised procedures to carry them out, and do not monitor what is happening, schooling is ineffective. Chance in our society is not on the side of girls. Good schooling could be. A sexually differentiated schooling system inhibits and warps both boys and girls, gives both limited perceptions of themselves and of the other sex, and puts many girls in an inferior position of severely limited power. We have seen from most of the chapters so far very strong evidence of the differential treatment given to girls and boys, often unknowingly, and arguably thus more powerfully. A snapshot of the results in England and Wales can be clearly seen in the comparison of mean grades at the age of 16 in examination subjects. A large sample in Durham, investigated by Cornelius and Cockburn (1978, p. 52), demonstrates the differences very clearly. The graph opposite shows their findings, which epitomize those elsewhere.

It will be seen that the boys achieve a higher mean grade not merely in mathematics and science, but also in history and geography. And the girls? They achieve their high grades not only in the famous girl-oriented subjects of English and modern languages, but also in the

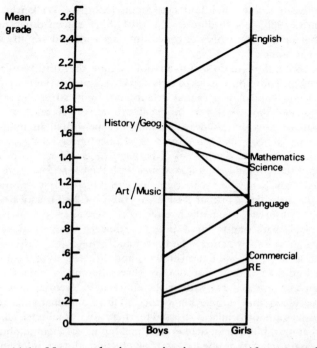

Figure 14.1   Mean grades in examinations at age 16, compared for subjects and sex

subjects less often mentioned: commercial studies and religious education. There in that diagram is the old conventional picture of the British girl: literate, with a smattering of a foreign language, with a future in an office, and the holder of the religious conscience. That balance is still to be found in school option arrangements. For instance, I worked once with a fourth- and fifth-year pattern that had a 'commercial' course entirely for girls. Most of the week was typing and office practice, but that was supplemented by home economics, art, and biology – all compulsory. What a fascinating package! Art was felt to be necessary because, it was argued, it was a feminine accomplishment, helping with creating, home-making, and a woman's appearance. Though why 'commercial girls' were obliged to do biology was less fully argued! That example is one of many which the Durham stereotype reveals.

However, differential treatment is not only shown in the timetabled subjects pupils end up studying in the option years. It lies at a much deeper and more subtle level. Lisa Serbin, Carol Dweck and Dale Spender in particular have pointed to the different ways in which teachers behave to boys and girls. It is often difficult for us to accept that we do all of us to some extent or other thus vary our approaches. However, the more carefully classrooms are analysed the more obvious it is. Even studies of infant classrooms (compare Walkerdine and Eynard, 1980; Walkerdine et al., 1981) have shown differences in teacher behaviour, which of course interact with and amplify differences at home.

Not only, though, do we unconsciously allow the attitudes of society to influence our approaches to girls and boys, but also there are particular school control devices that we slip into. In the stress and business of a school day, it is very noticeable how readily teachers under pressure use sex stereotypes as a handle to cope with ill discipline. In a ballroom dancing class, for instance, I once observed the (woman) instructor snap at a group of girls that if they did not stop fooling around they would be made to dance with the boys! There are many primary teachers who say that you have to 'keep the boys motivated', but the girls 'will work on their own'. In a so-called practical science lesson I observed, two badly behaved girls were allowed to give up the practical work, and 'do a project' (that is, copy sections from magazines) on cosmetics. The reprimands, the style of criticism, the sarcasm, the praise, the punishments and the rewards of the ordinary give-and-take of the classroom are very different for girls and boys. From 5 to 16, teachers use their perception of differential interests as a stereotyping and amplifying device. These and many more such examples are the results of stressed teachers not just falling back on sex stereotypes, but almost deliberately making use of them to obtain the necessary classroom peace and quiet, and thus reinforcing and elaborating them. Indeed, the harder things are for teachers in the school, the more these prejudices rise to the surface. It is difficult not to use any handy tool for control and motivation. Some classrooms in some schools are such desperately difficult places that teachers are seriously tempted to exploit anything – even if it offers only short-term help.

Can we change schools in the way that they reinforce and create stereotypes? In considering the possibilities, there are two helpful points:

1. *Schools do have power over their pupils.* It is not, of course, a complete power, but effective and extensive teaching demonstrably alter pupils' capabilities. Elizabeth Fennema makes an important point (page 165) that girls who study mathematics actually learn mathematics: the boy–girl difference in mathematics results is partly at least a difference in their exposure to teaching. This is so obvious that it is frequently overlooked. It is, however, clearly demonstrated by Neville Bennett's research into primary schools (Bennett, 1976), for he found that the pupils in classes that were so managed that the pupils spent more time on learning tasks actually learnt more! Similarly, the important Rutter research (Rutter et al., 1979; Rutter, 1980) demonstrates the wide range of a school's effects on pupils. The extent of the school's effect is controlled by the method and effectiveness of managing the school, and the effectiveness of the classroom teaching. It is a reasonable supposi-

tion that the weak school is one which, because it has little positive effect according to its own policies, allows the prejudices of society to show through. A strong school brings more pupils up to a higher threshold, and thus alleviates these external effects. For instance, poor primary mathematics teaching is likely to allow the societal pressures to produce a greater sex differentiation in mathematics results than effective mathematics teaching. Similarly, ineffective teaching of foreign languages in the early years of a secondary school is likely to allow a vacuum for normal stereotyped attitudes to flourish.

2. *Schools can change themselves.* There is a tendency for teachers to react as if things are possible elsewhere, but not in 'our' school, because of others – the L E A, the head, colleagues, the area, the parents, etc. Thus schools lapse into impotence from the fear that there is nothing that can be done to change things. If a school has a proper planning mechanism (and if it has not the first step is to create one), considerable organizational, pastoral and curriculum changes can be achieved. More generally the ethos, the procedures and the details of teacher approach can be adjusted.

# Principles for change

Although each school system or school will have to develop its own detailed approach, there are I believe a number of general principles which need considering to establish the most profitable balance. I shall outline eight principles, discussing each first in the form of questions.

1. *Should we treat the question of sexual differentiation as a separate problem or should we regard it as a central part of the main educational problem?*
Conscientious and concerned schools often act like many a bureaucratic body. When for some reason (usually a combination of external publicity and an eloquent teacher or two inside) the school becomes aware of a 'problem', it sets up a committee. Thus some hard-working schools have language committees, multi-ethnic committees, community committees, and wonder whether they ought now to add a sex differentiation committee. In the U S A, where within-school planning is rare and the more usual method of arriving at a curriculum is to buy in programmes, this centrifugal tendency is demonstrated by Federal or State programmes which are introduced to cope with problems as additions to the main courses: bolt-on optional accessories, whether for bilingualism, minority groups or gifted children.

All these approaches institutionalize the very problem they are set up to solve: the issue becomes a separate, extraneous matter for enthusiasts. For instance, although the aim of a language across the curriculum policy is to permeate the entire curriculum with an understanding of language, the separateness can be increased, and the school take this on merely as an extra with little or no change to the mainstream.

Schools in the vanguard of change have attempted the same mechanism with the question of sex differentiation: they set up special committees, usually with an unrepresentative membership, and in so doing separate the problem of the stereotypical education of girls from the more central problem of underachievement and from the school's overall curriculum planning. This not only weakens the approach, but probably risks making even worse the very problem the school is trying to solve. On the whole, although I accept that there are times when a special committee can have value, especially for a limited diagnostic task, I should prefer to feed this concern into the central planning mechanism of the school, and not hive it off as a separate issue.

2. *Are we searching to give 'equality' or to right the inequality of the past by giving girls extra help – 'affirmative action'?*
There is a deep ideological issue here, one that is clearly articulated from a feminist viewpoint, but which is often obscured by others who will express willingness to 'put things right', but miss the point made by Dale Spender (on page 98) that this might be preparing women for 'a man's world', without making adjustments all round.

The first question is whether we just give 'equal' opportunities, or whether, because of the legacy of the past, this requires compensatory education. For instance, it is clearly inadequate merely to give girls *access* to, say, physics or engineering options. At the moment, and following the effects of societal pressures and the legacies of the education of earlier years, it is pretty clear that very few girls will take up the option or have the pre-experience to make good use of it. To put this right requires some form of special action, of compensatory action. This may take the form of special pre-tuition, special persuasion, or even special all-girl facilities.

There are many dangers in such action, not the least of which is the risk of a male backlash, the equivalent of the Bakke case in the USA, in which a white student, refused a place by a university which had filled its quota, sued the university for illegal racial discrimination against him. However, despite risks, and accepting that the ultimate goal is equality, I recommend positive affirmative action now, though hopefully this could be phased out, as it should not eventually be required.

3. *In defining the question, should we focus essentially on the plight of girls, or see our problem more widely as that of sex differentiation?*
The title of this book makes my own views clear: to see the problem as exclusively one affecting girls is both inaccurate and denies long-term success even for that narrower aim.

First, the present situation is demonstratively bad for boys as well as girls. At the simplest level it drives boys away from modern languages and even English literature at school. More than that it clearly gives to boys an inaccurate picture of what it is like to be a woman – and indeed a man. It is this which no doubt lies behind the driving away from many careers in 'the caring professions' boys who could be fulfilled and successful in them. In economic terms and in status terms the dearth of women as doctors, headteachers, engineers and directors is serious; but in many other ways, personal and public, it is equally bad that so few men are infant teachers, librarians, nurses and social workers.

Secondly, the pattern does a great deal of harm to boys – and to society – in the images it creates of life. Just as colonialism can be seen as being bad for the rulers as well as the ruled, so sexism is bad for the dominators as well as the dominated. For instance, Stevi Jackson (1980) shows that sex education as taught in schools is sexist. In her paper the viewpoint is that of the woman, but it comes through equally strongly how much harm it is doing to boys in the inadequate and inaccurate portrayal of human sexuality.

4. *Are we to work mainly with the girls, or with categories of pupils at risk?*
The problems I outlined earlier (pages 3–4), of fleeing from newly defined stereotypes only to embrace older ones more closely, are particularly sharp in this question. For instance, if the issue of verbal participation is considered, we have to avoid the trap of presuming that this is entirely one for girls. There are, of course, quiet boys, and even in single-sex classes the group tends to drive some pupils into themselves – and those can be girls or boys. If we consider difficulties of spatial visualization, while some would argue that there are sex differences in all cultures (Jahoda, 1980), none would argue that the difficulties are limited to the girls. On one test, investigators found a mean score of 12·13 for boys and 8·73 for girls in Scotland and 7·05 for boys and 4·65 for girls in Ghana (ibid, page 429). In both schooling systems there are many pupils of the higher scoring sex who need great help. Similarly, although most girls are apparently forward in foreign language lessons, the problem is not essentially one of girls versus boys, but rather pupils who have good auditory perception and suitable learning attitudes and ones who do not.

Thus compensatory action should not be limited to one sex or the other, but to those who are having difficulty. If many pupils, mostly girls, suffer in discussion lessons, discussion strategies need teaching, with especial help towards those observed to be 'out of it'.

5. *Should a school try to alter its activities in response to recognizable girl/boy expectations, or should it ignore them in the curriculum provision, and try to change the expectations by direct approach? In other words, should you work with or against the stereotype?*
Clearly for some (but by no means for all) of the pupils in school there seem to be recognizable and established 'boy interests' and 'girl interests', and recognizable 'boy weaknesses' and 'girl weaknesses', and clearly we have to acknowledge some polarity. However, I am unhappy about exploiting these and using them for classroom effect. I should prefer to play down the sex-stereotypical responses by searching for androgynous material, topics and approaches. Otherwise we find ourselves shaping the curriculum and selecting the learning materials according to the very stereotypical results we are trying to avoid. For instance, our response to the usually lower status of 'girls' subjects

should not be merely to raise their status, but to blur the labelling. The fact that in a certain mixed school the 'girls' subject of home economics has low status need not be responded to by endeavouring to give it more, but to struggle to remove it from its 'girls' label, and to the extent that it keeps its sex-stereotypical image to de-emphasize it.

6. *Where we recognize stereotyped attitudes in our pupils, with whom should we work?*

The immediate reaction of most of us in schools is to direct our attention to the deprived group. Thus, when a school realizes that its girls are not opting for the physical sciences, the natural response is to endeavour to drum up enthusiasm by exhorting the pre-option girls. This is no doubt necessary, and produces some good. However, it leaves untouched the causes of those girls' attitudes, and some part at least comes from the attitudes of the boys. Therefore, as Elizabeth Fennema demonstrates (Chapter 11), to alter the relationship between girls and the previously sex-stereotypical activities, it is frequently more effective to work on the *boys'* attitudes – for it is their views that are the most powerful and which strongly affect the girls. You cannot support the girls without altering the boys' perceptions, for much of the girls' self-image, it can be shown, is taken from the prejudices of the boys in the school.

7. *To which aspect of schooling do we direct our attention?*

It is tempting for some to see a single species of villain. In fact the stereotyping of society works into schooling through every channel, and there is no single aspect of schooling, still less any single group of people, who are largely to blame. There are those who blame options, teacher prejudice, published material, teaching style, career structure, and so on.

Care has to be taken that as far as possible actions carry more than one payload, that is they achieve other desirable aims as well. For instance, it is obvious that craft, design, and technology should be compulsory for all pupils for the key years of secondary schooling. More than that, I should argue for its position in the curriculum in the elementary years. However, this is not a decision merely to change the image of the activity, but also because of the value of this practical work for its own sake and as a support for other subjects.

8. *As all aspects interlink, a multi-faceted approach is required. At what level in the school system or within the school should the question be focused?*

Eileen Byrne makes the vital central point: unlimited delegation leads to planned non-provision. Subsequent attempts to work a non-sexist policy across a school which has already devised its programmes independently are always difficult and usually unsuccessful. Unless there is whole-school planning there is no real possibility of building ambitions such as those which are the concern of this book into the basis of the work. Each school should have a whole-school planning mechanism, and this should start with a clear statement of the objectives of the school. Only if this is done is there a set of criteria against which to judge the subsequent decisions. Thomas Tallis School in London is an example of a school which has built the aim of sex equality into the stated objectives of the school, and therefore also created the obligation to report annually to the governors on this aspect of the school's work.

Ideally I believe that such objectives ought also to be built into the plans of the school system, whether US School Board or UK Education Authority. Perhaps the most powerful level would be the consortium of schools that work in the same area, with the same families and pupils. (I expand on this grouping of a community of schools in the final section of Marland, 1980.) In some LEAs in the UK, such as Suffolk and Rochdale, attempts are being made to create through-planning. Small US School Districts have that already. Only if the objectives are thus system-wide can they really be fulfilled. The Inner London Education Authority has laid a general obligation to review the underachievement of girls on all schools, but this, though a start, does not oblige schools to incorporate such aims into their declared policies.

These eight questions lead me to suggest that we all need to work from the eight principles I have derived from them:

1. Approaches to solving sexual differentiation should be located in the central educational aims
2. Affirmative action is required, at least at first and in some aspects ('action beyond access')
3. The problem to be solved should be seen as one from which both boys and girls suffer
4. Attention should be given to pupils with problems in certain aspects of schooling, rather than always to sex categories
5. Strenuous efforts should be made not to use, and thus increase, stereotypes in the efforts to remove them
6. Stereotypes have to be tackled by working with both the victims of the stereotypical view and the other group, for the first are affected by the second
7. All aspects of schooling need to be simultaneously tackled
8. Work is required at all levels in schooling from the system management to the classroom teacher.

## Support for the school

The autonomy of the UK school in organization, responsibility structure, curriculum planning and teaching style places a considerable burden on the teachers, who are also planners and administrators. Eileen Byrne in Chapter 13 demonstrates the weakness of this. It also makes the question of what kind of external support might be helpful very difficult. But support there must be. In the United States and Canada, federal, state, and school board control is far tighter and the nature of the support is in one respect simpler: curriculum, teaching material and organization can be heavily influenced by those outside the school, leaving teachers' attitudes and classroom style as the main element requiring outside support.

In the UK I should hope for the following kinds of support:

1. *Central*

   The task of the Department of Education and Science, the Schools Council (or its successor bodies), and publishers is vital:

   (a) To provide national analysis against which individual schools and groups of schools can judge their own situation.

   (b) To provide analyses of tests and teaching material and annotated lists of resources. Publishers, the Schools Council (or its successors) and the National Book League need to cooperate on this.

   (c) To provide analysis of aspects of the curriculum that presently increase differentiation and accounts of possible variations.

2. *Local*

   (a) Local education authorities, while leaving the details of curriculum planning to schools, should discuss and agree guidelines for school organization and curriculum.

   (b) Similarly LEAs or consortia of LEAs could establish task forces that could be invited in by a school to report to the school on aspects of the question. Do our teaching materials show a bias? Is our library suitably stocked? Is our option system stereotypical? How do our classroom styles match up?

   (c) In-service education opportunities are most important, and so far there have been very few opportunities in the UK for teachers to consider the issues of this book. School-focused in-service work would be especially valuable, for in this way a whole staff can consider its work, (see Bolam, 1982).

# Monitoring and evaluation

Intervention requires knowledge not only of the aim but also of what is happening. Too much school discussion of what to do is based on only the broadest and vaguest generalizations about the situation to be improved. If you do not know what is happening you waste efforts intervening inappropriately.

Too little work is done on making ideas happen in schooling. As Marten Shipman puts it in his authoritative book on in-school evaluation: 'Curiously, there is much published work on the aims of education, helping teachers to decide on targets. There is little on how to hit them.' (Shipman, 1979, p. ix) He argues that evaluation is the duty of those who have autonomy in schools.

As a head myself I have often found myself and my colleagues ignorant about what is really happening. Do girls come into our secondary school with the same mathematics range of attainments as boys? Are the differences between the sexes in examination results the same for all ethnic groups in the school? Are there sex differences in attendances, in suspension rates, in staying on, etc.? And if so, how do the differences in this school compare with the differences in others locally or with national figures? I have found that half the 'facts' I am told which I can later check prove to be wrong – but in advance there is no way of telling which half! Dale Spender shows (Chapter 7) how her expectations about male and female use of language were not met by the facts.

The basic starting-point is to ensure that all school statistics are kept in separate girl/boy columns, in each case with the raw figures followed by a percentage (as the balance will often not be even). For instance, the first-preference intake figures for one year into North Westminster Community School is set out like this, showing the differences in the ability spread of the boys and the girls at that time.

| | Marylebone House | | Paddington House | |
|---|---|---|---|---|
| | Boys | Girls | Boys | Girls |
| Ability band | 1 2 3 | 1 2 3 | 1 2 3 | 1 2 3 |
| Sex | Boys | Girls | Boys | Girls |
| Totals | 11 48 22 | 3 15 13 | 3 14 21 | 3 18 15 |
| % of that sex in house | 14 59 27 | 10 48 41 | 8 37 55 | 8 50 42 |
| Sex totals | 81 | 31 | 38 | 36 |
| Sex totals as % of house | 72 | 28 | 51 | 49 |
| House total | | 112 | | 74 |

Similarly, whatever figures have been kept hitherto should be kept in this way. The scrutinizing of a time series will reveal whether there are questions to ask, such as:

Are option take-up figures changing?
Are girls better attenders?
Are boys doing better at A level?

In the setting up of new monitoring tests and in the interpretation of all test results there needs to be an awareness of an appropriate response to the vagaries of all modes of testing, especially, of course, the sex differentiation of the tests used: do they create differences that do not exist or mask differences that do?

This uses existing data collection, and simply ensures that it carries information about sex. The next stage is to identify what I call 'significant categories', that is those groups of pupils which one would expect to have girls and boys represented in them equally if there were no school pull towards sexual differentiation. Defining such 'significant categories' is in fact asking questions about the possible sexual differentiation of the school, whereas looking at the existing data is a less active task.

Such categories might include:
top fifteen percentile in standardized tests at certain ages
bottom fifteen percentile

those gaining five O-level ABC or CSE grade 1
those gaining no examination passes
those gaining any A-level passes
those gaining three A-level passes
those in top third-year sets for specified subjects
those in top fifth-year sets for specified subjects
those absent more than 00 sessions in a term
those referred to education welfare officer
those participating in specified extra-curricular activities
and so on.

This task could be the responsibility of one senior person and related to sex equality (as it is in one Norwich school), and indeed the Equal Opportunities Commission so recommends: 'Schools could consider having a member of staff responsible for reviewing potentially discriminatory practices; analysing the sex differences in the take-up of subjects and courses; advising the staff on current research developments, new materials, etc.' (EOC, p. 16). However, I should prefer this role to be part of wider in-school monitoring.

Such monitoring is only a preliminary, for it shows aspects of the school's work about which questions might be asked. If the figures are different in their sexual composition from the norm of that year or section of the school, the school has to say: 'Is there a question that needs posing?' The normal questions are:

Are these figures significant, or just chance? (Time series over the years are helpful in answering this.)

If the figures reveal a significant difference, how might this difference have come about?

In what ways might we intervene to adjust the balance in the future?

Such monitoring leads to programmes of action: crash courses, special persuasion, new approaches, different arrangements. It is a tool towards evaluation, for if the aims of the school from this point of view have been clearly articulated, efforts must be made to establish to what extent they have been achieved.

'Peer-group evaluation' is a simple method of considering how a school is doing. It is broadly similar to the way a CSE Examinations Board reacts to a Mode III proposal; how, on a larger scale, the Council for National Academic Awards (CNNA) evaluates courses in higher education in the UK, or the regional accreditation boards assess schools in the USA. The school invites a small panel, which might include teachers from other schools, local residents and educational workers in other fields, to visit from time to time to assess aspects of the school according to the agreed brief. (For a fuller account, see Shipman, 1979, pp. 55–9.) Such a group would be particularly valuable for the more intangible aspects of our concern, such as learning materials and classroom procedures. If the report is based on a brief prepared by and agreed by the staff, and if the report is in the first instance to the teachers, issues of professional autonomy are not seriously problematic.

All this is easier for a school that already has a programme of monitoring and evaluation. For those who have not, I have to recommend that both are vital tools in ensuring that a school moves towards reducing the deleterious effects of sex differentiation.

The changes required are difficult, for they are not only in terms of procedures, planning, and organization, but require changes in attitudes which lie deep in each person's own character and background. But since the late 1970s a host of important groups have started in all countries. In the US, for instance, the 'Sex Equity Project' of Richland Community College is an example of local groups organizing regional conferences. In the UK the setting up by the Schools Council of a Sex Differentiation Working Party is of great significance. Publishers, youth organizations, unions, curriculum planners – a whole range of people – are working at the issue from a variety of points of view.

This book is addressed to those who influence schools. It has hoped to put knowledge and ideas at their disposal. Teachers, parents, advisers, publishers, librarians and governors and the pupils themselves could change schools.

# References

Bennett, Neville (1976). *Teaching Styles and Pupil Progress*. Open Books.

Bolam, Ray (ed.) (1982). *School-focussed In-service Education*. Heinemann Educational Books.

Cornelius, M.L. and Cockburn, D. (1978). 'Influences on pupil performances', in *Educational Research*, vol. XXI, no. 1, pp. 48–53.

Equal Opportunities Commission (n.d.). *Do You Provide Equal Educational Opportunities?* Manchester: EOC.

Jackson, Stevi (1978). 'How to Make Babies: Sexism in Sex Education'. Women's Studies International Quarterly, vol. 1, no. 4, pp. 342–52. Pergamon Press.

Jahoda, Gustav (1980). 'Sex and ethnic differences on a spatial-perceptual task: some hypotheses tested'. *British Journal of Psychology*, vol. LXXI, part iii, pp. 425–35.

Marland, Michael (ed.) (1980). *Education for the Inner City*. Heinemann Educational Books.

Rutter, M. (1980). 'Secondary-school practice and pupil success', in Marland, Michael (ed.). *Education for the Inner City*. Heinemann Educational Books.

——, Mortimore, P. and Olsen, S. (1979). *Fifteen Thousand Hours*. Open Books.

Shipman, Marten (1979). *In-School Evaluation*. Heinemann Educational Books.

Walkerdine, V., Corran, G. and Eynard, R. (1981). *Cognitive Development and Infant School Mathematics*. Final report to the Leverhulme Trust.

—— and Eynard, R. (1980). *Girls and Mathematics in the Nursery School*. Progress Report to the Leverhulme Trust.

# Annotated Bibliography
## Emily Patterson and Michael Marland

This is not a full bibliography of all the references in each chapter, for it omits any books in which the topic is not really central. Further it is not a bibliography of education in general nor feminism in general, but is strictly limited to works that consider the relationship between sex differentiation and schooling. A small selection of essential books for the teacher working in the school has been marked with an asterisk*.

AHLUM, Carol and FRALLEY, Jacqueline (1976). *High School Feminist Studies*. New York: The Feminist Press. ISBN 0 912670 24 X.
Covers three main areas: history (primarily women in US), literature and interdisciplinary studies (emphasis on US), with a chapter on textbook analysis.

ARBIB, Patricia (1978). *Sexism and Schools*. New South Wales: NSW Department of Education. ISBN 0 7240 3824 8.
Examines sexism within Australian communities and especially within the school context, drawing out issues over which teachers have control. Appendices.

ASSOCIATION of Assistant Mistresses (1976). *Promotion for Women Teachers: an Account of Three Conferences held in 1975 to mark International Women's Year*. AMMA.
After giving the relevant statistics, this report considers such topics as barriers to promotion, applications and interviews, and the procedure for appointment of staff.

BARCLAY, Lisa K. (1974) 'The emergence of vocational expectations in preschool children'. *Journal of Vocational Behavior*, vol. IV, no. 1, pp. 1–14.

BELOTTI, Elena Gianini (1975). *What Are Little Girls Made Of? The Roots of Feminine Stereotypes*. Writers and Readers. ISBN 0 904613 06 2
Translated from the Italian. Discusses early socialization and education of girls.

BERRILLS, R. (1977–78). 'Sex bias in mathematical education'. Abstract

3/1366 in *Register of Education Research in the U.K.*, vol. III.

BLACKSTONE, Tessa and FULTON, Oliver (1975) 'Sex discrimination among university teachers: a British–American comparison'. *British Journal of Sociology*, vol. XXVI, no. 3, pp. 261–75.
Differences and similarities in rank, pay, promotion and subject areas are drawn from the statistics of national surveys conducted in 1969.

—— and WEINREICH-HASTE, Helen (1980). 'Why are there so few women scientists and engineers?' *New Society*. February. pp. 261–75.
Analyses the ways girls learn to underachieve.

BLOCK, J.H. (1976). 'Issues, problems, and pitfalls in assessing sex differences: a critical review of the psychology of sex differences'. *Merrill-Palmer Quarterly*, no.22, pp. 283–308.

BOARD OF EDUCATION. *Differentiation of the Curriculum for Boys and Girls Respectively in Secondary Schools*. HMSO, 1923.
This is the less known half of the report of the Hadow Committee, the better known part being on 'psychological tests of educable capacity'. Although many of the arguments are based on data later to be regarded as inaccurate, there is a great deal of forward thinking, for example, on mathematics, physics, and literature.

BRADLEY, Judy and SILVERLEAF, Jane (1979). 'Women teachers in further education'. *Educational Research*, vol. XXII, no. 1, pp. 15–21.
The effects of academic and professional qualifications, geographical mobility, aspiration, marital status and subject area on promotion are cited from a National Foundation for Educational Research project.

BRADSHAW, Jan, DAVIES, Wendy and DE WOLFE, Patricia (1981). *Women's Studies in the UK*. Women's Research and Resources Centre. ISBN 0 905969 11 1.
As well as details on women's studies and courses, suggestions on how to start a course. Bibliography.

BRIMER, A., MADAUS, G.F., CHAPMAN, B., KELLAGHAN, T. and WOOD, R. (1978). *Sources of Difference in School Achievement* Windsor: NFER Publishing. ISBN 0 85633 155 4.

BRYANT, Margaret E. (1979). *The Unexpected Revolution: a Study of the Education of Women and Girls in the Nineteenth Century*. University of London Institute of Education. ISBN 0 85473 086 9.
Study of the significance and revolutionary characteristic of changes in the education of women and girls in the nineteenth century. Argues that historians, in generally neglecting the significance of such changes, failed to prepare the Western world for the Women's Liberation Movement of the last decade.

BURSTYN, Joan N. (1980). *Victorian Education and the Ideal of Womanhood*. Croom Helm. ISBN 0 389 20103 0.
Study of the opposition to female entry to the universities.

BYRNE, Eileen M. (1978). *Equality of Education and Training for Girls (10–18 Years)*. Collection Studies: Education Series No. 9. Brussels: Commission of the European Communities.
A report on the inequality girls face in second level education and its socio-political impact. Based on an inquiry in 1977–78.

*—— (1978). *Women and Education*. Tavistock. ISBN 0 422 75960 0 (hardback); ISBN 0 422 75970 8 (paperback).
Examines the whole range of education for girls and women with the goal of using education for change. Appendix. Bibliography. Indexes.

CADOGAN, Mary and CRAIG, Patricia (1976). *You're a Brick, Angela! A New Look at Girls' Fiction from 1839-1975*. Gollancz. ISBN 0 575 02061 X.

CARDEN, Maren Lockwood (1977). *Feminism in the Mid-1970s. The Non-establishment, the Establishment and the Future*. A report to the Ford Foundation. New York: Ford Foundation. ISBN 0 916584 04 6.

CATER, Libby A. and SCOTT, Anne Firor, with MARTYNA, Wendy (1976). *Women and Men: Changing Roles, Relationships and Perceptions*. New York: Aspen Institute for Humanistic Studies. ISBN 0 915436 21 3.

CENTRE FOR SCIENCE EDUCATION (1975). *Girls and Science Education: Cause for Concern?* Centre for Science Education.
Six papers from a 1975 conference at the Centre for Science Education, Chelsea.

CHABAUD, Jacqueline (1970). *The Education and Advancement of Women*. Paris; UNESCO. ISBN 0 92 3 100842 0.

CHANDLER, E.M. (1980). *Educating Adolescent Girls*. Allen & Unwin. ISBN 0 04 370097 7.
A book for the practitioner: research findings and material drawn from recent work by teachers in school alongside theoretical approaches. The importance of education for girls is looked at in the context of their future roles as members of the work force and as mothers of the next generation.

CHILDREN'S RIGHTS WORKSHOP (1976). *Sexism in Children's Books: Facts, Figures and Guidelines*. Writers and Readers. ISBN 0 904613 22 4.
Includes three informative articles on illustrations in picture books and role models in reading schemes, and the text of McGraw-Hill's guidelines for equal treatment of the sexes in their publications.

CLARRICOATES, Katherine (1978). '"Dinosaurs in the classroom": a re-examination of some aspects of the "hidden" curriculum in primary schools'. *Women's Studies International Quarterly*, vol. I, no. 4, pp. 353-64.
Language, preference of students determined by sex, lesson content and promotion of sex stereotyped behaviour are pointed out as methods teachers may use to control their classes.

CLEMENT, Jacqueline Parker (1975). *Sex Bias in School Leadership*. Evanston, Ill.: Integrated Education Associates. ISBN 0 912008 10 5.
Discusses the small number of women in educational leadership roles, and the federal government's attempts to regulate the participation of women in economic life. Bibliography. Appendices.

COMMITTEE of Inquiry into the Engineering Profession. (1980). *Engineering Our Future* HMSO. ISBN 0 11 512497 7.
Summary of the Report of the Committee chaired by Sir Monty Finniston. Recommendations include changes required in schools.

CONNOR, J.M., SCHACKMAN, M. and SERBIN, L.A. (1978). 'Sex-related differences in response to practice on a visual spatial test and generalization to a related test'. *Child Development*, no. 49, pp. 24-9.

—— and SERBIN, L.A. (1978). 'Children's responses to stories with male and female characters'. *Sex Roles*, no. 4, pp. 637-45.

—— SERBIN, L.A. and SCHACKMAN, M. (1977). 'Sex differences on children's response to training on a visual-spatial test'. *Developmental Psychology*, no. 13, pp. 293-4.

—— SERBIN, L.A. and ENDER, R.A. 'Responses of boys and girls to aggressive, assertive and passive behaviors of male and female characters'. *Journal of Genetic Psychology* (in press).

CORNELIUS, M.L., and COCKBURN, D. (1978). 'Influences on pupil performance'. *Educational Research*, vol. XXI, no. 1, pp. 48–53.

—— and —— (1978). 'Pupil performanc in school mathematics: some factors of influence'. *Bulletin: The Institute of Mathematics and its Applications*, vol. XIV August-September, pp. 220–2.
Home background, sex, and age are examined as influences on 16-year-old students from the Derwentside District of County Durham.

COUSSINS, Jean (1977). *The Equality Report: One Year of the Equal Pay Act; the Sex Discrimination Act; the Equal Opportunities Commission.* NCCL Rights for Women Unit. ISBN 0 901108 61 8.

DALE, R.R. (1969). *Mixed or Single-sex School? A Research Study in Pupil–Teacher Relationships.* Routledge & Kegan Paul; New York: Humanities Press, 1969. ISBN 0 7100 6282 6.

—— (1971). *Mixed or Single-sex School? Volume II, Some Social Aspects.* Routledge & Kegan Paul; New York: Humanities Press. ISBN 0 7100 7024 1.

—— (1974). *Mixed or Single-sex School? Volume III, Attainment, Attitudes and Overview.* Routledge & Kegan Paul; New York: Humanities Press. ISBN 0 7100 7744 0.
A comparison of coeducational and single-sex schools based on a range of research in Great Britain. Bibliography. Index. Appendices.

—— (1975). 'Education and sex roles'. *Educational Review*, vol. XXVII, no. 3, pp. 240–8.
Promotes the attitude that individual differences are more important than sex differences.

DAVEY, Angela (1980). *Ballet Shoes or Building Site? The Role of Books, Reading and Libraries in the Encouragement of Girls to Take Up Careers in Engineering* Birmingham: Birmingham Library School Cooperative. ISBN 0 906945 02 X.
Study conducted with the cooperation of the Engineering Industry Training Board. Looks at attitudes to careers for girls in this field, and at the way girls are portrayed in a wide range of children's books. Summarizes findings of a survey carried out into childhood reading of girl technicians in the engineering industry, of girls studying for a diploma in business studies, and of a control group with no special interest in technical subjects. Bibliography.

DAVIES, L. (1977–78). 'Deviance and sex roles: the nature of girls' reaction to schooling'. Abstract 3/1947 in the *Register of Educational Research in the U.K.*, vol. III.

DEEM, Rosemary (1978). *Women and Schooling.* Routledge & Kegan Paul. ISBN 0 7100 8958 9.
Chapters range from the 'Entry of women into mass education' and 'Patterns of contemporary curricular discrimination' to 'Women as teachers' and the 'Possibilities of change'. Bibliography. Index.

*—— (ed.) (1980). *Schooling for Women's Work.* Routledge & Kegan Paul. ISBN 0 7100 0576 8.
Collection of papers demonstrating the continual existence of gender stereotyping in primary and secondary schooling, and the endeavours by schools to prepare women for domestic labour and a narrow range of female-dominated occupations.

DELAMONT, Sarah (1980). *Sex Roles and the School.* Methuen. ISBN 0 416 71320 3.
A sociological study of the everyday life of schools based on extensive participant-observer research. Very many vivid examples of the ways in which teacher expectation influences the construction of sex roles are given.

*DEPARTMENT OF EDUCATION AND SCIENCE (1975). *Curricular Differences for Boys and Girls*. Education Survey 21. HMSO. ISBN 0 11 270381 X.

Study of primary, middle, secondary and further education in single-sex and mixed schools to determine 'which curricular differences and customs contributed to inequality of opportunity for boys and girls' by HM Inspectors. Appendix.

—— (1976). *Sex Discrimination Act 1975*. Circulars 2/76 and 20/76. London and Cardiff: Department of Education and Science.

—— (1978). *Primary Education in England: a Survey by HM Inspectors of Schools*. HMSO ISBN 0 11 270484 0

This detailed survey of the work of primary schools in the UK has important data on curriculum differentiation for boys and girls, HMI commitment to removing this (for example, in section 8.29), and male/female staffing figures.

—— (1980). *Girls and Science*. HMSO. ISBN 0 11 270534 0.

A report of an inquiry carried out by HM Inspectors into the teaching of science to girls in coeducational comprehensive schools, and an assessment of the factors influencing their choice of science subjects.

DEPARTMENT OF HEALTH, EDUCATION AND WELFARE. (1975). 'Nondiscrimination on basis of sex'. *Federal Register*, vol. XXXX, no. 108, part 2, pp. 24128–45, Washington, D.C.: US Government Printing Office. Rules and regulations affecting education programmes and activities receiving or benefiting from Federal financial aid.

DEVON EDUCATION DEPARTMENT (1978). *A Discussion Paper on Sex Equality in Education: Curriculum in the Primary School*. Exeter: Devon Education Department.

The report of a working party set up by the Devon LEA to consider the guidance that should be given to primary schools following the 1975 Equal Opportunities Act. As the first major LEA response, this is an important document. Bibliography.

DIXON, Bob (1977). *Catching Them Young: Sex, Race and Class in Children's Fiction*. Vol. 1. Pluto Press. ISBN 0 904383 50 4.

Looks at what attitudes and ideas writers convey to children in popular fiction and how those attitudes and ideas are conveyed. A companion volume looks at political ideas. Bibliography. Index.

DONLON, T.F. (1973). 'Content factors in sex differences on test questions'. *Research Memorandum*, Princeton, N.J. : E.T.S.

DRIVER, Geoffrey (1977). 'Cultural competence, social power and school achievement: West Indian pupils in the West Midlands'. *New Community* Journal of the Commission for Racial Equality, vol. V, no. 4, pp. 353–59. Includes specific comparison between West Indian girls' and West Indian boys' test results, and the social factors influencing them.

DWECK, Carol S. (1977). 'Learned helplessness and negative evaluation'. *Educator*, vol. 19, no. 2, pp. 44–9.

Examines changes in children's performances in relation to failure, classroom feedback, cognitive-motivational differences and sex differences.

—— and COETZ, Therese E. (1978). 'Attributions and learned helplessness', in J. Harvey, W. Ickes and R. Kidd (eds). *New Directions in Attribution Research*, vol. II, pp. 159–79. New York: Halsted. ISBN 0 470 98910 6.

Helpless and mastery-oriented children are examined through past and current research, and the value of attribution training stressed.

DWYER, C.A. (1974). 'The influence of children's sex-role standards on reading and arithmetic achievement'. *Journal of Educational Psychology*, no. 66, pp. 811–16.

—— (1975). 'Comparative aspects of sex differences in reading', in D. Moyle, (ed.), *Reading: What of the Future?* Ward Lock.

—— (1976). 'Test content and sex differences in reading'. *The Reading Teacher*, no. 19, pp. 271–80.

—— (1979). 'The role of tests and their construction in producing apparent sex-related differences', in M.A. Wittig and A.C. Petersen (eds.). *Sex Related Differences in Cognitive Functioning* New York: Academic Press. ISBN 0 12 761150 9.

DYHOUSE, Carol (1976). 'Social Darwinistic ideas and the development of women's education in England, 1800–1920'. *History of Education*, vol. 5, no. 1, pp. 41–58.

—— (1977). 'Good wives and little mothers: social anxieties and the schoolgirls' curriculum, 1890–1920'. *Oxford Review of Education*, vol. 3, no. 1, pp. 21–35.

—— (1978). 'Towards a "feminine" curriculum for English schoolgirls: the demands of ideology, 1870–1963'. *Women's Studies International Quarterly*, vol. I, no. 4, pp. 297–311. Pergamon Press.

'Surveys various social and ideological pressures on girls' schools in England over the last century to re-shape the curriculum in order to make more provision for domestic training; to emphasize the importance of women's reproductive and domestic "vocations" at the expense of intellectual, professional or other occupations.'

—— (1980). *Girls Growing Up in Late Victorian and Edwardian England*. Routledge & Kegan Paul. ISBN 0 7100 0821 X.

Looks at the way in which the role of young girls at the start of the century was shaped by the society in which they grew up, how school reinforced the pattern, and the influences on the curriculum offered in elementary schools.

EAVES, Aubrey. (1978). 'Equal opportunities for men and women'. *Trends in Education*, no. 4, pp. 7–10.

Concludes there is little evidence of inequality of opportunity in the educational system.

EDDOWES, Muriel (1983). *Humble Pi: the Mathematics Education of Girls*. Longman for the Schools Council.

A joint Equal Opportunities and Schools Council project which clearl; describes the present situation in the UK and sets out practical ways in which schools can help more girls be successful in maths.

ELLIOTT, John (1974). 'Sex role constraints on freedom of discussion: a neglected reality of the classroom'. *New Era*, vol. 55, no. 6, pp. 147–55.

Case-history of teacher's attempts to develop discussion of controversial issue with adolescents of mixed ability.

ENGINEERING INDUSTRY TRAINING BOARD (1977). *School Learning and Training*. Watford, Herts: EITB. ISBN 0 85083 334 5.

An interim report on research over the four-year period 1971–75. Objectives of this EITB project were to examine school methods and subsequent industrial participation and performance and form links between educational institutions and industry. Emphasis was on last year at school and early training.

*EQUAL OPPORTUNITIES COMMISSION. (1980). *A Guide to Equal*

*Treatment of the Sexes in Careers Materials.* Manchester: EOC. ISBN 0 905829 32 8.
Practical guidelines for wording of resources and interviews. Appendix. Bibliography.

—— (1977). *Report of Formal Investigation into Equal Provision of Secondary Education as between the Sexes in the area of the Local Education Authority of Tameside Metropolitan Borough, 1976–77.* Manchester: EOC.

—— (1979). *Education of Girls: a Statistical Analysis.* Manchester: EOC.

—— (1981). *Grants for Equality.* Manchester: EOC. ISBN 0 905829 40 9.
Details of research and educational activities funded by the Equal Opportunites Commission from 1976 to 1981.

ERNEST, John (1976). *Mathematics and Sex.* Santa Barbara, California: Mathematics Department, University of California.
A brief report on women and girls in mathematics from early student attitudes in the classroom to actual career participation.

ESSEN, Juliet, FOGELMAN, Ken and GHODSIAN, Mayer (1978). 'Long-term changes in the school attainment of a national sample of children'. *Educational Research*, vol. XX, no. 2, pp. 143–51.
In a study based on data from the National Child Development Study which examined the extent to which the same children performed relatively well, or poorly, at each stage of their school career, the authors show that mathematics differences between sexes have important features hidden by considering only the mean.

ESTLER, Suzanne E. (1975). 'Women as leaders in public education'. *Signs*, University of Chicago Press, vol. 1, no. 2.

*EVERLEY, Barry (1981). *We Can Do It Now 4–16: a Report of Some Good Practices in Science, Technology and Crafts in Schools.* Manchester: Equal Opportunities Commission. ISBN 0 905829 43 3.
Points out that it is vital to introduce science and technology into the school curriculum as early as possible in order to provide girls with the experience necessary for the development of technical skills, and to prevent the formation of prejudices. Advice ranges from the kind of science resources to specific career advice. Appendices. Bibliography.

FAIRWEATHER, H. (1976). 'Sex differences in cognition'. *Cognition*, no. 4, pp. 231–80.

FENNEMA, E. (1974). 'Mathematics learning and the sexes: a review'. *Journal for Research in Mathematics Education*, vol. 5, p. 126.

—— (1975). 'Spatial ability, mathematics and the sexes', in E. Fennema (ed.) *Mathematics Learning: What Research Says About Sex Differences.* Columbus, Ohio: ERIC Centre for Science, Mathematics and Environmental Education College of Education, The Ohio State University.

—— (1978). 'Influences of selected cognitive, affective and educational variables on sex-related differences in mathematics learning and studying', in L.H. FOX et al. *Women and Mathematics: Research Perspectives for Change – NIE Papers in Education and Work, No. 8.* Washington, D.C.: National Institute of Education.

—— (1979). 'Women and girls in mathematics: equity in mathematics education'. *Educational Studies in Mathematics*, vol. X, pp. 389–401.
After looking at cognitive, affective and educational variables, concludes 'All variables appear to be directly related to the stereotyping of Mathematics as a male domain.' Bibliography.

—— and SHERMAN, J.A. (1977). 'Sex-related differences in mathematics achievement, spatial visualization and affective factors'. *American Educational Research Journal*, vol. 14 no. 1, pp. 51–72.

—— and —— (1978). 'Sex-related differences in mathematics achievement and related factors: a further study'. *Journal for Research in Mathematics Education.* vol. 9, p. 189.

FINLAYSON, Douglas S. (1973). 'The goal structure of teachers in comprehensive schools'. *Education Research*, vol. XV, no. 3, pp. 188–93.

FOX, L.H., FENNEMA, E. and SHERMAN, J. *Women and Mathematics: Research Perspectives for Change.* NIE Papers in Education and Work No. 8. Washington, D.C.: National Institute of Education, 1978.

FRANSELLA, Fay and FROST, Kay (1977). *On Being a Woman: a Review of Research on How Women See Themselves.* Tavistock. ISBN 0 422 76080 3. Includes a section on 'Children's views of teachers', which is complemented by other sections containing data on what attitudes children bring to school and those they leave with. Bibliography. Indexes.

FRAZIER, Nancy and SADKER, Myra (1973). *Sexism in School and Society.* New York: Harper & Row. ISBN 0 06 042172 X. Part of a series developed particularly for educators, this explores overt and hidden sexism at all stages in education and makes proposals for change. A sex bias questionnaire for teachers and administrators is included to focus thought on actual school practices. Bibliography.

FROSCHL, Merle, HOWE, Florence and KAYLEN, Sharon (eds) (1975). *Women's Studies for Teachers and Administrators: a Packet of Inservice Education Materials.* Old Westbury, N.Y.: The Feminist Press. ISBN 0 912670 21 5. Has four major components: (1) a cassette of four speeches given at The Feminist Press' national conference 'Re-educating a Generation of Teachers'; (2) Women's Studies Inservice Course outlines; (3) samples of curriculum materials and (4) resource list.

GARDNER, P.L. (1974). 'Sex differences in achievement, attitudes, and personality of science students: a review'. *Science Education: Research*, pp. 231–60.

GATES, Barbara, KLAW, Susan and STEINBERG, Adria (1979). *Changing Learning, Changing Lives: a High School Women's Studies Curriculum from the Group School.* Old Westbury, N.Y.: The Feminist Press. ISBN 0 912670 47 9. Designed for the working-class young woman and developed over five years by The Group School, a certified, alternative high school in Cambridge, Mass. Bibliography.

GERSONI-STAVN, Diane (1974). *Sexism and Youth.* New York: Bowker. ISBN 0 8352 0710 2. A large compilation of essays, papers, reports and studies focused on initial and early programming. Index.

GIRLS' PUBLIC DAY SCHOOL TRUST (1972). *GPDST 1872–1972, A Centenary Review* GPDST. ISBN 0 903357 00 3. A brief celebratory history of one of the major British organizations pioneering education for girls, with a few pages on each of the schools still working in 1972.

GOOD, Thomas L., SIKES, J. Neville and BROPHY, Jere E. (1973). 'Effects of teacher sex and student sex on classroom interaction'. *Journal of Educational Psychology*, vol. LXV, no. 1, pp. 74–87. Concludes that male and female teachers behave differently in some ways, although they show similar patterns in their treatment of boys and girls.

GRAF, R.G. and RIDDELL, J.C. (1972). 'Sex differences in problem solving as a function of problem context', *Journal of Educational Research*, no. 65, pp. 451–2.

GRAY, Charlotte (1977). 'Behaving according to plan'. *Where*, March, pp. 69–71.

Ways in which parents and the educational system reinforce sex-role stereotypes are briefly discussed. Suggestions for parental action in combating the above are given.

GRAY, John, MCPHERSON, Andrew and RAFFE, David (1979). 'Collaborative research in Scotland: a new departure'. *Educational Research*, vol. XXI, no. 3, pp. 178–85.

GROSS, Neal and TRASK, Anne E. (1976). *The Sex Factor and the Management of Schools* New York and Toronto: Wiley-Interscience. ISBN 0 471 32800 6.

Based on a survey of male and female public (state) elementary school administrators in the same positions in the States, the primary objective being to determine if sex determines promotion prospects.

HANNON, Valerie (1981). *Ending Sex-Stereotyping in Schools: a Sourcebook for School-Based Teacher Workshops* Manchester: Equal Opportunities Commission. ISBN 0 905829 26 3.

Makes suggestions about the content and format of courses and workshops on increasing equality of opportunity, and lists a range of the resources available.

HARDING, Jan (1979). 'Sex differences in examination performance at 16 + ', *Physics Education*, vol. XIV, pp. 280–4.

HARMAN, Harriet (1978). *Sex Discrimination in Schools: And How to Fight It* National Council for Civil Liberties. ISBN 0 901 108 73 1.

Small manual on strategies for combating sex discrimination in Britain. Geared towards the teacher's role in the education structure. Text of the Sex Discrimination Act 1975 included.

HARNEY, E. (1977–78). 'Sexism in pre-school and primary school literature and its effects on the socialization of the child'. Abstract 3/0636 in the *Register of Educational Research in the U.K.*, vol. III.

HARRISON, Barbara Grizzuti.(1973). *Unlearning the Lie: Sexism in School* New York: Liveright. ISBN 0 87140 559 8.

Sensitive, personal account of parental interest in a private, American school being sex-role conscious in the classroom. Comments on resulting tensions related to the women's movement, racism, classism. Bibliography.

HARTLEY, D.J. (1977–78). 'Sociological aspects of sex differences among children in infant schools'. Abstract 3/0483 in the *Register of Educational Research in the U.K.*, vol. III.

*HARTNETT, Oonagh, BODEN, Gill and FULLER, Mary (eds) (1979). *Sex-Role Stereotyping* Tavistock. ISBN 0 422 76780 8.

A collection of papers from the international conference on sex-role stereotyping sponsored by the British Psychological Society. Includes education and intervention strategies to reduce sex-role stereotyping in educational programmes. Indexes.

HARVEY, T.J. (1979). 'Mixed ability teaching in physical science', *Educational Research*, vol. XXII, no. 1. pp. 60–1.

A short report on a study of 240 children in physical science in mixed-ability classes. Usefully shows not only the mean differences, but comparative differences between different ability levels.

HEALY, Maura and MARLAND, Michael (eds) (1983). *Sexual Differentiation and the Teaching of English* York: Longman for Schools Council.
The report of a working party established by the English Committee of the Schools Council. Focuses on general teaching approaches (choice of topics, classroom discussion), literature (bias, range available), and examinations (set texts, the language of examinations, oral examinations). Bibliography.

HEARN, Michael (1979). 'Girls for physical science: a school based strategy for encouraging girls to opt for the physical sciences'. *Education in Science*, April, pp. 13–16.
A description of pupil and parent strategies, as well as utilization of the careers officer, non-science staff, and girl scientist, as developed in a London mixed comprehensive school.

HENLEY, Nancy and THORNE, Barrie (1975). *He Said/She Said: An Annotated Bibliography of Sex Differences in Language, Speech, and Nonverbal Communication*. Pittsburgh, Pa.: KNOW. ISBN 0 912786 36 1.

HOFFMAN, Mary M. (1975). 'Assumptions in sex education books'. *Educational Review* vol XXVII, no. 3, pp. 211–20.
Argues that sex education books generalize from extreme cases to moralize about chastity and to promote a sexist view of society. Bibliography.

HOLLAND, Janet (1981). *Work and Women*. University of London Institute of Education, Bedford Way Papers, no. 6. ISBN 0 85473 119 9.
Subtitled 'a review of explanations for the maintenance and reproduction of Sexual Divisions', this study, mainly focusing on aspects of work, has extremely useful considerations of the relationship between education and these work divisions.

HOWE, Florence (1971). 'Sexual stereotypes start early'. A KNOW reprint from *Saturday Review*, 16 October, pp. 1–7.
Adaptation of speech in which curricular development, education and re-education of teachers and counsellors, and revised textbooks are called for.

ILEA INSPECTORATE (1982). *Equal Opportunities*. Inner London Education Authority. ISBN 7085 0001 3.
A committee report whose terms of reference were to 'make recommendations on ways of promoting equality of educational opportunity for boys, girls, and young people'. Includes valuable statistical analysis and balanced recommendations.

INNER LONDON EDUCATION AUTHORITY (1975). *Careers Opportunities for Women and Girls* ILEA. ISBN 0 7085 0006 4.
Pamphlet looks at the present employment situation for women and girls, and gives recommendations to improve this area. Appendices.

JACKLIN, C.A. (1978). Review of L.H. Fox, E. Fennema and J.Sherman, *Women and Mathematics: Research Perspectives for Change* NIE Papers in Education and Work, in *Journal for Research in Mathematics Education*, vol. IX, no. 5, pp. 387–90.
Social factors, cognitive abilities and possible biological differences are related to girls and mathematics. A favourable review of special interest to teachers.

—— (1979). 'Explaining sex-related differences in cognitive function', in M.A. Wittig and A.C. Petersen (eds). *Sex-Related Differences in Cognitive Functioning: Developmental Issues* New York: Academic Press. ISBN 0 12 761150 9.

—— and MACCOBY, E.E. (1978). 'Social behavior at 33 months in same-sex and mixed-sex dyads'. *Child Development*, no. 49, pp. 557–69.

—— MACCOBY, E.E., and DICK, A. (1973). 'Barrier behaviour and preference: sex differences (and their absence) in the year old child'. *Child Development*, vol. XLIV, pp. 196–200.

—— and MISCHELL, H. (1973). 'As the twig is bent – sex role stereotyping in early readers'. *School Psychology Digest*, vol. II, no. 3, pp. 30–8.

JACKSON, Stevi (1978). 'How to Make Babies: Sexism in Sex Education'. Women's Studies International Quarterly, vol. 1, no. 4, pp. 342–52. Pergamon Press.

An important analysis of the content and approach of sex education in schools, based on questioning young people as well as studying the books available, in which the author reveals the absence of information on sexuality, especially that of women. The author convincingly argues that, by emphasizing reproduction rather than sexuality, the teaching is male orientated and strongly sexist.

KAMM, Josephine (1965). *Hope Deferred: Girls' Education in English History* Methuen.

—— (1972). *Indicative Past*. Friends of the Girls' Public Day School Trust. A history of the GPDST schools, of great interest for the first phase of education of girls in England.

KELLY, Alison (1975). 'A discouraging process: how women are eased out of science'. Paper presented at conference, 'Girls and Science Education', Chelsea College, Edinburgh University, 19–20 March 1975. Paper on the psychological and sociological factors that influence girls (in the field of science) outside of educational institutions.

—— (1975). 'Why do girls study biology?' *School Science Review*, vol. 56, March, pp. 628–32.

—— (1976). 'Women in physics and physics education' in J.L. Lewis (ed.). *New Trends in Physics Teaching*, vol. 3. Paris: UNESCO.

—— (1978). *Girls and Science: an International Study of Sex Differences in School Science Achievement*. Stockholm: Almquist and Wiksell. ISBN 0 91 22 00182 4.

*—— (ed.) (1981). *The Missing Half: Girls and Science Education* Manchester: Manchester University Press. ISBN 0 7190 0753 4. Collection of theoretical essays, research studies and personal accounts 'concerned to elucidate the origins of girls' underachievement in science and suggest ways to improve their performance'. Appendix. Index.

—— and WHYTE, Judith (1978). 'An affirmative action project on the science achievement of schoolgirls' research proposal to the EOC/SSRC Joint Panel on Women and Under-Achievement, April 1978.

KEYS, Wendy and ORMEROD, M. B. (1976). 'A comparison of the pattern of science subject choices for boys and girls in the light of pupils' own expressed subject preferences'. *School Science Review*, vol. LVIII, no. 203, pp. 348–50.

KING, Ronald (1971). 'Unequal access in education: sex and social class'. *Social and Economic Administration*, vol. V, no. 3, pp. 167–75.

LAMB, Felicity and PICKTHORN, Helen (1968). *Locked-Up Daughters*. Dunton Green: Hodder & Stoughton. ISBN 0 340 02594 8.

LARRICK, Nancy and MERRIAM, Eve (eds) (1973). *Male and Female Under 18*. New York: Avon. ISBN 0 380 29645 15 0. Collection of poetry and prose about being a boy or girl today. The writer's ages range from 7 to 18. Indexes.

LAWRENCE, Sarah Lightfoot (1977). 'Family-school interaction: the cultural image of mothers and teachers'. *Signs*, University of Chicago Press, vol. III, no. 2, pp. 395–408.

LLOYD, Barbara and ARCHER, John (eds) (1976). *Exploring Sex Differences* Academic Press. ISBN 0 12 453550 X.
A look at differences as interpreted by social psychologists, anthropologists, and biologists, most drawing on their research. Index.

LOBBAN, G. (1977). 'The influence of the school on sex-role stereotyping' in J. Chetwynd and O. Hartnett (eds). *The Sex-Role System*. Routledge & Kegan Paul. ISBN 0 7100 8722 5

LONGMAN U.K. SCHOOLS DIVISION and OLIVER & BOYD *Guidelines on Countering Racism and Sexism*.
For use by authors, editors, artists and in-house staff to assist in 'the production of material which is . . . positive and realistic'.

MACCOBY, E.E. and JACKLIN, C.N. (1973). 'Stress, activity and proximity seeking: sex differences in the year old child'. *Child Development*, vol. XLIV, pp. 34–42.

—— and —— (1974). 'Myth, reality and shades of gray: what we know and don't know about sex differences'. *Psychology Today*, vol. VIII, no. 7, pp. 109–12.

*—— and —— (1974). *The Psychology of Sex Differences*. Stanford: Stanford University Press. ISBN 0 8047 0859 2.
A major review of the present state of knowledge of all kinds of sex differences (and non-differences). Bibliography. Indexes.

—— and —— (1980). 'Psychological sex differences', in M. Rutter, (ed.). *Scientific Foundations of Developmental Psychiatry*. William Heinemann Medical Books. ISBN 0 433 28989 9.

MARTINI, Richard (1982). *Sex Differences and Achievement*. ILEA Research and Statistics RS 823/82.
Analysis of sex differences in the 1980 examination achievement in ILEA of the 15 to 16-year-old age-group, including results from single-sex and mixed schools, and sex differences in the entry rates of particular subjects.

MCLEOD, Jennifer S. and SILVERMAN, Sandra T. (1973). *You Won't Do; What Textbooks on U.S. Government Teach High School Girls*. Pittsburgh, Pa.: KNOW. ISBN 0 912786 25 6.

McROBBIE, Angela and McCABE, Trisha (eds) (1981). *Feminism for Girls: an Adventure Story*. Routledge & Kegan Paul. ISBN 0 7100 0961 5.
Presents feminist perspectives on aspects of adolescence, including careers, romance, 'doing' English literature at school, being a black girl in today's society.

MEIGHAN, Roland and DOHERTY, Jim (eds) (1975). 'Education and sex roles'. *Educational Review*, vol. XXVII, no. 3. Whole issue has articles on this theme.

MILES, Betty (1975). *Channeling Children: Sex Stereotyping in Prime-Time TV*. Princeton, N.J.: Women on Words and Images. ISBN 0 9600724 2 X.

MILES, H.B. (1979). *Some Factors Affecting Attainment at 18 +: Study of Examination Performance in British Schools*. Oxford: Pergamon Press. ISBN 0 8024 678 8.

MILLER, Cassey and SWIFT, Kate (1977). *Words and Women*. Garden City, N.Y.: Anchor Books. ISBN 0 385 04858 0.

MILTON, G.A. (1957). 'The effects of sex role identification upon problem solving skill'. *Journal of Abnormal and Social Psychology*, no 55, pp. 209–13.

—— (1959). 'Sex differences on problem solving as a function of role appropriateness of problem content'. *Psychological Reports*, no. 5, pp. 705–8.

MITCHELL, Juliet (1971). *Woman's Estate* Harmondsworth: Penguin Books. (Reprinted 1973, 1974, 1976) ISBN 0 14 02 1425 9.

—— and OAKLEY, Ann (eds) (1976). *The Rights and Wrongs of Women* Harmondsworth: Penguin Books. ISBN 0 14 02 1616 2.

A collection of academic essays representing a variety of ideologies with several chapters on education, including Pauline Marks on 'Femininity in the classroom' and Tessa Blackstone on 'The education of girls today'.

MITRANO, Barbara S. (1979). 'Feminist theology and curriculum theory'. *Journal of Curriculum Studies*, vol. XI, no. 3, pp. 211–20.

Advocates a stronger feminist influence in curriculum theory and the need for dialogue betwen feminist theologians and reconceptualist curriculum theorists.

MOIR, E. (1976). 'Nice Girls Don't'. *Momentum* vol. 1. no. 2.

—— (1976). 'Sex differences in activities'. *Scottish Journal of P.E.*, vol. 4, no. 3.

MOLLER, Susan Okin (1980). *Women in Western Political Thought*. Virago. ISBN 0 86068 169 9.

Looks for the causes of inequality in the traditions of political philosophy permeating Western culture and its institutions.

MONTEITH, Moira (1979). 'Boys, girls and language'. *English in Education* vol. XIII, no. 2, pp. 3–6.

As a result of seven lessons with 10-year-old boys and girls, the author observes that boys use more specific language which relates more to the world outside school. Stereotyped attitudes seemed to be fixed for both girls and boys at this age.

MORTIMORE, Peter (1980). *ILEA Secondary School Staffing Survey Report No. 1* ILEA Research and Statistics Branch.

Analysis concerns age, sex, experience, qualifications, and subject specialization of teachers. Wherever possible, comparisons with national figures are included. Of particular interest is division of special responsibility between male and female teachers.

MURPHY, Roger J.L. (1978). *Sex Differences in Objective Test Performance* Unpublished Associated Examining Board Research Report. RAC/56.

MUTRIE, Nanette (1981). 'Women's attitudes towards school physical education programmes'. *Women Speaking*, July – September.

Practical recommendations for improving physical education for girls.

NATIONAL COUNCIL OF TEACHERS OF ENGLISH (1975). *Guidelines for Nonsexist Use of Language in NCTE Publications*. Urbana, Ill.: NCTE. Stock No. 19719.

NATIONAL UNION OF TEACHERS RESEARCH PROJECT (1980). *Promotion and the Woman Teacher*. National Union of Teachers/Equal Opportunities Commission. ISBN 0 900560 66 5.

A study of the present distribution of posts in the UK, and an analysis of such factors as motivation, break in service, and career patterns.

NICHOLSON, John (1979). *A Question of Sex*. Fontana. ISBN 0 00 635710 5.

NICHOLSON, Joyce (1977). *What Society Does to Girls*. Virago. ISBN 0 86068 021 5.

A brief look at the way society affects girls and boys at different stages of development, and the results this produces in adult life. Bibliography.

OAKLEY, Ann (1975). *Sex, Gender and Society*. Temple Smith. ISBN 0 8511 7020 X.

The author looks at the differences between male and female and if they really exist or are caused by biological or cultural influences.

ORMEROD, M.B. with Duckworth, D. (1975). *Pupils' Attitudes to Science: a Review of Research*. Windsor: NFER Publishing. ISBN 0 85633 077 9. Bibliography.

ORMEROD, M.B. et. al. (1979). 'Girls and physics education'. *Physics Education*, vol. XIV, pp. 271-7.

*PHI DELTA KAPPA*, vol. LV, no. 2 (October, 1973).
Entire issue is devoted to 'Education and the Feminist Movement'. Includes articles on elementary school, secondary-school curriculum, and physical education.

POWELL, Robert C. (1979). 'Sex differences and language learning: a review of the evidence'. *Audio Visual Language Journal*, vol. XVII, no. 1, pp. 19-24.
Comparisons between the examination performances of boys and girls in European languages, with conclusion that 'setting by sex is beneficial at least on the basis of increased positive attitudes'.

PROJECT ON EQUAL EDUCATION RIGHTS (PEER) (1977). *Stalled at the Start. Government Action on Sex Bias in the Schools*, New York: PEER/NOW Legal Defense and Education Fund.
PEER was established, as part of the NOW Legal Defense and Education Fund, to monitor governmental work in enforcing laws designed to protect students and personnel in public schools. This pamphlet evaluates the US Department of Health, Education and Welfare's enforcement of Title IX.

RAGLAND, Barbara G. *Sex Bias Activities for Teachers*. Greenville, NC: General Assistance Center, School of Education, East Carolina University.
A series of questionnaires, such as 'Sexism in American schools', 'Language, magazines and the real world', and a 'Checklist for evaluative sexism in curriculum materials'. Bibliography (nonsexist children's books).

RESTAK, Richard M. (1979). *The Brain: the Last Frontier* New York: Doubleday. ISBN 0 385 13405 3.
Discusses physiological brain differences between girls and boys. Concludes that there are differences in addition to culturally induced ones.

RICKS, Frances A. and PYKE, Sandra W. (1973). 'Teacher perceptions and attitudes that foster or maintain sex role differences'. *Interchange*, vol. IV, no. 1, pp. 26-33.
A survey of sixty secondary-school teachers revealed teacher preference for 'male teachers and male students' and 'the reluctance of most teachers to facilitate sex role behaviour changes'. Suggestions as to how the education system can aim for a new role balance. Bibliography.

RIVERS, Caryl, BARNETT, Rosalind and BARUCH, Grace (1979). *Beyond Sugar and Spice: How Women Grow, Learn, and Thrive*. New York: G. P. Putnam's Sons. ISBN 0 399 12164 1.
Working mothers, girls' play behaviour, sexuality and conflict, the female 'phenomenon of dropping back' are all investigated.

SAARIO, Terry Tinson (1976). *Title IX: Now What?* A Ford Foundation reprint from Allan C. Ornstein and Steven Miller (eds). *Policy Issues in Education*. Lexington, Mass.: Lexington Books/D.C. Heath.
Looks at background of the US 'Title IX', its achievements so far, the relationship between legislation and practice, and ways ahead for more complete implementation.

—— (1978). 'Sexism, inequality, and education'. *Harvard Educational Review*, vol. XLVIII, no. 2, pp. 267–83.

An essay review of four books which is a clear statement of the state of study of sexism in schools in 1978. It makes a plea for action by 'federal government, courts, and state legislatures, and in every school in the nation'.

——, JACKLIN, Carol Nagy and TITTLE, Carol Kehr (1973). 'Sex role stereotyping in the public schools'. *Harvard Educational Review*, vol. 43, no. 3, pp. 386–416.

An investigation of sex-role stereotyping in elementary school basic readers, educational achievement tests and differential curricular requirements for males and females.

SANDRA, Margaret. (1977). *The Language of Sex*. Teaching London Kids. ISBN 0 90030 280 1.

SCHOOLS COUNCIL AND INNER LONDON EDUCATION AUTHORITY (1983). *Equal Opportunities: what's in it for boys?* Schools Council. An unusual but important argument that boys suffer educationally by being expected to follow a traditional pattern of behaviour.

SCHOPP-SCHILLING, Hanna-Beate (1978). *The Changing Roles of Women and Men in the Family and in Society*. Report on an International Conference, Aspen Institute, Berlin, 27 February – 3 March, 1977. New York: Aspen Institute for Humanistic Studies.

Contains sections on sex-role stereotyping on the primary and secondary levels in addition to other relevant topics. Appendices.

SERBIN, Lisa A. (1978). 'Teachers, peers, and play preferences: an environmental approach to sex typing in the preschool', in Barbara Sprung (ed.). *Perspectives on Non-sexist Early Childhood Education*. New York: Teachers College Press. ISBN 0 8077 2547 1

Teachers who have reinforced sex-role stereotypes in the past can reverse these patterns effectively when they become aware of them.

—— (with M. Sadker, S. Greenberg, D. Ulrey and I. McNett) (1977). 'Toward a non-sexist school'. *American Education*, April, pp. 7–9.

——, CONNOR, J.M., BURCHARDT, C. and CITRON, C.C. (1979). 'Effects of peer presence on sex-typing of children's play behaviour'. *Journal of Experimental Child Psychology*, no. 27, pp. 303–9.

——, CONNOR, J.M. and ILER, I. 'Sex-stereotyped and non-stereotyped introductions of new toys in the preschool classroom: an observational study of teacher behavior and its effects'. *Psychology of Women Quarterly* (in press)

—— and O'LEARY, K.D. (1975). 'How nursery schools teach girls to shut up'. *Psychology Today*, December.

——, O'LEARY, K.D., KENT, R.N. and TONICK, I.J. (1973). 'A comparison of teacher response to the pre-academic and problem behavior of boys and girls'. *Child Development*, no. 44, pp. 796–804.

——, TONICK, I.J. and STERNGLANZ, S.H. (1977). 'Shaping cooperative cross-sex play'. *Child Development*, no. 48, pp. 924–9.

SEX EQUITY PROJECT (1978). *Action Beyond Access*, vol. 1, no. 1, pp. 1–8. Decatur, Ill.: Richland Community College.

Newsletter designed 'to assist educators in striving towards sex equity in vocational education'. Conference dates, lists of materials, relevant statistics and short articles were in this first issue.

SEXISM IN EDUCATION COMMITTEE, NEW SOUTH WALES MINISTRY OF EDUCATION (1977). *Report of the Committee on Sexism in Education*. New South Wales: New South Wales Ministry of Education. ISBN 0 7240 3456 0.

A thorough study of all aspects of New South Wales education, including teacher education, staffing, organization and curriculum.

SHARGEL, Susan and KANE, Irene (1974). *We Can Change It!* San Francisco, Calif.: Change for Children.
This pamphlet contains an annotated bibliography of non-sexist and non-racist children's books, with discussion on ways they can be used in the classroom or home.

SHARPE, Sue (1976). *'Just Like A Girl': How Girls Learn to be Women.* Harmondsworth: Penguin Books. ISBN 0 14 02 1953 6.
The ideas of a group of racially mixed, London girls is the basis for a discussion on the kinds of problems girls and women deal with in a sexist society.

SHERMAN, J. and FENNEMA, E. (1977). 'The study of mathematics among high school girls and boys: related factors'. *American Educational Research Journal*, vol. XIV, no. 2., pp. 159–67.

—— and —— (1978). 'Distribution of spatial visualisation and mathematical problem solving scores: a test of the sex-linked hypothesis' *Psychology of Women Quarterly*, vol. VI, no. 3, pp. 157–67.

SHIRT, Kathleen (1979) 'Sexism'. *Journal of Curriculum Studies*, vol. XI, no. 3, pp. 270–2.
A review of four books which 'make a useful contribution to feminist discussion': *Women and Men*; *What Society Does to Girls*; *Women's Studies in the U.K.*; and *Women and Schooling*.

SMITHERS, A. (1978). 'Girls in science' Paper given to the Findlay Society, University of Manchester, 15 March 1978.

SOCIAL DEVELOPMENT UNIT, NEW SOUTH WALES MINISTRY OF EDUCATION (1979). *Submission to the Teacher Education Inquiry with Particular Reference to the Position of Women and Girls in Education and Affirming the Principle of Equality of Opportunity.* New South Wales: New South Wales Ministry of Education.
Considers social changes affecting education, the state of pre-service teacher education, and the state of inservice training. Appendices.

—— (1980). *Sport in Schools: the Participation of Girls; a Discussion Paper.* New South Wales: New South Wales Ministry of Education.
Covers the historical development of sport in Australia, assumptions underlying the sport involvement of each sex, and social factors influencing involvement in school sport. Bibliography.

SPENDER, Dale (1978). 'The facts of life: sex differentiated knowledge in the English classroom and the school'. *English in Education*, vol. 12, no. 3, pp. 1–9.
Talking, writing and reading are examined as ways by which a teacher's dissemination of knowledge varies according to the student's sex.

*—— (1980). *Man Made Language* Routledge & Kegan Paul. ISBN 0 7100 0675 6.
A feminist study of language, its rules and uses. Argues that it is through the patriarchal language that much of women's subordination is structured. Suggests moves towards women encoding their own meanings. Bibliography. Index.

*—— (1981). *Men's Studies Modified*. Pergamon Press. ISBN 0 08 026770 X.
A symposium on 'the impact of feminism on academic disciplines', which is of great help in curriculum planning. It is particulary good on the social sciences.

*—— (1982). *Invisible Women: the Schooling Scandal*. Writers and Readers

in association with Chameleon Editorial Group. ISBN 0 906495 94 6.
Documents the exclusion of women from knowledge produced by men.
Focuses on how education and school play a significant role in perpetuating
male dominance and control. Appendix. Bibliography.
*—— and SARAH, Elizabeth (eds) (1980). *Learning to Lose: Sexism and
Education* The Women's Press. ISBN 0 7043 3863 7.
Collection of essays offering a practical critique of existing practices and
accounting for the continuing underachievement of girl students in school
and the under-representation of women teachers at higher levels of education. Includes numerous classroom exercises, suggestions and teaching
aids. Appendix. Bibliography.
SPRUNG, Barbara (1975). *Non-sexist Education for Young Children*. New
York: Citation Press. ISBN 0 590 09605 2.
Contains examples of activities based on experience in four New York city
volunteer child-care centers, and sources for a variety of non-sexist
materials. Bibliography.
SPRING, Margery Rice (1981). *Working-class Wives: their Health and Condi-
tions* Virago Reprint Library. ISBN 0 86068 158 X.
First published in 1939, this classic work 'stripped off the veil of indifference
and ignorance which concealed the hardships of millions of women'.
STACEY, Judith, BÉREAUD, Susan and DANIELS, Joan (eds) (1974).
*And Jill Came Tumbling After: Sexism in American Education*. New York: Dell.
ISBN 0 440 32111 5.
STANWORTH, Michelle (1981). *Gender and Schooling: a Study of Sexual Divi-
sions in the Classroom*. Women's Research and Resources Centre. ISBN
0 905969 07 3.
Looks at the ways that gender divisions are established at school.
Bibliography.
STERNGLANZ, S.H. and SERBIN, L.A. (1974). 'Sex-role stereotyped
in children's television programs'. *Developmental Psychology*, no. 10,
pp. 710–15.
STIMPSON, Catharine (ed.) (1978). 'Women, science and society'. *Signs*,
University of Chicago Press, vol. IV, no. 1.
STINTON, Judith (ed.) (1979). *Racism and Sexism in Children's Books*.
Writers and Readers. ISBN 0 906495 18 0.
SUTHERLAND, Margaret B. (1978) 'The Galton Lecture, 1977: Educating
girls – "To repair the ruins of our first parents" ', in W.H.G. Armytage
and John Peel (eds). *Perimeters of Social Repair*. Academic Press, pp. 105–119.
ISBN 0 12 062750 7.
Changes in modern society are cited as basis for changes in the ways educational systems view and educate girls.
*—— (1981). *Sex Bias in Education*. Oxford: Basil Blackwell. ISBN
0 631 12617 1.
Account of the progress towards sexual equality in the educational system,
and of the possible causes for differences in achievement and subject choice
– including physiological, psychological and social influences, the 'hidden
curriculum', and the influence of employment prospects.
TAYLOR, J. (1979). 'Sexist bias in physics textbooks'. *Physics Education*,
vol. XIV, pp. 277–80.
THORNE, Barrie and HENLEY, Nancy (1975). *Language and Sex*. Rowley,
Mass.: Newbury House. ISBN 0 88377 043 1.
TOBIAS, Sheila (1978). *Overcoming Maths Anxiety*. New York: Norton.

ISBN 0 393 06439 5.
Discusses learned reactions to maths that produce avoidance and their relationship to early sex sterotyping. Also discusses methods for coping. Appendices.

US DEPARTMENT OF HEALTH, EDUCATION AND WELFARE (1978). *Taking Sexism out of Education: the National Project on Women in Education.* NEW Publication No. (OE) 77–01017. Washington, DC: US Government Printing Office. Stock No. 017–080–01794–6.

UNIVERSITY OF LONDON EXAMINATION BOARD (1974). *World Affairs from 1919 to the Present Day.* University of London Publications Office. Being syllabus C, A/O level, subject number 826, of the GCE History papers. Section E is one of seven options of which candidates have to choose one: 'Women in Society in Britain Since 1850'.

VETTERLING-BRAGGIN, Mary (ed) (1981). *Sexist Language.* Littlefield, Adams and Co. ISBN 0 8226 0353 5.
A wide-ranging collection of essays on aspects of language, including key historical analyses.

WALDEN, Rosie and WALKERDINE, Valerie (1982). *Girls and Mathematics: the Early Years.* University of London Institute of Education, Bedford Way, Papers no. 8. ISBN 0261 0078.
This brief booklet reviews the research and outlines the authors' own studies of infant classrooms and the relationship between teachers' approaches and mathematical learning. They find that many expected differences are not to be found. Girls 'can and will take up positions in play (such as construction play) normally ascribed to boys if they are not discouraged from doing so'.

WALKERDINE, V., CORRAN, G. and EYNARD, R. (1981). *Cognitive Development and Infant School Mathematics* Final report to the Leverhulme Trust.

——— and EYNARD, R. (1980). *Girls and Mathematics in the Nursery School.* Progress report to the Leverhulme Trust.

WARDLE, D. (1978) 'The education of women: sixty years on: the progress of women's education 1918–78'. *Trends in Education*, no. 4, pp. 3–7.

WEINER, Gaby (1978). 'Education and the Sex Discrimination Act'. *Educational Research*, vol. XX, no. 3, pp. 163–73.
Reviews research on primary, secondary and higher education levels, and literature and children's books, and their relation to the Sex Discrimination Act.

WEINREICH-HASTE, Helen (1978). 'Sex differences in "fear of success" among British students'. *British Journal of Social Psychology*, vol. XVII, pp. 37–42.
Uses a measure from the American study of Horner to test male and female undergraduates' attitudes towards success and failure. Males demonstrated greater anxiety towards failure.

——— and KELLY, Alison (1978) 'Science for girls?'. *Women's Studies International Quarterly*, vol. II, no. 3, pp. 275–93.
Asks why boys dominate science on a world-wide scale. Gives some answers, and concludes with strategies to de-sex science. Bibliography.

WITTIG, Michele Andrisin and PETERSEN, Anne C. (1979). *Sex-related Differences in Cognitive Functioning: Developmental Issues.* New York: Academic Press. ISBN 0 12 761150 9.
Written for 'advanced undergraduates majoring in bio-behavioral

sciences', this textbook reviews research on those aspects of cognitive functioning that have been linked to differences between the sexes. Index.

WOLPE, Ann-Marie (1976). 'The official ideology of girls' education', in M. Flude and J. Ahier (eds). *Educability, Schools and Ideology*. Croom Helm. ISBN 0 85664 411 0.

—— (1977). *Some Processes in Sexist Education*. Women's Research and Resources Publications. ISBN 0 905969 01 4.

Based on a study of a comprehensive school, the two papers are entitled 'Education – the road to dependency' and 'Sexuality and gender roles in a secondary school'. Bibliography.

WOMEN ON WORDS AND IMAGES (1975). *Dick and Jane as Victims: Sex Stereotyping in Children's Readers*. 2nd ed. Princeton, N.J.: Women on Words and Images. Slide show edition, 1976. ISBN 0 9600724 1 1.

Results of an analysis of 2760 stories in 134 children's readers. Jobs, domestic scenes, story themes and number of appearances by girls in stories reflected almost totally traditional role stereotypes.

WOOD, Robert (1976). 'Sex differences in mathematics attainment at GCE ordinary level'. *Educational Studies*, vol. II, no. 2, pp. 141–60.

Analysis of multiple-choice and free-response questions serve as basis for discussion of possible reasons for and significance of sex differences.

—— (1978). 'Sex differences in answers to English Language comprehension items'. *Educational Studies*, vol. IV, no. 2, pp. 157–65.

The wide differences in examination results in English Language analysed, and the effects of different subject matter of passages and different styles of questioning related to sex differences in scores.

WYNN, Barbara (1979). 'Domestic subjects and the sexual division of labour' in HARGREAVES, O., WATSON, T.J. and WOLFE, R., *Schooling and Society: Open University Reader E202*. Milton Keynes: Open University Press.

ZIMMET, Sara Goodman (1976). *Print and Prejudice*. Dunton Green: Hodder & Stoughton. ISBN 0 340 21026 5.

Chapter 8 considers sexism in children's literature, comics and schoolbooks.

## Classroom materials

BRISTOL WOMEN'S STUDIES GROUP (eds) (1979). *Half the Sky: an Introduction to Women's Studies*. Virago. ISBN 0 86068 086 X.

A collection of extracts from a variety of sources designed to be used in Women's Studies Courses mainly for adult students, but also for older secondary-school pupils. Of particular relevance are the first two chapters on education and early stereotyping. Bibliography. Index.

CAMPBELL, R.M. (ed.) (1969). *Face to Face*. Macmillan. ISBN 0 333 10060 3.

English textbook for the 14 to 17-year-old age-range, with topics related to growing up, careers, marriage. Extracts from classics, modern novels and non-fiction, selected to throw light on the 'dramatic struggles for girls' education and emancipation'. Conventional pattern of comprehension, summary and composition.

COUSSINS, Jean (1979). *Taking Liberties: a Teaching Pack for Boys and Girls on Equal Rights*. Virago. ISBN 0 86068 038 X.

Eighteen work cards for classroom use on legal questions about rights of the sexes. Questions and suggestions for discussion topics and projects.

CURRY, Jennifer (1971). *The Faces of Woman*. Harrap. ISBN 0 245 50405 2.

A collection for class use of literary excerpts, poems, and lists of songs and artwork by and about women. Exercises are at the end of each chapter. Suitable for pupils aged 15 + .

GROOMBRIDGE, Joy (1971). *His and Hers: an Examination of Masculinity and Femininity*. Harmondsworth: Penguin Books. ISBN 0 14 08 0279 7.
Part of the *Connexions* series of topic books for students in schools and colleges of further education, this includes discussion material on concepts of masculinity and femininity. Has a section on education.

HOFFMAN, Nancy and HOWE, Florence (1979). *Women Working: an Anthology of Stories and Poems*. Old Westbury, N.Y.: The Feminist Press. ISBN 0 07 020431 4.
Thirty-four stories and poems with biographical introductions to the authors for reading by older pupils. Divided into oppressive work, satisfying work, family work and transforming work sections. Index.

HUNT, Janet (1978). *Measure for Measure: For the Discussion of Sex Discrimination*. Nuneaton. National Association of Youth Clubs. ISBN 0 901528 87 0.
A set of six discussion cards with a booklet of notes for discussion-group leaders. Covers the main aspects of sex discrimination. Although designed primarily for British youth clubs, could be used for school classrooms with secondary-age pupils.

JONES, Anne, MARSH, Jan and WATTS, A.G. (1974). *Male and Female: Choosing Your Role in Modern Society*. Cambridge: Hobsons Press. ISBN 0 86021 002 2.
Part of The Careers Research and Advisory Centre (CRAC) lifestyle series. Suitable for classroom exercises for school pupils of about 14 + .

McROBBIE, Angela and McCABE, Trisha (eds) (1981). *Feminism for Girls*. Routledge and Kegan Paul. ISBN 0 7100 0961 5.
A collection of essays and stories devised for young women readers thinking about all aspects of feminism. Very suitable for a school library.

STERLING, Dorothy (1979). *Black Foremothers: Three Lives*. Old Westbury, N.Y.: The Feminist Press. ISBN 0 07 020433 0.
Biographies of Ida B. Wells, Mary Church Ferrell and Ellen Craft, all activist in American civil rights events, designed primarily as class reading for older pupils.

VINCENT, Monica (1982). *A Woman's Place?* Longman. ISBN 0 582 52410 5.
A reader for students who require a controlled vocabulary. The author discusses in a lively way with many illustrations the role of women in Western society. Very suitable for school libraries.

# Reading lists

ARTEL, Linda and WENGRAF, Susan (1976). *Positive Images: a Guide to 400 Non-sexist Films for Young People*. San Francisco: Booklegger Press. ISBN 0 685 65283 1.

CHILDREN'S RIGHTS WORKSHOP (1979). *Children's Book Bulletin*. Children's Rights Workshop.

CISSY (Campaign to Impede Sex Stereotyping in the Young) (1979). *Non-sexist Picture Books*. CISSY. ISBN 0 906713 00 5.
Bibliography of predominantly British titles divided into those recommended without reservation and those which have various kinds of reservations. Useful addresses and publications section also. Appendix.

DIXON, Bob (1982). *Now Read On, Recommended Fiction for Young People.* Pluto Press. ISBN 0 86104 383 9.

Complementary to *Catching Them Young*, this is designed as a practical list of books which the compiler judges to be the best children's fiction published in Britain up to the end of 1980 which have positive attitudes to sex, race, and class.

EVANS, Mary and MORGAN, David (1979). *Work on Women: a Guide to the Literature.* Tavistock. ISBN 0 422 77140 6.

Bibliography covering family, education, work, sexuality, welfare, history and literature from a feminist perspective.

FROSCHL, Merle and WILLIAMSON, Jane (1977). *Feminist Resources for Schools and Colleges: a Guide to Curricular Materials.* Rev. edn. Old Westbury, N.Y.: The Feminist Press. ISBN 0 912670 14 2.

In addition to books, articles, conference reports, multi-media, organizations and programmes and guidelines for institutions implementing US' Title IX, contains lists of education bibliographies and publishers.

GUTTENTAG, Marcia and BRAY, Helen (1976). *Undoing Sex Stereotypes. Research and Resources for Educators.* New York: McGraw-Hill. ISBN 0 07 025380 3 (hardback), ISBN 0 07 025381 1 (paperback).

The results of a research project that involved assessing children's attitudes towards sex roles before and after an intervention programme in the classroom. Lists many classroom resources, predominantly American. Bibliography. Indexes.

HULME, Marylin A. (1977). *Sourcebook for Sex Equality: Small Presses.* New Brunswick, N.J.: Training Institute for Sex Desegregation of the Public Schools, University Extension Division, Rutgers University.

—— (1978). *Sourcebook for Sex Equality: In-Service Training.* New Brunswick, N.J.: Training Institute for Sex Desegregation of the Public Schools, University Extension Division, Rutgers University.

JOHNSON, Laurie Olsen (ed.) (1974). *Nonsexist Curricular Materials for Elementary Schools.* Old Westbury, N.Y.: The Feminist Press. ISBN 0 912670 25 2.

Divided into two sections: for the teacher and for the classroom, with various exercises, a student workbook and a student bibliography.

OLIN, Ferris and HULME, Marylin A. (1976, 1977). *Fair Play: a Bibliography of Non-stereotyped Materials*, vols. 1 and 2. New Brunswick, N.J.: Training Institute for Sex Desegregation of the Public Schools, University Extension Division, Rutgers University.

ROSENFELT, Deborah Silverton (ed.) (1976). *Strong Women: an Annotated Bibliography of Literature for the High School Classroom.* Old Westbury, N.Y.: The Feminist Press. ISBN 0 912670 40 1.

Has a cross-topical index with subjects: adolescence, female sexuality, women in the arts and professions, women and political commitment, third world women and working-class women.

STONES, Rosemary and MANN, Andrew (1979). *List of Non-Sexist Children's Books*, Spare Rib.

Covers picture and story books, younger readers, older readers and young adults. Indicates titles which are particularly good.

WHITE, Bob (1977). *Non-sexist Teaching Materials and Approaches.* New Childhood Press.

A listing of pamphlets, articles, books, handbooks, games, films, resource centres, organizations, etc., with an introduction entitled 'Sex stereotyping and the teacher'.

# A Note on Legislation

Both the United Kingdom and the United States have legislation that provides a background to the concerns of this book.

In the United Kingdom there is the Sex Discrimination Act of 1975. The key section is 22:

It is unlawful in relation to an educational establishment falling within column 1 of the following table, for a person indicated in relation to the establishment in column 2 (the 'responsible body') to discriminate against a woman –
(a) in the terms on which it offers to admit her to the establishment as a pupil, or
(b) by refusing or deliberately omitting to accept an application for her admission to the establishment as a pupil, or
(c) where she is a pupil of the establishment –
    (i) in the way it affords her access to any benefits, facilities or services, or by refusing or deliberately omitting to afford her access to them, or
    (ii) by excluding her from the establishment or subjecting her to any other detriment.

(The table referred to lists the different kinds of establishments and specifies the 'responsible body'.)[*]

In the United States the relevant legislation is Title IX, part of the 1974 Education Ammendments, which became law in the United States on 21 July 1975 (Public Law No. 93–568, 88 Stat. 1855). Its key statement is:

No person in the United States shall, on the basis of sex, be excluded from participation in, be denied the benefits of, or be subjected to discrimination under any education program or activity receiving federal financial assistance.[**]

[*] For a commentary, see Equal Opportunities Commission, *Do You Provide Equal Educational Opportunities?* (Manchester: EOC, n.d.).

[**] For a discussion of the law, see Terry Tinson Saario, 'Title IX: now what?', in A.C. Othstein and S. Miller (eds), *Policy Issues in Education* (Lexington: Lexington Books, D.C. Heath, 1976); also available in a reprint for the Ford Foundation, Office of Reports, 320 East 43 Street, New York, N.Y. 10017.

# The Contributors

JACKIE BOULD
*Research Associate, Counselling and Career Development Unit, University of Leeds, UK*
After experience in the Careers Service and industry, Jackie Bould took a B. Tech. in Industrial Technology and Management from Bradford University. She then became Information Officer and Careers Officer for the Bradford Careers Service for three years, before taking her present post in 1977, in which she is researching into sex stereotyping in schools. She has run courses and given training for youth workers, careers officers, social workers and teachers.

EILEEN M. BYRNE
*Lecturer in Education, University of Queensland, Australia*
Eileen Byrne has over eighteen years' practical experience of local education authority adminstration, and was at one time one of England's only three women Deputy Chief Education Officers. She has first-hand experience of both school and college organization, of further education and training, of in-service education of teachers, and school building and design, as well as of curriculum planning. Her doctoral thesis on the rationale of educational resource allocation in local education authorities was published by the National Foundation for Educational Research in 1974 as *Planning and Educational Inequality*. In recent years she has been Education Consultant to the Commission of the European Communities and UNESCO. Dr Byrne has worked on a major six-country project for the Commission on the transition from school to working life in the disadvantaged regions of the Community. She has lectured to postgraduate education students at several UK universities, and has developed some special work at this level in the New University of Ulster. She is the author of *Women and Education* (Tavistock, 1978) and of *Equality of Education and Training for Girls* (Commission of the European Communities, 1979, Education Series No. 9 of *Studies*), which was presented to the Eleventh Standing Conference of European Ministers of Education, 10–13 June 1979, as

a formal contribution of the Commission of the European Communities.

## CAROL S. DWECK
*Professor of Human Development, Harvard University, USA*
Carol Dweck's central research interest has been with the relationship between achievement-related cognitions and behaviour. In her analysis of failure she has found many sex-related differences, and developed the concept of 'learned helplessness'. After some years at the University of Illinois, Urbana, Champaign, she moved to Harvard, where she is working on achievement. She has published many papers (listed in the bibliography) and is co-author of *Personal Politics* (Prentice-Hall, 1973).

## ELIZABETH FENNEMA
*Associate Professor, Department of Curriculum and Instruction, University of Wisconsin, Maddison, USA*
From 1950 until 1962 Elizabeth Fennema divided her time between elementary school teaching and homemaking, with some time also as a research assistant. Her first degree was in Science in Psychology, her Master's in Science in Education, and in 1969 she added a Ph.D. in Curriculum and Instruction in Mathematics Education. Since 1962 she has taught at the University of Wisconsin, but has also been a mathematics consultant for various school districts, and from 1974 until 1976 directed the NSF project, Relations between Mathematics Learning, Sex, Spatial Visualization, and Social/Cultural Factors. From 1975–1979 her Professorship was specifically on the Women's Studies Programme. Her very many papers and articles range over aspects of the analysis of mathematics teaching and learning and its relationship to sex differences. She is a member of many professional organizations and a reviewer for the key journals in mathematics education. From 1974 to 1976 she chaired the 'Research on Women in Education' group of the American Educational Research Association, and in 1976 organized the Second Annual Midwest Conference on Women in Education.

## BARRIE HOPSON
*Director, Counselling and Career Development Unit, University of Leeds, UK*
Barrie Hopson's first work after his BA in Psychology and Sociology was designing and constructing psychological tasks as a Research Officer for the National Foundation for Educational Research in 1964. A year later he started his work with the Vocational Guidance Research Unit at Leeds as Research Associate. He then lectured in psychology, and from 1969 to 1976, when he took his present post, he was Director of the Vocational Guidance Research Unit. He has been a visiting professor in Germany, Sweden, and America, and written important books on vocational guidance, including (with John

Hayes) *Careers Guidance: the Role of the School in Vocational Development* (Heinemann Educational Books, 1972).

## CAROL NAGY JACKLIN
*Senior Research Associate, Department of Psychology, Stanford University, California, USA*
Carol Jacklin's Ph.D. was from Brown University in Experimental Child Psychology. She has done research and taught in aspects of developmental psychology in Wisconsin, Connecticut (where she originally took her BA and MA), West Valley College, Brown University, and since 1971 at Stanford, where she has worked with Dr Eleanor Maccoby. In addition to the very well-known *Psychology of Sex Differences* (Stanford University Press, 1974), Carol Jacklin has written, on her own or with Eleanor Maccoby, a variety of articles, a number of which are listed in the bibliography. She is Consulting Editor to *Contemporary Psychology*, *Psychology of Women*, and *Infant Behaviour and Development*, and is in considerable demand as a reviewer and as a keynote speaker at major conferences.

## BARBARA LICHT
*Assistant Professor of Psychology, Florida State University, USA*
After receiving her Ph.D. in clinical psychology in 1980 at the University of Illinois, Urbana, Champaign, Barbara Licht has taught courses at undergraduate and graduate level in child development and educational psychology and supervised student therapists on cases involving children with learning and/or behavioural problems. Her research continues on the cognitive-motivational factors that contribute to children's achievement, the achievement-orientations of children with learning disabilities, and sex differences in children's achievement-related beliefs and behaviours.

## MICHAEL MARLAND, CBE
*Headmaster, North Westminster Community School, Inner London Education Authority; Honorary Professor of Education, Warwick University, UK*
Has taught in secondary schools since 1957 and has been Head of English, Director of Studies, and Headmaster (of Woodberry Down School) before opening his present school in 1980. His many publications include anthologies and textbooks for pupils, papers and articles on the teaching of reading and literature, and school organization. He is General Editor of *Longman Imprint Books* and *Heinemann Organization in Schools Series*. His recent books include *Education for the Inner City* (Heinemann Educational Books, 1980) and *Departmental Management* (Heinemann Educational Books, 1981). He has been heavily involved in in-service education for many years, and founded Organization in Schools Courses. His national responsibilities have involved membership of the Bullock Committee on the teaching of reading and the uses of language, the Schools Council's Whole-Curriculum Working

Party, and its English Committee, of which he was Chairman. He chaired the National Book League's Use of Books in Schools Working Party, has been Vice-chairman of the Committee of Enquiry into School Book Supply. He is a member of the Education and Human Development Committee of the Social Science Research Board, and the Chairperson of the National Association for Pastoral Care.

## EMILY PATTERSON
*Urban Centre Library, Langston, Oklahoma, USA*
After her BA in Political Science at Central State University, Wilberforce, and work in the public library system, Emily Patterson took her Master's in Library Science at Buffalo University. She has worked in a Community College Library in Houston, Texas, and for two years in England for the National Book League and Organization in Schools Courses. Her present position is Social Sciences Co-ordinator at the Tulsa Urban Centre of the University of Langston. She has written short stories and poetry.

## LISA A. SERBIN
*Associate Professor of Psychology, Concordia University, Montreal, Quebec*
Lisa Serbin has published well over twenty papers on aspects of the psychology of young children in relation to the sex-stereotyping of teachers, stories, television programmes and the environment generally. Her first degree was in Psychology at Read College, Portland, Oregon, and she took her Ph.D. in 1972 at State University of New York, with a dissertation on 'Sex differences in the pre-school classroom: patterns of social reinforcement'. From 1972 to 1978 she remained at the State University of New York as Research Associate, Co-director of laboratory school, and Assistant Professor of Psychology, moving to Concordia in 1978. She has been involved in three research projects related to this book: The Development of Gender Salience in Pre-school Children; Mathematics, Visual-spatial Ability and Sex Roles; and Modifying Sex-related Behaviours and Cognitive Skills. Some of her many research papers are listed in the bibliography.

## DALE SPENDER
*Lecturer in Women's Studies MA Course at the Institute of Education, London University, UK*
Following her BA and Dip. Ed. at Sydney University, Dale Spender started teaching in New South Wales in 1965, being Head of English at a High School from 1971 to 1973. She then lectured in Education at James Cook University in North Queensland. In 1976 Dale Spender became a lecturer at the University of London Institute of Education. *Women's Studies International Quarterly* was founded by her, and she still edits it and the Pergamon Press *Athene Series*. Her many papers and articles include 'Educational research and the feminist perspective' and 'Bibliography: language and sex'. Her books include *Man-made*

*Language* (Routledge & Kegan Paul, 1980), *Learning to Lose* (with Elizabeth Sarah, Women's Press, 1980), *Men's Studies Modified* (Pergamon Press, 1981), *Invisible Women: the Schooling Scandal* (Writers and Readers, in association with Chameleon Editorial Group, 1982) and *There's Always Been a Women's Movement This Century* (Routledge & Kegan Paul, 1983).

## MARGARET B. SUTHERLAND

*Professor of Education, and Chairman of the Board of the Faculty of Education, University of Leeds, UK*

After Glasgow University and Jordanhill College of Education, Margaret Sutherland taught French and German in Glasgow secondary schools. She then went to Queen's University, Belfast, as lecturer in Education, later becoming Reader. In 1972 she took the Chair of Education at Leeds. Margaret Sutherland's main interests are comparative education and educational psychology. She is past Chairman of the Education Section of the British Psychological Society and past President and former Chairman of the British Section of the Comparative Education Society in Europe. She edits the *British Journal of Educational Studies* and, as well as many articles and the chapter cited in the Bibliography, is author of *Everyday Imagining and Education* (Routledge & Kegan Paul, 1971). In 1977 she gave the Galton Lecture 'Educating girls – to repair the ruins of our first parents', and in 1981 published *Sex Bias in Education* (Basil Blackwell).

# INDEX